Services in the Global Market

Services in the Global Market

Edited by
Jacques Nusbaumer

Kluwer Academic Publishers
Boston/Dordrecht/Lancaster

Distributors

for the United States and Canada: Kluwer Academic Publishers,
101 Philip Drive, Assinippi Park, Norwell, MA 02061

for the UK and Ireland: Kluwer Academic Publishers, MTP Press Limited,
Falcon House, Queen Square, Lancaster LA1 1RN, UK

for all other countries: Kluwer Academic Publishers Group, Distribution
Centre, P. O. Box 322, 3300 AH Dordrecht, The Netherlands

The views expressed in this book are those of the author and do not in
any way commit the organization that employs him.

Library of Congress Cataloging-in-Publication Data

Nusbaumer, Jacques, économiste.
  Services in the global market.

  Bibliography: p.
  Includes index.
  1. Service industries.   I. Title.
HD9980.5.N88   1987   338.4'6   87–4053
ISBN 0–89838–198–3

Contents

Preface   vii

1   Introduction   1

2   The Brave New World of Intelligence   5
    Utility, disutility, and value   5
    What makes services valuable?   13
    The three-factor theory revisited   19
    The international dimension   29

3   Trade Classifications and Trade Determinants   39
    Defining and classifying services   40
        Testing times for comparative advantage   50
        H-O and services   58

4   Definitions, Functions and Regulations   69
    What is "labor"?   86
    Tradeability   91
    Functions   93
    Regulations   98
    Data problems   101
    Concluding remarks   106

5   Facts and Figures   109
    Banking   109
    Telecommunication and data services   121
    Insurance and reinsurance   129
    Transport   135
    Professional, business, and scientific services   142
    Distribution services   150
    Final consumer services   152
    Government services   156

6   The Internationalization Process   163
     From trade to integration   165
     From integration to networking   170
     Services and developing countries   175

7   Technology and Trade, Two Sides of the Same Coin   181
     The new look of international trade   183
     Trade regulation in a new environment   185
     Scope and coverage of international trade regulations   189

8   A New Framework for Trade in Services: Rationale, Methodology, 195
     and Scope
     GATT and services: a bird's eye view   196
     Could GATT apply?   198
     The story of the shoe   210
     FLK, LIK, and international economic relations   214

9   By Way of Conclusion   225

Bibliography   231

Index   243

Preface

Service activities are at the heart of a major economic revolution taking place all around us. This new economic revolution is equivalent to the Industrial Revolution in the eighteenth century, the rise of the guilds in the Middle Ages, and the shift from a hunter/gatherer economy to an agricultural/pastoral economy at the dawn of recorded history when organized agriculture first led to the development of towns and the invention of writing. In this new revolution, computers, factory robots, and completely automated factories are rapidly reducing the need for physical labor in production. At the same time, sophisticated agricultural machinery, fertilizers, pesticides, and biogenetic engineering have reduced and will continue to reduce the physical labor involved in growing food. In the new economy that will emerge from this revolution, most people will earn their living by working in services.

Like all revolutions, the new economic revolution is troublesome because it brings with it major changes in everyday life, both at home and in the workplace. Change creates uncertainty about the future and ambiguity in the interpretation of economic trends. The new revolution is also troublesome because it adds to the complexity of economic organization and removes more people from the direct production of physical goods. In the new economy, more and more jobs will be based on the application of specialized knowledge and the manipulation of information with computers, a long step away from "real" jobs like growing wheat and assembling cars.

The new economic revolution is also transforming the organization of the international economy. Production is becoming more international. A typical home computer, for example, contains parts manufactured in over a dozen countries and services generated in another dozen countries.

These globally produced goods compete in global markets, perhaps best illustrated by airport shops around the world that display the same electronic gadgets, fashion apparel, or liquor. The internationalization of manufacturing has been matched by an equivalent internationalization of services.

The internationalization of economic activity is based on growing trade in so-called business services, many of which are knowledge- and information-intensive services used by businesses. Few people have direct exposure to the world in which (1) computers link foreign exchange trading in Singapore, Tokyo, New York, and London; (2) computers in Amsterdam process data for companies located in Sweden; (3) lawyers and financial advisors in New York advise clients from Abu Dhabi; (4) high school graduates in Korea summarize American laws for a computer database in the United States; (5) engineers and architects in India design buildings and roads being built by an American construction company with Korean labor in the Middle East; (6) models from France pose in Greece for an American advertising company preparing ads for Japanese publications; (7) Italian craftsmen design cars for American and Japanese car companies; and (8) Philippine management consultants and accountants help to unravel the financial mysteries of a failed business in Hong Kong. All these activities, in one way or another, involve trade in services, and without them the international economy could not function.

In recognition of the growing importance of such trade in services, GATT trade ministers agreed at a meeting in Punta del Este in September, 1986 to launch negotiations on trade in services. They agreed that "...the negotiations in this area shall aim to establish a multilateral framework of principles and rules for trade in services, including elaboration of possible disciplines for individual sectors, with a view to expansion of such trade under conditions of transparency and progressive liberalization and as a means of promoting economic growth of all trading partners and the development of developing countries."

The issues are complex and the negotiations will be difficult. In agreeing to start negotiations, however, the trade ministers took a giant step toward facing up to the trade policy issues posed by this new economic revolution.

Jacques Nusbaumer has made a major contribution to the negotiations by providing us a methodical and incisive analysis of trade in services. He has brought to this task the meticulously detailed analysis of a scholar and the practical insights of a practicing trade official. The book leads the reader through a thorough examination of the characteristics of services, the organization of service industries and service markets, the role of services in the world economy and the nature of trade in services, and the domestic policy issues that arise in services and the implication for trade in services. The final chapter addresses itself to the key principles underlying current GATT rules for trade in goods and offers some insights on how they might be applied to trade in services.

Economists are just beginning to probe trade in services, having defined services as nontradeable in the past. Mr. Nusbaumer offers a full discussion of the theoretical contributions that have been made by economists in recent years and lays down his own theoretical treatment of the subject. He supports and supplements the work of other theorists in some areas, and refutes it in other areas. He thus leaves the reader with a thorough familiarity of the economic literature.

The theoretical analysis of services is supported by extensive observations about the real world, on a sector-by-sector basis. The book thus provides a valuable bridge between the world of the theorist and the world of the practitioner, and sets the stage for the concluding chapter dealing with the negotiation of trade rules for services.

Agreement on the application of the trade principles discussed in chapter 7 to trade in services would represent an important step toward improved management of the increasingly integrated world economy. International service transactions are ultimately the glue that holds the world together, and a world in which such service transactions can take place more freely will be one that works much better for everyone. Agreement on some principles will not solve all problems, but it will give policy managers better guideposts for dealing with the detailed issues that arise on a daily basis. Adoption of the principles should leave considerable room for national preferences on regulatory methods and goals, while providing more explicit recognition of the basic fact that economic progress is based on increased interdependence among nations.

GEZA FEKETEKUTY
Counselor to the
U.S. Trade Representative

To Tamara

1 INTRODUCTION

This book is about the workings of market economies in the information age. Knowledge-based activities, assisted by rapidly evolving information technology, have become the mainspring of economic growth. Their impact on production processes, consumer behavior, and socioeconomic structures has begun to attract the attention of economists and policy-makers alike. They are now seen by the latter as possible outlets for factors displaced from sunset industries. Supply-side economics and deregulation have unleashed tremendous creative potential in many production fields previously neglected as alternative sources of wealth and welfare.

As a result of these developments, much more has been written about services in the last 5 years than in the previous 200. However, a coherent view of the economic role of services is only slowly emerging because the analytical problems are daunting, and the statistical data are scarce and inaccurate. There is as yet no consistent theory of value for services, nor is there widespread agreement on the applicability of traditional trade theory to services. There are few if any conventional indicators of the quantity of services output, and almost as many definitions and classifications as there are writers on the subject.

The rapidity and ease of modern communication are increasingly forcing service suppliers to compete on a world scale. Barriers to entry into

1

national services markets exist, and more can be created, but the pressures of competition make protectionism in this field more and more outmoded because services can no longer be treated as a separate sector of activity. The impact of services on production, trade, and distribution of goods is being increasingly felt, to the effect that services have become a major determinant of the overall economic performance of any country. Consequently, it is no longer appropriate to consider them as "non-traded goods" and to study them in the narrow framework of the national economy.

This book stresses the global dimension of services activities, and as such it places in its proper perspective the analysis contained in the previous book by this author: *The Services Economy: Lever to Growth* (Kluwer, 1987). Since the theory is still in the making and the facts are still largely unknown, it would be awkward to pretend that the analysis is thereby in any way completed. By the same token, the time is not ripe to attempt to compose a standard textbook on this complex subject. Part of this book is therefore devoted to new theoretical analysis in areas which were touched upon, but not elaborated upon, in the previous book. This relates in particular to the theory of value and to the theory of comparative advantage. The points made on these questions in chapters 2 and 3 are brought together in the second half of chapter 8, where an interpretation is given of the determinants of international trade in services, based on a distinction between "locked-in knowledge" (LIK) and "foot-loose knowledge" (FLK).

Although ideas, like technology, are rapidly evolving in the field of services and it is difficult to present a "state of the art" without running the risk of being rapidly overtaken by events, a lot of thinking has taken place and a lot of technical material—some of it unpublished—has been made available in recent years: it has therefore appeared useful to bring all this together in one place, and this is the second objective of this book. All writers on the subject have faced—and are still facing—the same fundamental difficulty, i.e., the dearth of data. Much of what has been written has of necessity taken the form of deductive reasoning based on casual observation of market behavior. Therefore, those parts of the book that describe the production and trade characteristics of services also present a compendium of ideas about observed phenomena. This is true regarding not only the definition and classification of services discussed in chapter 4 but also the analysis of the impact of new technologies on the internationalization of services activities contained in chapters 5 and 6.

The decade of the 1980s will be marked by the first attempt of the international community to negotiate a set of multilateral principles and rules governing trade in services. This will take place in the context of the

Uruguay Round of Multilateral Trade Negotiations launched at the GATT Conference of Punta del Este in September 1986. Such an exercise, the outcome of which will greatly influence the operation of the world trading system in the next decades, raises issues which appear far more complex than those relating to trade in goods dealt with in the General Agreement on Tariffs and Trade. Although it is not possible at this stage to predict how they will be resolved, it is necessary to draw attention to them, and this is done in chapter 7 and the first half of chapter 8.

There is a logical sequence in handling the subject matter of this book, which is to look first at the fundamentals, second at the practice, and third, at the framework of international relations. Inevitably, however, many questions remain unanswered, and the conclusions briefly presented in chapter 9 are necessarily tentative. The pieces of the puzzle can be assembled in many different ways, and it is not until more analysis and more data will have been made available that economists can be expected to reach consensus on at least some major concepts, as they have done with regard to production and trade in goods despite their notorious inclination to disagree with each other. In order to reflect the presently somewhat disjointed character of economic theory in the field of services, the intention of the author has been to keep each chapter of this book as self-contained as possible. Nevertheless, there are some common threads of thought that run through all aspects of the subject matter and that have been purposely emphasized. This has been done at the cost of some repetition which, he hopes, the thorough reader will forgive. (This author happens to think that repetition is often more useful than cross-references to previous passages of the text which are never easy to find.)

In closing these remarks, I would like to have been in a position to line up a long list of names of persons to whom I owe acknowledgment. Many of the ideas contained in this book have been tested in discussions with other researchers listed in the bibliography, with participants in conferences and seminars on services, and with operators and government officials. However, most of them have never seen any part of this book in draft, and to give their names here would quite improperly appear to associate them in one way or another with its contents. Let them therefore be thanked anonymously for their invaluable contribution to the process of thought which has led to this result. A special debt of gratitude is owed, however, to Geza Feketekuty, who agreed to read the whole manuscript and has accepted the risk of writing its preface. I also wish to thank wholeheartedly Miss Meera Anklesaria, who has typed and retyped successive drafts of the manuscript with unequalled talent and patience.

The views expressed in this book are entirely my own, and cannot in any way be attributed to the GATT secretariat.

2 THE BRAVE NEW WORLD OF INTELLIGENCE

Economics is a science of social change. Man lives by doing; his destiny is to create. The art, artifact, or mode of doing is what determines his control over his natural environment and his freedom to live, whether the product of his efforts is tangible or intangible. Joining hands to do things improves results. Hence, the social dimension of work is omnipresent and especially worthy of attention; this is the unique claim to virtue of economists.

Utility, Disutility, and Value

Utility is the well-being created by man's actions. Wealth is accumulated utility which can be stored for future use beyond the owner's or the beneficiary's lifetime. *Disutility*, the converse of well-being, is also the result of man's actions. Since negatives cannot be accumulated, disutility per se cannot be stored, but it can lead to a permanent—once and for all or continuous—reduction of wealth.

Utility becomes *value* when it is exchanged in the market place among different producers or owners of it, and disutility becomes *cost* to whoever must exchange well-being against it as a condition of obtaining value.

5

Windfall utility and disutility which bypass formal market mechanisms are *external economies* and *diseconomies*.

As far back as we can go in man's history, we find evidence of the creation and accumulation of wealth in tangible forms. For a long time, in the absence of a language or writing medium, this was the only way in which utility could be transmitted from one period to another and from one generation to another. Therefore, the notion of utility was quite naturally associated with the ownership of tangible goods, and the plastic arts remained the most reliable vehicle for the transmission of culture.

With the advent of literacy and the discovery of practical means for the recording and transmission of ideas, these have become a source of wealth in their own right. The utility contained in ideas and their practical implementation can henceforth be stored and accumulated in books, magnetic tapes, text processing diskettes, videotapes, cinematographic films, etc., and used at will as a source of market value. Therefore, there is no longer any reason to accord, as in the past, particular attention to the production of tangible goods as opposed to that of intangible sources of well-being, in the short or long run. This goes to say that in modern economies, all productive activities play a similar economic role, i.e., there is none that is more "basic" than another and none that is more "residual" than another. A distinction can still be made, however, between those activities which produce utility in tangible forms and those which produce purely intangible utility. The latter are what are commonly called *services*.

If utility is looked at as the final goal of all productive activity, all products, tangible and intangible, can be incorporated in simple demand functions related to the wants and desires of final users. Total utility is seen then as a combination of market values and positive externalities (external economies), i.e., utility paid for and unpaid for. From this standpoint, it is more important to identify the ways in which physical materials and nonmaterial acts concur to produce utility which can be marketed for a price than it is to distinguish between goods and services. Thus, the particular organization of work in a given economic environment, as between the production and distribution of marketable physical goods and nonmaterial services and the production of positive externalities, determines the efficiency of human effort, both within that environment and in relation to other economic environments. As George Stigler [1962] put it: "...economics is the study of the operation of economic organizations, and economic organizations are social and rarely individual arrangements to deal with the production and distribution of economic goods and services."

The fact that goods and services produce utility can be recognized in general terms, but this does not suffice to determine the relationship between the total utility created by each type of product and its market value. Thus, knowing his/her way through the countryside may have special utility to an individual traveller but no market value. On the other hand, a loaf of bread has utility for the hungry person and also has market value. While in broad terms both forms of utility are comparable, since both produce well-being, in specific terms the value of knowing one's way is made up of different elements than the value of satisfying one's appetite.

In analyzing services, it is necessary to identify those elements which are the main determinants of their market value and to consider to what extent these may differ from the elements which constitute the market value of goods. Insofar as they are different, it can be argued that the economics of services differs from the economics of physical production. Insofar as they are alike, it should be possible to lay the foundation of a general theory of value which encompasses both goods and services and overcomes the limitations of previous theories of values that have addressed only market phenomena as they relate to the production and sale of goods. In this case, a common definition of value would apply to both tangible and intangible products sold on the market place—there being no fundamental economic distinction between goods and services except for the intangibility of the latter that would only be seen as a physical, not an economic, characteristic of services.

Explaining value in terms of concrete constituent elements is tantamount to explaining production processes in terms of the raw materials which they transform and combine to create marketable products as well as of the modes of extraction and cultivation of the raw materials themselves. The concrete elements that make up the value of individual services from the supply side are not necessarily, and in fact have no reason to be, the same as those that make up the value of goods, since these elements differ even among goods. Thus, a brick is made of clay; a loaf of bread is made of wheat flour, water, and yeast. Similarly, a lawyer's advice is made of the applied knowledge of law; a priest's sermon is made of faith and of the knowledge and understanding of sacred texts. Tangible products have different weights, sizes, etc. Intangible products have different contents in information and quality, the latter depending to a large extent on the quality of performance of the renderer of the service. To distinguish between goods and services generally, one must therefore look for *common* supply characteristics.

The particular modes of production of services differ from the modes of production of goods in the way they affect the relationships between economic agents, as well as the sociopolitical structures within which these agents deploy their activities. For example, in the absence of means of reproduction, storage, and transportation of services, the intangible character of the latter dominates the way in which they are rendered. In such situations, the supplier of a service embodies the store of raw materials, the means of production, and the means of distribution of the service. His simultaneous presence with the consumer of the service is required for a market transaction to take place. By comparison, a shoe can be manufactured in one place and sold in another without requiring the presence of the manufacturer or of one of his designers or engineers at the point of sale. Therefore, in the cases of the services in question, the personal relationship between seller and buyer—and the sociopolitical framework in which they take place—automatically extends into a personal relationship between producer and consumer, whereas in the case of shoes the relationship between the latter remains totally impersonal. Differences between goods and services are, however, often only a matter of degree. A book can be written in one place and sold in another, whereas a sophisticated machine tool can be manufactured in one place and sold in another only with the assistance of engineers from the manufacturing firm for the installation, maintenance, and perhaps even running, of the machinery. Services can be transported over telecommunication wires or transmitted through satellite.[1]

Our habits of thinking leave us with the notion that services are only intermingled with goods to the extent that the labor services of goods producers are embodied in physical objects. This reflects a very narrow view of the production process. Many services which play an important role in goods production and distribution are produced and consumed without the intervention of goods or even of a material support. A porterage service uses only the hands and feet of the porter. A legal service uses a minimum of physical goods (basically pen, paper, and telephone). In addition, the use of the term *service* to describe labor in general is very misleading because in present-day economic thinking, services are commonly understood to be *products* in their own right and not simply the effort of producing. It is true that because services are intangible, service products are less clearly defined than goods, i.e., they cannot be measured in terms of length, height, width, weight, etc., as goods can. Nonetheless, *service acts* which give rise to an immediate creation of utility are not comparable to *working acts* which only create utility so to speak by proxy through their embodiment in goods acting as utility carriers. The problem is complicated, however, by the fact that there is no clear segregation between goods-producing workers and services-producing workers in any economy. The work of the shop-hand and the value of the engineer are both integrated into the value of the automobile. Indeed, parcels of the work of machinery and equipment used in the automobile plant are incorporated in the value of the automobile. Where does one draw the line?

This issue is similar to the one that arises in connection with the quality of goods. There may exist side by side (and in real life there do exist) goods of almost identical description except for the quality of their make or their performance. Statistically, such goods are often counted as units of the same product, and it is only the evolution of the quality of identical goods through time which is deemed to give rise to problems of interpretation as to the true value of production. This problem has been recognized for a long time, and it has become known as the "index number problem."[2] Since there does not exist sufficient information about changes in the quality of goods over time, except in particular circumstances, adjustments for quality are made by manipulation of price data and, in the short term, it is simply assumed that the index number problem does not exist. Nonbelievers in economics would argue that the lumping in the same basket of goods which are not identical in terms of quality is pure fiction. Economists, however, describe it as a statistical convention. At the moment, no agreed conventions exist for the classification of services or even for the definition of what is a "service" and what is not. There is a vague feeling that the worker on the shop floor should not be classified as a service provider, whereas the engineer should. Such a problem would not need to be addressed if economic activities were organized in terms of goods-producing enterprises only, without there being in existence firms or individuals that cannot show any tangible result for their efforts. But the evolution of modern societies is exactly the opposite. We see more and more people being employed and more and more value being created in nongoods-producing sectors.

A special feature of today's modern economies is that more goods are being produced while fewer and fewer people seem to be involved in that production. This is not only a question of industrial or agricultural productivity. At the same time that more goods are being produced, more people are involved in intangible production. Of course, being involved in intangible production does not mean something totally distinct from involvement in the production of goods. To a large extent, the production of services is a question of definition, in the sense that only if services are produced by independent enterprises are they identified as separate products. All sorts of services are being produced in the institutional framework of goods-producing enterprises or administrations such as state-run industries, without its ever being known whether such activities have any relevance of their own to the gross national income of a country. Institutional distinctions between goods-producing and service-producing enterprises are only the beginning of the story. They throw no light on the processes leading to the creation of value in any particular economic environment. The doorman of a bank plays no recognized role in the economic process until and unless he becomes an employee of a private security firm. The lawyer of an automobile manufacturing enterprise has

Figure 2–1. Rates of growth of services output and goods output, selected developed countries, 1972–1984.

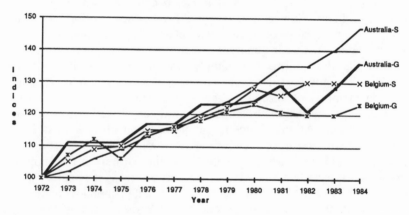

a. Australia, Belgium;

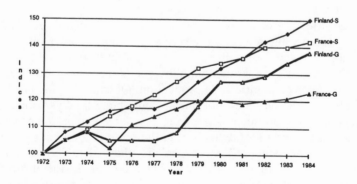

b. Finland, France;

much less social and economic significance (statistically speaking) as an employee of that enterprise than if he were the owner of his own law firm. Further, it is wrong to assume that if one suddenly sees the lawyer leave the goods-producing enterprise to establish his own law firm, the recorded value of goods production will decrease. On the contrary, the value of goods production may increase as a result of the lawyer producing more competitive and hence cheaper law services for manufacturers, while at the

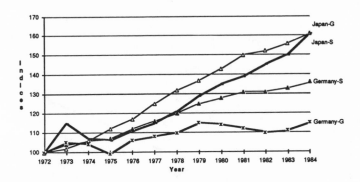

c. Germany, Japan;

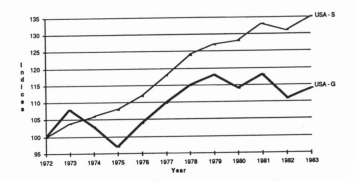

d. United States.

Source: OECD, 1986. National Accounts, Vol. II. Paris. OECD
Notes: —Including government services and "other" non-market services; excluding construction and imputed bank service charge
—Constant prices—Indices: base 1972 = 100
Australia: 1979–80 prices; Belgium, Finland, Germany and Japan: 1980 prices; France: 1970 prices; United States: 1975 prices.

same time, the gross national product of the country concerned will rise due to the independent lawyer's producing more lawyer outputs per unit of input.

There are, however, two disturbing facts that seem to belie this perception. First, while historically services output appears to have increased faster than goods production (figure 2–1), there also appears to be a trend for output per man to fall over time in the services sector (figure 2–2). This can be explained either by the relative labor-intensity of

Figure 2–2. Rate of increase of real output per man in services and in goods, selected developed countries, 1972–1984.

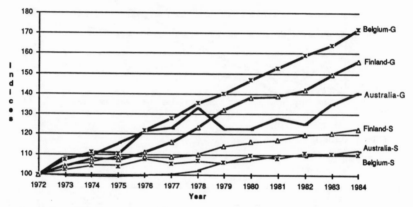

a. Australia, Belgium, Finland;

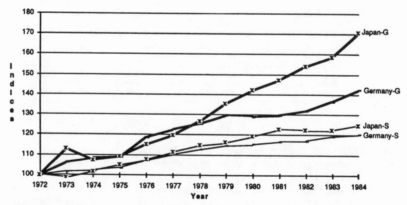

b. Germany, Japan;

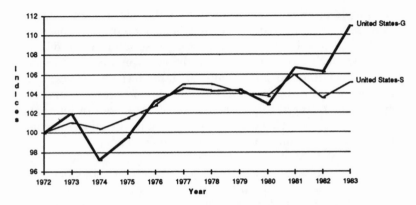

c. United States.

Source: OECD, 1986. National Accounts, Vol. II. Paris. OECD
Notes: —All persons employed
　　　 —Constant prices—Indices: base 1972 = 100

services or by the "disappearance" of services output from GDP data. The first explanation can be sustained by reference to units of value created per unit cost of labor input in services activities. The second explanation rests on the nature of service output which (being both intangible and invisible and being such as to produce utility beyond that of the immediate users— externalities) normally goes unrecorded to varying degrees. These are fundamental questions to which most of the rest of this chapter will be devoted.

What Makes Services Valuable?

The utility created by services consists of information and communication. These give rise to value if they can be sold for a price to users. Insofar as the information provided by services can be broken down into homogeneous units, and on the assumption that service markets are competitive, the price of a service will equate the sum of its constituent units valued at the marginal cost of producing one extra unit in each case. The same applies to communication functions of services if such functions can be broken down into homogeneous units. The assumption of homogeneous units implies that there are, in the short run, no discontinuities in the production of services. It also implies that a given type of service, like a pair of shoes, produces more or less the same amount of utility for different consumers, i.e., that services are standardized, not personalized. Only under those conditions is it possible to reap economies of scale in the production of services since such economies reply on the lower unit costs of producing a greater amount of identical units of a product. Armed with these assumptions, it is possible to reconstitute in the area of services the essential tenets of the theory of price and of the theory of international trade applied to goods. However, a close look at reality raises some doubts about such an extension of traditional economic theory.

The contents of a shoe are a sole, uppers, and laces made up of different materials, and the shoe is made to fit feet of different sizes but of more or less standard shape. The contents of a service can be broken down into two main categories of elements. First, there is the element of applied physical force, which is the main component of the service rendered by unskilled laborers. Second, there is the element of knowledge and experience (information) which informs the acts of workers providing services of a less purely physical, or of an essentially intellectual, nature. While physical force may be considered as a fairly homogeneous raw material, information varies in character according to the type of service being performed; knowledge is not a fungible good. So far, we may not have discovered much difference with goods, since various kinds of information may be compared to various kinds of materials entering into the manufacture of finished goods such as steel, aluminium, leather, cotton, etc. Still, even within fairly narrowly defined categories of services, the question arises whether information can be broken down into homogeneous functional parts which, when added together, produce predictable results. For example, it is far from certain that any given amount of pleading in court by a lawyer will always automatically produce the release of the accused.

The third element contained in services is physical capital, which has particular importance in some services based on the use of technologically advanced equipment, such as telecommunication and data-processing services, and also for less technologically advanced activities but which traditionally rely on heavy capital equipment and infrastructure, such as road transport, shipping, and aviation. In speaking of the intangible character of services, the input of physical capital is often overlooked. The impression may thus be given that economies of scale may be reaped in the production of services, whereas, in fact, the economies of scale are reaped through the use of efficient equipment which allows more services to be either transported, communicated, or processed in a given time span and with a given amount of financial investment. The services themselves which benefit from these technological advances may not be any less labor-intensive to produce.

If we now try to analyze the value of services in Ricardian terms,[3] we can break it down into three main constituent elements: labor, human capital, and physical capital. The distinction between human capital, or what we have previously called knowledge, and labor or physical capital may be somewhat artificial depending on where one draws the line between skilled and unskilled work on the one hand, and embodied and disembodied knowledge on the other. However, the notion of human capital is clearly perceived by anyone who understands that a man who can read and write is likely to perform better in a given job than a man who can do neither, and that a sophisticated machine tool is likely to produce more results in a given time span than a shovel. Also, the distinction between various types of human capital may be difficult to perceive at first sight. Information constitutes the common characteristic of all human capital, which is more or less sophisticated depending on the degree to which the raw information is processed. Yet it is clear that information varies in character and that various combinations of information are used as inputs into different services. Knowledge can be a simple acquaintance with facts, or it can be the result of very elaborate thought processes which confer upon it considerable leverage for the production of utility.

In general, the various proportions in which human capital, labor, and physical capital are incorporated in a service, determine the value of the service in the market where these different factors must be procured. As we shall see later (chapter 8), this is one reason why the theory of international trade that holds for goods appears at first sight to be extensible to services. However, the nature of knowledge (in particular its easy transferability) introduces a different dimension into the production equation, which makes it more difficult to reconcile traditional trade theory with the theory of the exchange of services.

As in the case of goods, the particular configuration of factors used for the production of services depends not only on the availability and cost of the factors but also on the nature of the service being provided. Thus, some services are by nature human-capital intensive, others are physical-capital intensive, and yet others are labor-intensive. Nonetheless, whatever the degree of human capital or physical capital used, services tend to employ a large amount of labor. Whether this is due to the nonstorability of services as one would presume, or is only seen as a particular feature of services production because of the fact that the actual volume of services rendered is not properly measured, is a crucial issue which needs to be resolved before any conclusion can be drawn regarding the productivity of factors used in services production or the role of services in national production generally. At first sight, it appears reasonable to argue that for the same volume of output of services, the productivity of labor increases as both human capital and physical capital increase and vice versa. But this simply begs the question of what is to be understood by a given volume of output of services.

Even if differences in the quality of services are interpreted as quantum differences, it remains unclear how much utility a particular service act can create over time. In the case of goods, a distinction is often made between durable and nondurable goods. Nondurable goods such as food produce utility at a given point in time or over a very short period, whereas durable goods produce utility during an extended period. Services being intangible, the temptation is to assume that all services only produce short-run or immediate utility and to discount the more diffused, "environment"-creating effects of services on individuals, social groups, and on the economy as a whole. Many of these diffused effects are not measurable but clearly recognizable, and in some economies there may be no market value for them. They are what economists call "public goods" or by other names such as "social overhead," "externalities," "unrequited output," etc. The existence of a bus service is not only directly useful for bus travellers but also as a *possibility* given to would-be travellers who expect to find a need for the service eventually. The existence of a police force is more important as a potential source of utility, by giving a sense of security to the population, than as a producer of immediate utility in the sense of arresting criminals. One of the charms of large cities is the number of theaters one can go to even if one never leaves one's armchair in front of the fireplace. There is a fundamental difference between goods and services in this respect, although the line between the two should not be drawn too sharply, because some goods directly produce externalities and sometimes in the most unexpected fashion. Thus, the New York skyline in a distinct source of utility for city lovers, as is the sight of a regatta for sailing fans. Services perform communication and information functions, and in so doing they establish linkages between goods and people which provide leverage, i.e., external economies, to the actions of individuals and groups of individuals in their social environment. Much of this leverage effect goes unrecorded in money terms even in perfectly competitive, fully monetized economies, giving rise to an indefinite amount of unrecorded value in existing data on gross national product which may, in conjunction with other factors (in particular the failure to take separately into account various inputs of human capital), explain the apparent low productivity of labor in services in modern economies.

Two reasons for approaching the question of the value of services from the supply side are, therefore, the constraint imposed by the nonexistence of market prices for many services, and the fact that many services create utility in the form of externalities, that is, not in the form of value as traditionally defined. The absence of a market price for many services is a particular problem related to their invisibility and their intangibility. The contours of a service vary with the personality of the service provider. Unless service providers can be standardized, or be made to look standard, the services they provide will not be comparable in quality and therefore will not, or should not, earn the same price in a competitive market. Therefore, one extra unit of service will not create one extra unit of utility comparable to the previous unit, giving rise to a discrete utility curve. Consequently, the analysis of services on the basis of marginal utility in consumption breaks down, as does all demand analysis which assumes equal increments of utility over a given income scale.

Externalities created by services make it necessary to think in terms of the *intrinsic* contribution which they make to the process of economic development, whether this process is conceived in terms of tangible or of intangible production. Thus relating services to wealth creation in the broadest sense provides a point of reference for approximating their real role in accumulation and distribution, irrespective of fluctuations in their price according to the vagueries of the market.

In concrete terms, this means that the value of services is made up of the *value of the factors* (including knowledge) used to produce them as well as of the *utility of the functions* (whether or not valued at market prices, i.e., whether or not considered as service products or external economies) they perform in different economic systems and social environments.

As we have seen, the factors that enter into the production of services are themselves either tangible or intangible. Unskilled labor and physical capital are tangible units, the availability of which in a given market can be measured with relative precision and subjected to traditional supply/demand analysis. Human capital, as pointed out above, is not so easily measured although there is a tradition of breaking down education and training curricula into recognizable portions corresponding to general levels of skills. While such breakdowns and the content of the resulting portions vary from one society to another and over time within the same society, at any given point in time there is little ambiguity concerning the skill content of given levels of education and training. In fact, the World Bank publishes literacy and skill statistics which give a fairly good idea of the level of scientific and technological development of the average unit of population in different countries. Similarly, pioneers in the theory of

human capital such as Gary Becker and Harold Mincer have used standardized education and training levels as reference quantities for developing
their theories.[4]

Primary, secondary, and tertiary education and specialist training at
technical or professional level command different factor prices in the
market. There are also recognized monopoly elements in knowledge and
information which are due either to the very specialized nature of the
knowledge or information in question or to institutional factors, such as the
use of patented technology by major computer firms or the corporatist
withholding and exploitation of information by doctors, lawyers, and other
professionals. Such monopoly elements can be taken into account in
estimating the value of factor inputs in the service activities concerned.
Thus, at least between countries with roughly equal levels of economic
and social development, comparisons of knowledge-factor availabilities
based on proportions of the population with a primary, secondary, and
university education will produce patterns of factor endowments which fit
certain commonly made observations about these countries' economies.
For example, the fact that more than one-half of the Japanese population
has a secondary education and more than one-third a university education
provides an intuitively correct explanation for the success of Japan in
assimilating foreign technology and in rapidly moving from the stage of
copying to that of inventing in many advanced fields of science. At the
same time, it has often been remarked that the economies of many
developing countries have difficulty "taking off" because of illiteracy
and/or lack of indigenous technical skills.

The second component of the value of services, i.e., the utility of the
functions they perform in the economy, can be transferred either to other
service products or to tangible wealth. Just as service products can be
intermediate or final,[5] service functions are intermediate if they serve to
enhance the supply of wealth by other producers of goods or services, or
final if they assist consumers in acquiring utility from the goods or other
services they purchase. However, whereas service products can be either
complementary to or substitutes for other goods or services, service
functions are by essence complementary to other outputs because the
utility they transfer to these outputs cannot exist without them. For
example, the utility created by the sight of a regatta cannot exist without
the sailboats and the sporting event that produce the sight. Although the
value of service functions is elusive whenever they take the form of public
goods with a quasi-indefinite production range and an indefinite consumption domain, it is this author's intuitive conviction that the role of services
in economic development is at least as important in the form of functions as
in the form of products.[6]

The Three-Factor Theory Revisited

Before giving examples of service products and service functions which will allow a clearer distinction between them in terms, respectively, of the value which they add to total national product and of their contribution to social welfare, let us examine, with the aid of figures 2–3, 2–4, and 2–5, the contribution of the three major classes of factors identified above to the production of services. In figure 2–3 we have the three factors depicted in a three-dimensional diagram, where each factor substitutes for each one of the other two in the proportion given by the relevant price ratio (the slopes of the lines K_1L_1, K_1H_1, and H_1L_1), and where the plane circumscribed by K_1, L_1 and H_1 is the locus of possible factor combinations for the production of a given amount of service X. As more of X is produced, the plane extends outward from the origin. With constant elasticity of substitution between factors, the locus of production of X will be like a bowl, the base of which touches the plane at a point determined by the factor price ratios.[7]

In figures 2–4 and 2–5, the same three-factor situation is depicted but with one important variant, namely, that the elasticity of substitution between factors changes as output increases ($X_2 > X_1$), thereby affecting

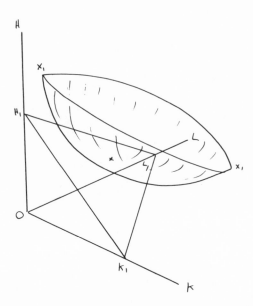

Figure 2–3. Factor price ratios in services

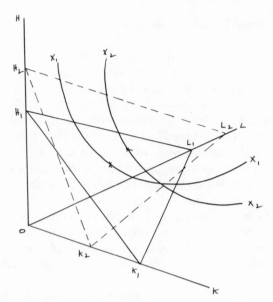

Figure 2–4. Factor price ratios in services

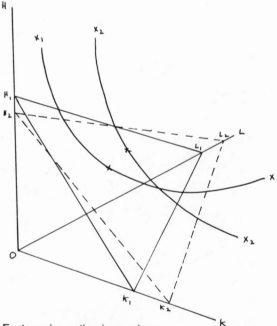

Figure 2–5. Factor price ratios in services

factor price ratios. On the assumption that the supply elasticity of the factors is at least equal to one, the price ratios will change inversely to the relative demand for factors; otherwise they will change directly with the demand. Two possible combinations of factor prices are shown in figures 2–4 and 2–5. Different situations will, of course, prevail depending on the particular service being produced and on the availability of different factors in the market where it is produced, so that the assumption in figure 2–3 that the technical substitution possibilities just match the market price ratios is a very strong one. In fact, the solid representing the locus of output can take many different shapes which are difficult to represent graphically.

It is also conceivable that, within a given range of output, the relationship between factors is one of complementarity rather than substitution. The case of complementarity between human capital and labor is one that has often been assumed by economists because the delivery of services generally requires the physical presence or intervention of the economic agent producing the service who acts as a carrier of utility. However, at higher levels of quality, that is, for services which involve a greater amount of information and a greater degree of elaboration of data, and which can be called information or knowledge-intensive services, the possibility of substitution of human capital for labor may increase, insofar as accumulated knowledge can be recorded, stored, and delivered outside the presence of the generator of the service, i.e., without any labor input on his part beyond that necessary to produce the service. This is the case of what J. Bhagwati [1984, 1986] has called "disembodied" services.[8] Human capital and physical capital may, on the contrary, be substituted less easily in the production of sophisticated types of services, since machines which can imitate the movements of the human brain have not yet been invented.[9] The substitutability of physical capital for unskilled labor has long been known to be high in services, particularly in the least sophisticated unskilled labor (maids).[10] Be that as it may, it should be pointed out that there is a basic problem with defining the relationships between factors of production for a given service at different levels of output. When human capital is included, the addition of more human capital is likely to transform the nature of the service by increasing its quality.

Generally speaking, the reference to human capital as a separate factor of production provides a means of taking into account different qualities of labor in the estimation of the value of service products. This method is not a novelty. It has long been recognized that, while there is no definite and immutable scale of skills and it is the market that determines the relative price of labor at different skill levels, "highly-skilled" labor, however defined, has always been paid more than "low-skilled" labor and therefore has always transferred more value to commodities and services alike. Yet the notion of human capital is not limited to that of skill because it also encompasses the notion of durability. Now, as David Ricardo [1963] put it, "...suppose that the same quantity of labor was necessary to make [two] weapons (necessary to kill the beaver or the deer), but that they were of very unequal durability; of the durable implement only a small portion of its value would be transferred to the commodity, a much greater portion of the value of the less durable implement would be realized in the commodity which it contributed to produce" [chapter I, section III, p. 12]. The same reasoning can be applied to human capital as is here applied to physical capital. Low-skill service producers, i.e., producers which embody a small amount of human capital, transfer little value to the services they render, and those services are less durable. Moreover, it is in the case of low-skill services that one finds the most instances of simultaneity between production and consumption of services. Therefore, the notions of capital, durability, skill, and time all concur to produce a concept of value of services which is related to their knowledge intensity and the time during which they produce their effects. The services of a doorman exist only when he is standing by the door; those of an insurer can last a lifetime. Expressed differently, the little human capital contained in the services of a doorman is consumed by his simple presence at the door or by the act of opening the door which he performs, sometimes politely touching his hat, and sometimes not (less human capital), whereas only a small parcel of the human capital contained or embodied in the insurance broker is consumed by the act of drawing up and signing an insurance policy. Moreover, the insurance policy itself embodies a considerable amount of stored human capital and is a potential source of additional utility from the human capital it can set in motion in case of events giving rise to a claim by the insured.

Services also contain various amounts of physical capital, the value of which is transferred by the service provider in a nonvisible and nonreproducible form. To take up our previous comparison, the amount of physical capital contained in the act of opening a door is virtually nil, whereas the amount of physical capital contained in the production of an insurance policy can be quite sizable if the fixed assets of the insurance company, of the insurance broker, and of the telecommunications network on which the insurance policy may be ordered, are taken into account. Again, for common standardized insurance policies such as minimum automobile insurance, the amount of human capital and physical capital contained in the policy are less than those contained in a special insurance policy, for astronauts for example, due to the fact that (1) the standardized character of the insurance policy makes it possible for the insurer to reap economies of scale, and (2) the techniques of insuring for automobile accidents in accordance with legal minima have long become common knowledge whose market value is reduced by easy access to it, to the point of making it almost a free good in the more advanced financial communities.

Pursuing the argument along the lines of Ricardo's analysis of value, we note a striking dissimilarity between human capital and physical capital. Ricardo points out that some machines are more durable than others, and the less durable ones require more labor to be replaced. Therefore, "a rise in the wage of labor would not equally affect commodities produced with machinery quickly consumed, and commodities produced with machinery slowly consumed...every raise of wages therefore, or, which is the same thing, every fall of profits, would lower the relative value of those commodities which were produced with capital of a durable nature and would proportionately elevate those which were produced with capital more perishable. A fall of wages would have precisely the contrary effect" [Ricardo, 1963, p. 22].

This reasoning would not apply to human capital for two reasons:

1. Information, training, or knowledge are not perishable or hardly perishable, unless the economic agents suffer from amnesia or have left a particular type of activity for a long time, in which case they may need retraining. But even in this case, the cost of retraining is likely to be much less than the cost of initial training as we all know from common experience, for example with learning foreign languages, although admittedly the cost of retraining may bear a higher ratio to initial training for certain activities than for others.

2. Although the consumption of knowledge does not reduce its amount available to the service producer or its quality, knowledge can suffer from obsolesence by sheer interruption of the process of knowledge accumulation. Thus, once the learning curve of an economic agent flattens compared to that of other (possibly younger) agents, his stock of knowledge depreciates. This depreciation is a market phenomenon and not a natural or physical phenomenon.

The implication is that, in a society which is open to new sources of knowledge and which cultivates the acquisition, accumulation, and use (through innovation) of knowledge, human capital plays a *dynamic* role in the production processes and serves as a lever to economic growth. In contrast, machines play a passive role in production processes, during which they are consumed through wear and tear which requires labor to keep them in an efficient working condition. Consequently, as Ricardo put it: "...in proportion to the durability of capital employed in any kind of production the relative prices of those commodities on which such durable capital is employed will vary inversely as wages; they will fall as wages rise, and rise as wages fall; and on the contrary those which are produced chiefly by labor with less fixed capital or with fixed capital of a less durable character than the medium in which price if estimated, will rise as wages rise, and fall as wages fall" [1963, pp. 23–24]. The continued application of work effort to the maintenance of machines will not raise the value or the efficiency of the machines but merely serve to slow down their physical rate of depreciation. Human capital, on the other hand, as we have seen, increases continuously in line with work effort applied to maintain and develop it. Furthermore, it is the rise in wages (presumably of unskilled labor) that induces the use of labor-saving machinery and thus leads to the fall in the relative prices of goods and services produced with additional physical capital,[11] whereas it is human capital that determines the technical feasibility of such substitutions and the optimum allocation of resources between physical capital and labor in any given production process.

The emergence of human capital as the prime motive force behind economic progress becomes apparent as the rate of accumulation of knowledge accelerates and the stock of knowledge reaches a level that permits and indeed induces drastic transformations in traditional production methods. Thus, quantum jumps in human-capital accumulation have led to the industrial revolution of the nineteenth century and are leading to the information revolution of the second half of this century. This process of accumulation has reached such proportions as to call for a new definition of value reflecting the fact that the main constituting elements of production have changed both in terms of the distribution of output between services and goods and in terms of the constituent elements of services themselves.

In the late eighteenth century it is natural that the physiocrats should have attributed all the sources of value to agriculture and none to manufactures or other activities that were deemed to be habits of superfluous consumption. As industry became the mainstay of the economy, the manufacture of goods appeared to be the essential source of value and, instead of looking to the contribution of land-rent to wealth and welfare, economists turned to analyzing the relative contributions of labor and capital, relegating land to a secondary role. In the second half of the nineteenth century, when industry became predominant to the point of generating overproduction cycles, the focus of attention turned to solvent demand as a source of value, which led to consumer utility being adopted as the main yardstick of value in accordance with the theory developed by Alfred Marshall and John Hicks.

The theory of human capital as the main source of value presented above is not based on a new analytical approach, since it follows broadly the line of reasoning of David Ricardo, but it adapts that approach to the new producing circumstances of the modern world. The recognition or nonrecognition of the new role played by information and knowledge in the world economy will determine the correctness of development and trade policies of nations in the forseeable future. Until now, when the role of technology has been increasingly recognized, an artificial distinction has generally continued to be made between technology, knowledge, and services, whereas in practice the activities related to innovation, communication, and learning (which constitute the basic ingredients of services) are often indistinguishable as to the methods they use and the results they achieve. The theories advanced in this book essentially update the technology concept by broadening its meaning beyond the mere application of techniques for the physical transformation of raw materials and semiprocessed goods and the finishing of final goods to which it has been restricted to this day.

Following further on the tracks of Ricardo, it must be underlined that the emphasis being placed on human capital as a new factor of production and source of value does not, as the illustrations in figures 2–3 and 2–4 suggest, relegate physical capital and labor to some sort of economic museum. Indeed, as we shall see later, the development of human-capital resources impacts considerably on the development of physical capital itself and on the qualification of labor, even menial labor, generally raising the overall level of information and communication possibilities of societies as well as its production potentials or productivity in all fields of human endeavor. Another point that must be stressed (again following Ricardo [1963, section VI, p. 24]) is that the substitution of knowledge for the labor standard of value does not alter the fact that it is not possible to find a product (good or service) which could serve as an invariable standard measure of value or *numéraire*, because a variation in the price of information or knowledge would affect all products in different ways depending on the different combinations of factors (human and physical capital and labor) used in their production, and therefore the *standard* product itself. Only if the price of a product were artificially maintained by government intervention at a fixed level could that product serve as standard of value for all other products. This was the case for gold in the gold exchange standard system of Bretton Woods. It could be the case for university or high school or primary school degrees dispensed by a state (as in national government) education system, although the state also often passes on the changing costs of such education in the form of changes in

Table 2–1. Examples of indicators used to calculate the volume of production of services[1]

Type of activity	Unit of product	Indicators of value of production	Deflator
Hairdressing services	Permanent wave, etc.	Gross turnover at current prices	Price index for haircut, permanent wave, etc.
Medical services	Medical examination, work day in the hospital	Number of visits, of work days, amount of sickness insurance premiums	Price index for medical examinations, work days in the hospital, insurance premiums
Retail trade	—	Sales turnover	Price index for main categories of goods and services sold; consumer price index
	—	Gross profit margin for different categories of goods and services	Price index for different categories of goods and services sold
Banking services	—	Volume of sight and term deposits	Consumer price index; wholesale price index
	—	Number of checks cashed	Consumer price index or wholesale price index
		Net interests received	Index of purchasing power of gross receipts
Insurance	Insurance policy	Amounts insured: premiums paid	Volume index (number of premiums paid, etc.); general price indices (consumer or wholesale)
Air, rail, road, and sea transport	Passenger mile or ton mile	Number of passenger miles or ton miles transported; volume of freight; number of vehicles in circulation; fuel consumption	Index of wages paid. (In most cases the volume of output is calculated directly without reference to the price of the service rendered.)

Communications	Telephone conversation, telegram, letter, parcel	Number of telephone conversations, of telegrams, of letters and of parcels	Consumer price index or wage index
Storage and despatching	—	Volume or value of goods handled	Consumer price index
Public administration	—	Number of employees; number of hours worked	Index of wages paid; consumer price index
Education	—	Number of students or teachers; tuition paid	Wage and salary index, or consumer price index (in most cases the volume of output is calculated directly)
Domestic services	—	Number of employees	Consumer price index; wage index
Financial services, insurance, education, medical services, personal services, administration	—	N.B. In many countries the production of these services as well as others is estimated on the basis either of employment in the sector concerned or of total wages paid, adjusted with a general or specific wage index	

Source: Nusbaumer [1987].

Note: 1. Indications concerning the various methods used are mainly drawn from the following sources: V. R. Fuchs, *The Service Economy;* V. R. Fuchs (ed.), *Production and Productivity in the Service Industries;* Anthony D. Smith, *The Measurement and Interpretation of Service Output Changes;* Irving Leveson, *Productivity in Services, Issues for Analysis;* Derek W. Blades, Derek D. Johnston, and Witold Marezewski *Service Activities in Developing Countries,* OECD, 1974. Examples in the table only give a very small sample of the variety of indicators used by national and international statistical services.

tuition, fees, or income taxes. In practice educational achievements have been used as a standard of value for services activities such as engineering, law practice, medical services, accountancy, etc., because the prices of the corresponding diplomas either change only in small proportions and infrequently or represent such a small proportion of total income tax as to be perceived as invariable by the average tax-payer. If that is so, the only outstanding problem is to break down the continuous stream of acquisition of knowledge into conventional units like bars of gold of one kilo apiece, and to measure the *relative* values of all goods and services in such units.[12]

The difficulty of finding conventional units to evaluate the production of services is, however, a very serious one. The units of measurement currently used for various service activities do not have very much in common. An example of such units is shown in table 2–1.[13] None of the units in fact refers to a common substantive content of the services being measured. This is not surprising because the aim of statisticians in compiling units of services rendered is to not rank the various services in accordance with given valuation criteria, but to add them up in order to arrive at totals that can themselves be added up to totals of goods production. In the same way, they add up automobiles, apples, and pears to arrive at the total volume of output in a given economy or in the world economy. But, at least in economic theory, there is an implicit understanding that the totals reached represent either quantity (in the Ricardian sense) of labor incorporated in goods and services produced in the economy, or amounts of utility created by those goods and services (in the Marshallian sense).

There does not exist at present a body of economic theory that permits the referral of production totals to a concept of value which is specificially adapted to the predominant role that services have acquired in modern economies. In particular, no economist has yet attempted to evaluate the production of goods in terms of their knowledge-content, nor to rank them, for purposes of estimating the *real* value-added in an economy, on the basis of this criterion. Yet, in modern economies, not only do services account for the greater part of total value created and the greater part of employment but they also account for the greater part of the value of goods placed on the market. When services are supplied from within goods-producing enterprises (for example, engineers, accountants, advertisers, marketing specialists, etc.), they do not appear as separate activities in national accounts, and the problem of their valuation does not arise. On the other hand, when services are supplied by independent enterprises and sold either to other enterprises that are producing goods or services or directly to final consumers, the value added in these activities cannot be evaluated unless gross output and output costs can also be evaluated separately. Because of the lack of statistical conventions to evaluate in a consistent manner the gross output of various service activities, and because of the impossibility in most cases of counting units of services rendered, independent estimates of gross outputs are not available, and statisticians replace such estimates by estimates of the turnover of independent service enterprises or of the income of individual service providers such as doctors. This does not, however, supplant information on the unit price of services nor, therefore, on the amount of real value added in the production process per unit of output. In fact, it can be said that such statistical methods provide information on the sum total of service activities (total value-added calculated as a difference between turnover and total cost) without knowing what these totals comprise.

The International Dimension

In addition to playing a major role in national economies at all levels of economic development, but particularly in modern economies for reasons that will be discussed later, services play an increasingly important role in economic relations among nations. Not only do services account for a growing share of international trade but in addition, they are delivered in ever greater amounts through foreign investment or through other forms of presence of nationals of one country on the territory of another country. To speak of services in the international economy is to speak of the exercise of service activities in the context of the growth of global economic interdependence.

Interdependence is a catch-word for all forms of economic interchange taking place through buying and selling of goods and services across borders and through dirrect production by individuals or enterprises of one nation on the territory of another nation. This concept is apprehended by looking at the degree of self-sufficiency or its converse, the degree of dependency on foreign supplies and on foreign markets, of national economies. There are, of course, various factors that affect the significance of this indicator for different countries, depending on the size of their market, of their population, and their per capita income. Size is particularly important for certain services such as transport and telecommunication services (population determines the number of individual consumers in the market). In addition, the number of individuals to whom market information (and related services) must be delivered, and individual income determine the degree of solvency of the average consumer in the market. Another important factor influencing the degree of integration of a given economy in the world economy is the level of technological achievement of that individual economy. The reach of producers and distributors of goods and services will be considerably broadened if they have at their disposal modern means of transportation of materials, finished products, information, and knowledge. Tables 2–2 and 2–3 illustrate the evolution of the global market for goods and services during the last few years and the position of the main economies of the world in this respect. The raw data on imports and exports of goods and services and investment[14] should normally be adjusted for size of population, income per head, and technological achievement. But given the paucity of statistics, this cannot be done consistently for enough countries to make meaningful comparisons available. Nevertheless, two main findings emerge from the data available: (1) the degree of interdependence of major trading economies has increased rapidly over the period for both goods and services, although in the case of services the trend is apparently much less marked; and (2) the disparity between the degree of interdependence of major economies and economies at a lower level of development is large and increasing.

In the case of services, it should be kept in mind that the measure of interdependence based on data for cross-border trade in services and for direct investment in service activities gives an incomplete picture of

Table 2–2. Exports and imports of services and direct investment, world, main country groupings, and major countries (billions of SDR's)

Region or country	Year	Services[1]		Investments	
		Exports	Imports	Outward	Inward
World	1978	446	486	29	27
	1984	855	979	33	51
Industrial countries	1978	351	334	28	18
	1984	650	654	32	36
Developing countries	1978	95	152	1	8
	1984	205	325	—	15
United States	1978	76	60	13	6
	1984	166	157	4	22
France	1978	44	32	2	2
	1984	70	63	2	2
Germany, Fed. Rep.	1978	39	53	3	1
	1984	59	75	3	1
United Kingdom	1978	38	30	4	2
	1984	60	53	4	3

Japan	1978	22	17	2	—
	1984	54	69	6	—
Belgium—Luxembourg	1978	18	17	—	1
	1984	35	33	—	—
Italy	1978	21	15	—	—
	1984	39	32	2	1
Netherlands	1978	21	21	2	1
	1984	33	32	3	1
Spain	1978	12	5	—	1
	1984	25	12	—	2
Switzerland	1978	11	6	n.a.	n.a.
	1983	21	14	n.a.	n.a.
Saudi Arabia	1978	8	21	—	1
	1984	17	50²	—	5
Korea, Rep. of	1978	5	4	—	—
	1984	11	11	—	—
Singapore	1978	5	3	—	1
	1984	14	8	—	1
Mexico	1978	7	8	—	1
	1984	12	21	—	—
Brazil	1978	3	8	—	2
	1984	5	18	—	2
India	1978	3	3	—	—
	1982	4	6	—	—
Greece	1978	4	1	—	—
	1984	4	3	—	—
Yugoslavia	1978	7	5	—	—
	1983	5	7	—	—
Egypt	1978	2	2	—	—
	1983	5	5	—	1
Kuwait	1978	3	3	—	—
	1984	8	8	—	—
Chile	1978	1	1	—	—
	1984	1	4	—	—
Venezuela	1978	2	6	—	—
	1984	3	8	—	—
Panama	1978	1	1	—	—
	1984	6	5	—	—

Source: IMF. 1985. *Balance-of-Payments Statistics Yearbook, Part 2*, Vol. 36. Washington, D.C.: IMF.

Notes:

1. Defined as the sum of Shipment, Other Transportation, Travel, and Other Goods, Services, and Income.

2. Based on partial data.

— = significantly less than 1 billion SDR's.

Table 2–3. International transactions as a share of GDP,[1] world, main country groupings, and major countries (percentages)

Region or country	Year	Merchandise (exports)	Services (exports)	Investment (outward)
World[2]	1978	11.0	5.2	0.3
	1984	15.8	8.0	0.3
Industrial countries	1978	10.0	5.3	0.4
	1984	14.1	8.0	0.4
Developing countries	1978	14.7	5.1	—
	1984	21.2	8.1	—
United States	1978	6.9	4.6	0.8
	1984	5.8	4.5	0.1
France	1978	16.5	12.1	0.5
	1984	18.1	14.1	0.4
Germany, Fed. Rep. of	1978	22.4	7.9	0.6
	1984	25.5	9.4	0.3
United Kingdom	1978	17.6	12.4	1.3
	1984	21.0	13.8	0.9
Japan	1978	10.3	3.0	0.3
	1984	12.8	4.2	0.5
Belgium-Luxembourg[3]	1978	41.1	24.7	—
	1984	56.0	43.8	—
Italy	1978	21.9	10.4	—
	1984	20.0	11.0	0.6
Netherlands	1978	34.3	20.0	1.9
	1984	43.1	24.3	2.2
Spain	1978	10.0	10.7	—
	1984	43.1	24.3	
Switzerland	1978	29.2	16.9	—
	1983	26.0	22.8	—
Saudi Arabia	1978	52.7	14.3	n.a.
	1984	32.9	15.3	n.a.
Korea, Rep. of	1978	27.3	13.5	—
	1984	30.2	12.9	—
Singapore	1978	128.3	83.3	—
	1984	121.1	77.8	—
Mexico	1978	6.3	8.9	—
	1984	13.4	6.9	—
Brazil	1978	6.3	1.9	—
	1984	13.8	2.6	—
India	1978	5.7	3.3	—
	1982	6.2	3.0	—
Greece	1978	9.6	16.0	—
	1984	13.9	12.9	—

Yugoslavia	1978	12.4	18.9	—
	1983	24.5	13.2	—
Egypt	1978	7.9	10.5	—
	1983	12.5	17.9	—
Kuwait	1978	68.3	25.0	—
	1984	53.6	36.4	—
Chile	1978	18.2	9.1	—
	1984	18.0	5.0	—
Venezuela	1978	23.5	6.5	—
	1984	32.3	6.3	—
Panama	1978	10.0	50.0	—
	1984	32.0	120.0	—

Sources:
  IMF. 1985. Balance-of-Payments Statistics Yearbook, Parts 1 and 2, Vol. 36. Washington, D.C.: IMF.
  World Bank, 1986. *World Development Report 1986*. Washington, D.C.: IBRD.
  United Nations, 1984. *Statistical Yearbook, 1982*. New York: United Nations.
Notes:
  1. In some cases, GDP data estimated on the basis of benchmark figures and average annual growth rates in intervening years.
  2. Estimates based on World Bank, table A.3.
  3. Based on GDP for Belgium only.

economic integration because, as has been pointed out above, services are an integral part of the goods-production process. Therefore, the change in the service content of goods over time must be taken into account to measure the contribution of services to global interdependence. This can be done by looking at the value/weight ratio of traded goods. This ratio increases as the scientific and technological content of goods rises, since these components add value, but neither bulk nor weight, to the goods. Unfortunately, the only readily available data on value/weight ratio of goods entering international trade are unit value indexes, and these are influenced by too many factors (including erratic exchange rate fluctuations) to be reliable indicators of the phenomenon.[15]

Not only do services add value (but neither bulk nor weight) to international trade but they need *not* be exchanged across borders to be actually "traded," unless one limits the definition of trade to the simple transport of a valuable product between a point located inside one territory and a point located inside another territory. Traditionally, trade implies a change of ownership between the supplier resident in one nation and the buyer or consumer resident in another. In national accounting, trade also implies a change of ownership between the owner of a product and the buyer of it within the same territory, but this is not a common usage of the term when applied to transactions between residents of different countries (or customs territories), because economists dealing with international trade have usually assumed that goods are the normal object of exchange between different countries. However, in order to deal with exchanges in services or, expressed differently, international transactions of services, it is necessary to adapt the definition of "trade" to the realities of exchanges of invisible products and of transfers of knowledge between economic units. Such transfers of knowledge, being intangible in character, may be done over long distances, or only with the simultaneous presence of the transferer and the transferee, depending on the mode of transmission used. In general, transfers of knowledge require an understanding not only of the technical specifications of the knowledge being transferred but also of the characteristics of the recipients or the context within which the transferred knowledge is received and assimilated. This is why a presence in the market where knowledge intensive services are sold is often a sine qua non condition for "international trade" to take place. Therefore, given this technical aspect of international transactions in services, it is artificial to describe the ratio of services trade to services output in terms of the volume or value of services that cross international borders. The traditional separation between traded and nontraded goods in international trade theory needs to be adjusted to a situation where what is "nontraded" can nevertheless be the object of fierce international competition between producers.[16]

In order to circumscribe the notion of trade in services, it is also not sufficient to refer to exchanges of service products since such products are not the only source of creation of value from services activities that are also productive of value through certain functions performed by services in the economy. The distinction between service products and service functions lies in the lack of comparability between functions as compared to that of products. Service functions are effects of service activities on particular economic phenomena that differ from one service act to another and consequently cannot be standardized as service products can (however difficult such standardization may be in many circumstances). In addition to more or less standardized service products which can be exchanged in international trade, one of the most dynamic forces of international transactions in services is the role of services as functions in adjusting to economic change in the recipient country and in transforming the structure of linkages between various production and distribution channels on the one hand, and in creating networks of relationships between producers and consumers or users which play a dynamic role in the transfer of technology and in the elaboration of new adjustment processes in national economies, on the other. In addition, services perform linkage functions between different economies at different stages of development by establishing communication channels between individual economic agents whose activities are unrelated to the particular stage of development of the countries in which they operate.

There are several parameters involved in identifying particular service functions, which bring into play both the supplier and the recipient, user or consumer, of the service as well as the intensity of the servicing activity and the more or less durable character of the service provided. An example of such functions is the building of confidence among foreign exchange dealers, communicating worldwide through the telephone system, and handling millions of dollars of transactions on the basis of simple oral commitments. Another example is the establishment of personal relationships between airplane navigators and control-tower operators in numerous airports of the world, which provides a fundamental and essential element of flight safety on all major air routes. Functions are externalities which transcend pure market relationships and confer on the beneficiary economies a sprinkling of collective utility bearing no precise quantitative relation to the input of production factors entering the constitution of the function-creating service.

The Link with National Economic Progress

International economic interdependence, therefore, is made up not only of interchanges of goods and service products but also of functional linkages between economies that become interdependent because they gradually cease to be able to operate autonomously, in the sense of generating value, without the *direct* contribution of economic agents of foreign origin. The leverage provided by service functions internationally permit interdependent economies to develop concurrently, whereas those that remain outside the mainstream of global interchange condemn themselves to stagnation or retardation. The relationship between service functions and economic growth is often diffused and difficult to perceive. But in the same way that everybody is able to understand that a radio or a television set provides not only sound and image but also a special relationship with the culture they convey, it should not be difficult to understand that a banking service conveys economic and even moral criteria through the lending conditions and service requirements it imposes on borrowers.

Therefore, in order to understand the role of services in economic development, and in particular the special place of so-called "nontraded" *goods* in national economies, it is necessary to invoke the role of services in defining the context in which production processes take place and, in particular, in which economic growth reaches sustainable levels. A good starting point is to look at the importance of generally ill-defined services such as health and education in economic development. Whereas some economists would argue that from the point of view of efficiency of re-source use, the economy of a country like Bangladesh is better served by producing jute for export and importing rice than concentrating on pro-ducing rice and educating its work force, the introduction of the services dimension in the development process tips the balance in favor of the reverse solution. The primary function of development planners should be to make the best possible use of the most abundant economic resource of the nation, namely population. This does not necessarily involve using labor in the available numbers and skill levels to produce the goods or services which currently yield the highest rate of return. It may, on the contrary, involve making every effort to use the available work force to produce the wherewithal to increase the strength and ability to learn of that same work force, i.e., to produce rice rather than jute, taking into account the fact that the vagueries of power politics make it much less than certain that the additional real output per unit of input which can currently be

Figure 2–6. Change in the level of education of the Finnish work force, 1960–1995.

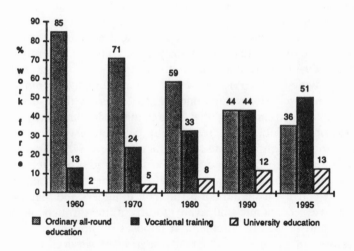

Source: The Finnish Business Challenge, Union Bank of Finland, Ltd; Helsinki, 1986

obtained in the form of jute will be used to purchase rice rather than guns.

Moreover, other considerations argue in favor of developing the skill capacities of the population, in view of the overall impact of knowledge-intensive work on production, compared to the simple addition of unskilled units of primary labor. The fact of the matter, as stated elsewhere, is that knowledge and the quest for knowledge have a dynamic of their own which can only be generated by establishing a base from which technology can be readily assimilated and innovative capacities enhanced. Economists often refer to a country's capacity to "absorb" new foreign investments without, however, relating such absorption capacity as much to the quality of complementary factors (human capital) as to the availability of primary labor, local finance, and infrastructure in the country concerned. This view of the world is gradually changing as it is increasingly realized that economic success stories such as those of Japan and Finland are essentially based on what Jotuni [1986] calls "the power of education." Figure 2–6, drawn from Jotuni's article, shows a dramatic change in the level of education of the work force during the last 20-year period of high and steady growth.

Notes

1. In chapters 3 and 4 more detailed distinctions will be made along these lines as a basis for classifying services as well as economic activities involving both services and goods.

2. The problem arises as a result of changes over time in the composition of groups of commodities for which volume, price, or value indexes are calculated, and from changes in the quality of individual items in any given commodity group. For price indices, the three forms in current use are Laspeyres, Paasche, and Fischer's "ideal" index. For an explanation of related methodologies, see Spiegel [1961 and later editions]. Other aspects of quality measurement, related to the theory of standards, are dealt with in Lecraw [1984] and De Vany and Saving [1983]. Quality of output is also a problem in macroeconomic theory, where various adjustments, based on scientific- and skill-content (or technology-content) of work are entered into regression equations, or in the analysis of error terms, to take changes in it into account [see Denison, 1967, 1974; Kuznets, 1960].

3. "The value of a commodity, or the quantity of any other commodity for which it will exchange, depends on the relative quantity of labour which is necessary for its production, and not on the greater or lesser compensation which is paid for that labour" [Ricardo, 1963].

4. Relevant data are found in the World Bank's annual World Development Report and in periodic reports on the economic situation of individual member countries (not generally available to the public). Seminal articles by Becker, Mincer, and others were published in an October 1962 supplement of the Journal of Political Economy entitled "Investment in Human Beings,"—how a collection piece and a tribute to the far-sightedness and modesty of a group of economists who spoke of services before everyone else, and never claimed to have opened the new era of "post-industrial economics."

5. For a categorization along these lines, see J. Nusbaumer [1987].

6. Dorothy Riddle [1986] gives an impassionate account of the role of services in development, particularly in chapters 2 and 3 of her book, which substantiates this intuition.

7. See Leamer [1984] for the theory underlying this graphic presentation.

8. Splintering and disembodiment are two aspects of a process wherein "goods splinter from services and services, in turn, from goods. . ., and the disembodiment of services splintering into goods extends alternatively to services becoming, not goods, but *long-distance services*" [Bhagwati, 1986].

9. Intensive research is underway in this area, however, particularly in the United States and Japan. (See Rothman [1986] and the description of the work of ICOT in chapter 3.)

10. For a systematic analysis of substitution between services and goods and its effects on employment, which follows the same line of reasoning as Bhagwati's, see Gershuny [1985] and Gershuny and Miles [1983].

11. "Thus then is the public benefited by machinery: these mute agents are always the produce of much less labour than that which they displace, even when they are of the same money value" [Ricardo, 1963, p. 23].

12. It should be stressed, as Ricardo did, that it is not relevant to know at what exact price different goods or services sell in the market, but rather in what proportions they will be exchanged: "It is of no importance to the truth of this doctrine whether one of these commodities sells for £1,100 and the other for £2,200, or one for £1,500 and the other for £3,000; into that question I do not at present enquire; I affirm only that their relative values will be governed by the comparative quantities of labour bestowed on their production" [1963, p. 26].

13. Reproduced from J. Nusbaumer [1986].

14. Available data on investment flows are scanty, and it is particularly difficult to distinguish between investment in goods and in services production. The data in the table should therefore be read with this caveat in mind.

15. An approximation of real changes in the value/weight ratio of goods traded may be obtained for some countries and specific classes of goods, with extensive statistical adjustments based on often imprecise data. This would not, in any event, suffice to give a broad view of the phenomenon described in the text, the proof of whose existence must therefore continue to rely on intuitive reasoning until the necessary data for empirical analysis become available.

16. Corden [1971] describes nontraded goods (which "would normally include services, distribution, building, and often parts of the production of power") as those "the price of which are not determined in the world market," but he adds that "the line between traded and non-traded goods is not always a clear one since world market conditions certainly *influence* the prices of non-traded goods. . ." [pp. 71–72]. The UNCTAD secretariat [1985] takes a more simplistic view of the question: by pointing out that only about 8% world services output is traded in the traditional sense of the term, it argues that it is more relevant to look at services in a national economic development perspective than as a trade issue. This appears to be deliberately ignoring the special characteristics of trade in services in order to artifically minimize their importance in international economic relations.

3 TRADE CLASSIFICATIONS AND TRADE DETERMINANTS

In textbooks on the theory of international trade, services are usually treated as "nontraded" or "nontradeable goods,"[1] although they are not goods at all, and this designation merely reveals the obsession with material production which has pervaded all economic analysis to this day. In discussing services as a special kind of product, therefore, the first question to ask is whether services are fundamentally different from goods, and if so, how. Only if common characteristics of services can be found which do not pertain to goods, is it possible to attempt a definition which reflects their specificity, and a classification according to the various ways in which they are produced and exchanged. It is a truism to say that services are intangible or nonmaterial, but clearly this affects the way in which their production is measured as well as the way in which services, once produced, are sold to users or consumers. Therefore, one essential common characteristic of all services is that they can be identified in terms of many parameters, except those which usually are used to identify goods, namely weight, size, density, fluidity, etc. Because one cannot put one's finger on a service, they have often been referred to as invisibles, although this designation may be confusing due to the fact that a service, when considered as the product of a specific economic activity, is often

39

indistinguishable from the service provider and he or she, at least, is visible.

Defining and Classifying Services

Paradoxically, the important thing about defining services is perhaps not to distinguish them from goods, but to see what economic functions they perform which may or may not be similar to the economic functions performed by goods. For example, it is quite conceivable that a concert would be a more effective means of putting someone to sleep than a sleeping pill, and in this case both the service and the good perform exactly the same function though by different means. An objection to this example might be that the function of a concert is not to put the listener to sleep, whereas the function of the sleeping pill is. However, goods which have a particular usefulness may also sometimes be used for purposes other than those for which they were manufactured. For example, an automobile may be considered as an art object, or a saw used as a musical instrument. These are very simple examples, taken from the economic past of modern societies, which is now very far removed from day-to-day reality. If one looks at the present content of production, one sees that the frontier between services and goods tends to become increasingly blurred as manufactured products contain more and more services in the form of applied human capital and require more and more services to be used in the form of complementary software or staff training, maintenance, repairs,[2] etc. One author has drawn the logical conclusion from this increasing integration of services and material products by referring to "compacks," or complex packages of goods and services, as being the typical outcome of modern production processes. Another way to approach this increasing intermingling between material and nonmaterial production is to speak of international trade as increasingly becoming trade in research and development (R&D) rather than trade in various kinds of commodities, reflecting the fact that an increasing proportion of the value added of traded goods consists of service products incorporated or embodied in those goods.

Taking the preceding observations into account, there are basically two ways in which a classification of services can be attempted: first, they can be classified according to the various types of functions they perform in the economy, i.e., financial function, trade function, transport function, etc. Second, they can be classified according to the various types of specialized knowledge that enter into their production, i.e., law, economics, medicine, etc. Yet another possible way of classifying services would be by the type of utility they provide: personal comfort, safety, movement, etc. In effect, however, this third classification refers to a subset of the functional classification, since basically all the elements of it fall into the subcategory of consumption function.

A more general way of classifying services is to rank them according to their *degree of processing*, just like goods are ranked in the United Nations Standard International Trade Classification (SITC), that is, irrespective of their particular functions or of the specialized knowledge they contain. Thus, like in the SITC, services that contain a greater amount of knowledge (general and specialized, including work experience and natural ability to do things) would be considered as being more highly "processed" than services that can be easily performed by economic agents with a comparatively low level of skills. In this case, the analogy with goods would be complete, in the sense that the classification of goods based on their degree or stage of processing relates to their mode of supply rather than to their mode of consumption. The factors used in their production, including the human-capital factor which is also used in the production of various services, determine the particular rank they occupy in the classification by degree of processing. In such a scheme, the particular use of services would be largely irrelevant since services, like goods, can easily be diverted from their traditional or intended use. For example, just like saws can be used to make music, music in stables can be used to stimulate the milk production of cows, and just like art books can be used to light a fire, soldiers can be used for pageantry.

The functional approach to the classification of services is nevertheless the one most frequently resorted to.[3] At first hand it may seem easy to implement, but it is more complicated in theory than in practice. In theory, all services perform one essential generic function in the economy, namely what some have called the "interlinkage" function, i.e., that of bringing together producers and consumers of goods and also of generating the network of interrelationships that constitutes what is commonly known as "the market" for both goods and services consumed for their own sake. On the other hand, there are various kinds of functions of services, such as the financial intermediation, the entertainment, the risk-covering, etc., functions which correspond to very specialized types of service activities and which do not appear to have very much in common. It is in relation to these functions that it is necessary to refer to various categories of specialized knowledge as indicators, but this begs the question of what makes services different from one another—the specialized knowledge they contain or the functions themselves.

In practice, providers of highly processed services embody a high share of fungible, generalized knowledge and a relatively small share of specialized, not easily transferable knowledge. Thus, lawyers usually understand a fair amount of economics, economists a fair amount of law, doctors a fair amount of statistics, etc., whereas a skilled machine tool operator is less likely to hold his own in an academic debate on the economic and social conditions of development with the lawyer, the economist, or the doctor. Thus distinctions between highly processed services based on contained specialized knowledge may lead to somewhat artificial classifications of activities, reflecting particular organizations of group interests rather than real functional difference. For example, in certain countries the category of financial services covers both banking and insurance, whereas in others these are quite separate; in still other countries the arts include handicraft production, whereas in others these two activities are considered as totally unrelated. Within and between these different categories, however delimited, only the degree of processing as defined above provides a common yardstick.

Consistently with the degree of processing approach, services can be categorized according to the role they play in production processes. In this regard, the classical distinction between primary, intermediate, and final products is fully relevant. Primary services are those that perform elementary linkage functions without particular reference to the scope or purpose of the activity they perform. All primary, unskilled labor services fall into this category. There is essentially no difference between the service of a bank porter or of a messenger boy carrying groceries between the shop and the entrance hall of a residence and from the entrance hall to the apartment of a tenant, and the service of a yard hand carrying a heap of wood from one side of a yard to another. Primary services are therefore synonymous with unskilled primary labor in any type of occupation, which can easily be shifted from one type of occupation to another. Indeed, primary services do not really belong to the category of services conceived as products of a specific activity or group of activities and are more akin to the traditional simple definition of "work" which subtends the theory of labor input of Ricardo, Marx, and other economists of the first half of the nineteenth century. In a sense, therefore, and certainly in the sense of distinguishing between service activities and service products, and goods-producing activities and goods as products, primary services do not belong to the category of services at all.

Intermediate services, on the other hand, are service products made up of the three elementary production factors entering into the making of such products, namely human capital, labor, and physical capital, in contradistinction to primary services which are made up essentially of labor without any adjunction of human capital (or so little) and physical capital (or so little). Intermediate services are the products of often complex production activities involving the collection and application of data and the elementary organization and structuring of these data into what is commonly known as information.

The information produced in the form of intermediate service products is the true raw material of final service products, which involve a more or less elaborate degree of processing or manipulation of information designed to adapt the raw database to the requirements of specific functions performed by the service providers. Therefore, to recapitulate, the distinction between primary, intermediate, and final services proceeds along the same lines of reasoning as the equivalent distinction made for goods, with a difference that when it is applied to service products, the categories are effectively reduced to the two latter ones, due to the fact that primary service products are synonymous with primary factor inputs in all production activities.

This difference is essentially a question of definition or convention, since in the realm of goods the distinction between primary and intermediate commodities is often arbitrary because so-called raw materials already involve a considerable degree of processing of basic natural resources extracted from the crust of the earth or cultivated or bred on its surface. For example, the really raw material in the case of copper mining is copper ore which contains a limited and variable percentage of copper per ton; similarly, the raw material called wheat has already undergone a considerable amount of processing before it is turned into grain. The real difference between services and goods regarding the classification of primary products is, however, that the physical nature of goods permits and even sometimes makes it necessary to identify linear processes of production based on the physical characteristics of the starting materials, whereas in the case of services there are no physical characteristics on which to base the definition of linear production processes; therefore, all relatively unsophisticated service acts are fungible in terms of their use to different economic ends. The point may be further elaborated by stating that, whereas nature furnishes different physical goods having specific shapes and chemical compositions, the particular chemistry that underlies various service acts resides not in the act itself but in the agent performing the act. Therefore, the only way to define a primary service product is to do so in terms of the knowledge-content of the act which gives rise to the product; hence a primary service product corresponds to a primary service act, i.e., unskilled and of unlimited application in an unlimited set of production activities. For example, pulling a string can be a service act if the string activates a bell in a court house, and it is an act of physical production if the string activates a sledge hammer in a steel factory.

The next logical step is to rank services according to the classification criterion suggestion above, namely by knowledge-content. This step is necessary to take in order to provide a consistent basis for analyzing international transborder transactions in services or to estimate or impute (in the absence of hard data) value-added in different service activities traditionally evaluated in terms of the factor input entering into them. No such classification can be arrived at without a considerable amount of theoretical and statistical research and, especially, without a large degree of international cooperation among economists, statisticians, and technicians, aimed at defining generally acceptable conventions constituting a common language among analysts and policy-makers. The development of conventions of this sort has taken years for the classification of goods entering international trade and for the classification of industries.[4]

All that can be done at this stage, therefore, is to suggest broad categories or classes of services in different fields of activities which more or less represent similar degrees of processing in terms of their knowledge-content. For this purpose, knowledge-content includes practical work experience and is not necessarily related to formal degrees of education. In any case, it is well known that educational systems differ from country to country, and that one of the most difficult areas of international cooperation is the equivalence of diplomas and other forms of professional qualification. Taking this into account, if educational systems are used as a basis for the classification of various stages of processing of services, the simplest approach, at least initially, consists in classifying services, where relevant, according to various levels of education reached by the service performers in any given educational system, without attempting a comparison among systems in terms of their educational content. One difficulty with classifying services in accordance with the level of education of the performers is that such a classification is de facto based on the assumed quality of the service provider and does not give a clear indication of the quality of the service provided. This difficulty seems unavoidable in all cases where there is total coincidence between provision of the service and its consumption, that is, where the performance of the service provider is indistinguishable in practice from the value of the service as defined by the quality of the agent producing it. It is impossible to escape from this ambiguity, particularly in the case of embodied services which contain little or no storeable information. In the case of goods, distinctions can always be made on the basis of the market value of the physical material from which similar goods are made. For example, a cigarette lighter made of ordinary steel is less valuable than the same lighter made of platinum because of the higher market value of the latter. By contrast, the artistic value of Dante's *Divine Comedy* is no less if it is printed on rough newsprint than on glossy white paper. Table 3-1 shows a rough classification by degree of processing which could be used for purposes of international recording of service transactions or for the classification of service activities in a national context. Only broadly defined categories of services are used since, as indicated above, considerable discussions among economists and statisticians will be necessary to arrive at precise conventions, and there is therefore no need at this stage to elaborate further.

Services in Goods

Having just attempted a classification of services by degree of processing, it is appropriate to dwell further on the relationship between services and goods and the impact of this relationship on international economic interchange, and in particular on the phenomenon of globalization of markets which is characteristic of modern international economic relations, or of what is more often referred to as economic interdependence. At the outset, it should be recalled that the concept of interdependenc has not been used in a way that takes fully into account the functional integration of different national economies, but rather has been based on the simple alignment of statistics on exports and imports of goods in relation to

Table 3-1. A tentative and illustrative ranking of services by degree of "processing," or knowledge-content, in ascending order

1. Babysitters; furniture removers.
2. Street and house cleaners.
3. Porters, guards.
4. Delivery, including mail, service operators.
5. Launderers, maids, chauffeurs, including small-scale transport operators.
6. Janitors; receptionists.
7. Private household employees, general purpose.
8. Escort service employees.
9. Cooks, gardeners, nurses.
10. Barbers, hairdressers, manicures.
11. Dry cleaning, dying and pressing service operators.
12. Street vendors.

Table 3–1.   (cont'd)

---

13. Waiters, sales attendants; general office staff.
14. Tourist guides.
15. Sports instructors; firemen; policemen.
16. Small-scale retailers and consumer equipment renters; caterers; restaurant/ hotel operators; franchisees.
17. Telephone and telegraph operators.
18. Radio communication technical operators.
19. Typists, stenographers; bank tellers; customs officers; rank military personnel.
20. Commission agents; auctioneers.
21. Office secretaries.
22. Storage and warehouse managers; wholesale, chain-store, and supermarket operators.
23. Travel agents; tourist agency operators; shippers and forwarders.
24. Dealers and jobbers, goods and financial assets; exchange dealers.
25. Merchanters, brokers; security brokers, real estate agents.
26. Land surveyors.
27. Computer operators and programmers; draftsmen; natural resource prospectors.
28. Flight controllers; flight navigators; ship pilots.
29. Insurance, bill collectors; adjustors.
30. Advertisers, copywriters; journalists; public relations specialists.
31. Security analysts; marketing specialists; actuaries, valuators, asseyors.
32. Insurance appraisers.
33. Skippers, aerial photographers, railway switching operators, printers.
34. Interpreters; translators; bookkeepers; statistical clerks.
35. Elementary school teachers; welfare workers; community service workers.
36. Accountants; auditors; notaries; patent attorneys.
37. Secondary school teachers; technical school instructors; detectives; priests.
38. Industrial designers; chartists.
39. Laboratory assistants; landscape architects; stylists; librarians.
40. Fashion designers; ballet teachers; film producers.
41. Military officers; university instructors; medical assistants; ship captains.
42. Solicitors; orchestra musicians.
43. Chartered accountants; administrators; managers; museum curators.
44. Engineers; university professors; lawyers; doctors; financial counselors; architects.
45. Scientific researchers.
46. Composers, painters, sculptors.

Note: Many of the job descriptions in the table appear in the Index to ISIC [United Nations, 1971]. In many instances the ranking of knowledge-content is, of necessity, based on subjective judgments. However, with more detailed information on individual activities and a basic set of conventional criteria, it should be clear that a reliable classification could be arrived at.

national production or on simple comparisons between total world exports of and total world production of goods. The dimension of economic integration introduced by the increasing intermingling of services and goods in production processes is much greater, as are the new prospects which this intermingling opens both for economic development and for social change.

Naturally, interdependence in goods-production processes is itself a factor of development and progress in the sense that the linkages established between physical production of one kind in one country and physical production of another kind in another country give rise to inter-changes between industrial, mining, and agricultural technology, which in themselves are carriers of knowledge and work experience, reciprocally raising the level of economic performance based on improved under-standings of transformation methods and marketing techniques. Goods traded between one country and another are thus natural carriers of knowledge and work experience.

However, the greater the proportion of the total value of the goods consisting of such knowledge and work experience compared to the materials of which the goods are made, the more trade is oriented toward the exchange of scientific, technological, and cultural values. The ability of human beings to communicate through such values is much greater than their ability to communicate through common tastes for simple material goods. Tastes for such goods may be constrained by set consumption patterns based on habit or tradition, both of which determine the appropriate shape, color, design, or sheer technical compatibility of the goods with the existing complex set of "keys" to consumer utility dictated by the existing cultural environment. For example, supermarket chains dis-tributing standardized products at fixed prices may conflict, at least in the initial stages of modernization of the distribution system, with traditional product-to-product quality comparisons and price-bargaining habits which constitute both a source of consumer insurance of getting value for money and a particular form of social relationship which is part of the enjoyment of living. Without venturing too far into the theory of consumer choice, it is suggested that very R&D-intensive consumer goods impose themselves more easily on remote and very culturally different consumers by the very fact that they supersede and overtake elementary consumer reactions based on visible physical characteristics of the goods. For example, a clock that simultaneously gives local time and time in another world location expands the consumer's world vision of time and constitutes an attraction in itself, as a result of the information and potential communication channel it provides.

The difficulty in comparing trade in services with trade in services embodied in goods is to disentangle one's reasoning patterns from traditional approaches which relate conditions of production to one another in the relatively rigid framework of comparative advantage analysis. True, the theory of international trade has evolved over the years to include more and more of the elements that make up the essential ingredients of modern production, namely technology, knowledge, and invention or innovation. However, economists still hark back to the classical factor-endowment analysis and the temptation is great to fit new production ingredients such as knowledge, work experience, technology, science, etc., and even art, into natural endowment patterns. Thus, in analyzing the economics of services, economists have tried to arrange various features of new processing methods, including human talent, into patterns of factor endowment very similar to those on which Ricardian theory was based.[5]

In this book, the approach to the description of production factors entering into services production has begun with a reference to Ricardian value theory. However, it is one thing to try and analyze the essential components of the value of services in terms of labor, physical capital, and human capital elements, and it is another to try to associate the availability of human capital with natural factor endowments, as if human beings were naturally more intelligent and cultivated in one part of the world than in another. Such a criticism could already be lodged against the theory of capital/labor endowments, since the accumulation of capital is not necessarily a phenomenon limited to particular parts of the world. It is, rather, the utilization of accumulated capital which has been associated with particular economic systems and therefore has appeared to be geographically influenced, hence described as a "natural" endowment. Capital has nonetheless been accumulated in all parts of the world for a long time; the fact that it has been used more for production than for pure future consumption (in the form of hoarding of gold or precious stones or land, or having slave or semislave labor) is due more to the dynamics of competitive behavior than the pure fact of having or not having accumulated wealth. The same can be said of knowledge and work experience, where, in given socioeconomic or sociopolitical circumstances, the hoarding of knowledge and work ability has been used to build cathedrals and kingly palaces rather than to produce shoes, textiles, or semiconductors. In a certain sense, therefore, the definition of economics given by G. Stigler [1962] should be expanded to include the motivations for economic activity since what truly determines the nature of economic life of a given society, and its success in producing more, is not only its ability to organize available physical and intellectual resources but also its motivation in using such resources.

Since we are concentrating here on international trade relations, there is a parallel distinction to be drawn between an essentially mercantilist approach to trade, which still pervades much of trading relations, and a more efficiency-minded approach that sees trade as a source of economic efficiency and growth. Individual producers or collective groups of individuals (nations) may strive to maximize their net returns from sales with a view to acquiring the means of buying more goods from abroad; others may aim to acquire in foreign markets the financial and technical means of developing their own processing and inventive capacities at home, with a view to being in a better position to fulfill their own needs rather than simply buying ready-made goods and services abroad. This second more dynamic approach to international trade has a particularly strong leverage effect on the globalization of service markets because it is the spreading of inventive ways of doing things and diversified ways of applying acquired knowledge that provides the developer and owner of the basic human capital with the means of making his discoveries and organizational talents profitable, rather than the simple selling of products for which the terms of trade happen to be favorable. Efficiency-minded nations thus create the demand which suppliers of human capital-intensive services need to develop.

International trade in services and services incorporated in goods may also be seen as a means of strengthening the hold of national producers on their own market. The development of knowledge-based and work-experience-based production and trade makes it possible to attain production and consumption autonomy irrespective of the national origin of the knowledge or experience. This is quite different from expanding production in areas where a country has a comparative cost advantage due to its physical factor endowments, for purposes of exchanging the output thus obtained against outputs similarly obtained by other countries. On the contrary, it is an approach which makes use of the fact that any good can be produced[6] anywhere and any service can be produced anywhere, provided that the available human capital is properly harnessed and, where necessary, enriched from abroad. Hence, the fungibility of human knowledge and experience is such that it is not in itself a limiting factor in production and, therefore, is not an element in determining the *comparative advantage* of any particular country or region.[7] Thus we are left with evaluating comparative advantages in terms of truly *natural* endowments of factors such as land and population, even discarding for purposes of the present analysis the accumulation of physical capital, since what defines physical capital as a production factor is a decision as to the use of accumulated wealth rather than the existence of wealth per se as a naturally given resource.

Testing Times for Comparative Advantage

These apparently iconoclastic comments about the traditional theory of comparative advantage as applied to services are not to be taken lightly. Even Edward Leamer [1984, p. xvii], in his thorough analysis of the sources of international comparative advantage,[8] finds that "...perhaps the most interesting finding is the reversed roles from 1958 to 1975 of knowledge capital and physical capital as sources of comparative advantage in manufactured products. In 1958 the most highly skilled laborers contributed to comparative advantage in all four manufacture aggregates, but in 1975 these workers contributed positively to only the most skill-intensive manufacture aggregate (chemicals). Conversely, in 1958 physical capital was the source of comparative advantage only in chemicals, but in 1975 it contributed positively to all four of the aggregates of manufactures." In fact, we may wonder why the terminology of comparative advantage theory continues to be used to describe situations that have nothing to do with the particular configuration of natural resources, including the physical existence of a large number of human beings with no particular skills to offer. The theory of comparative advantage as applied to international trade in goods has itself had to wrestle with the contradiction between modern conditions of manufacturing production and the basic, elementary conditions in which the theory was first enunciated, namely a situation where the advantage truly given by nature, such as the climate to grow wine or to grow wool (in Ricardo's classical example), were really the dominant factor directing the course of both production and trade. Now that the dominant factor has become knowledge, and it has been so for sometime, even in purely manufacturing processes (meaning processes geared solely to the transformation of raw materials into physical goods with different shapes and functions), neither the materials on which production is based nor the contribution of machines to the physical transformaion processes are the determining elements in establishing the relative competitive strengths of individual producers.

Nevertheless, the efforts made by economists to accommodate old theories to new economic phenomena can be illuminating, and it is therefore worth trying to analyze some recent attempts to apply comparative advantage theory to services.

In a recent article, Alan Deardorff [1984] analyzed three cases of trade in services between two countries and came to the conclusion that, at least in one case, the principle of comparative advantage did not appear to apply because the analysis of trade flows between the two countries revealed that it was the country with the higher autarchy price for services relative to the price of goods which was exporting the services to the other country. This situation arose because the first country had a technological superiority in producing both services and goods, i.e., it had a superiority embodied both in labor and management skills. As a result of this productivity gap, the first country could only export management skills (labor skills being considered as nontradeable) to the other country if, so Deardorff assumed, the first country managers, though paid more than in the second country, were not paid at a level corresponding to their difference in skill and therefore turned out to be cheap in comparison with the managers in the second country and in high demand there. In a critique of Deardorff's article, Ronald Jones [1984] pointed out that "...adjusted for quality units, managers have a relatively low autarchy price in (the first country) and this reconciles the trade pattern with comparative advantage."[9] This specific case presented by Deardorff and discussed by Jones is a particularly interesting one not only because it shows that with appropriate assumptions it is possible to apply mechanically the principle of comparative advantage to trade in services but also because it draws attention to one particular aspect of services trade which, in effect, makes the theory of comparative advantage irrelevant.

To begin with, in order to deal with a trade situation which often is found in real life, Deardorff finds it necessary to introduce differences in technology with identical factor endowments, thus deviating from the traditional Hekscher-Ohlin model, which assumes different factor endowments but identical production technology. Although developments of the theory of comparative advantage that followed Hekscher-Ohlin have put more and more emphasis on technology and knowledge factors in explaining trade flows, the situation in Deardorff's example is further complicated by the fact that the management services exported by the first country with the technological superiority are in fact "traded" by way of a movement of factors from the first to the second country. However, movements of factors cannot be used as an explanation of trade in the traditional sense of the word, since one explanation for trade is precisely that it substitutes for movements of factors from one production area to another.

This being said, a more interesting aspect of Deardoff's example is the assumption of technological superiority in one country. Such superiority is seen to be at the origin of the factor movement or "export" of management services from the first to the second country. However, Deardorff only assumes this trade to take place if the ratio of managers' pay between the first and the second country is lower than the ratio of their productivity. This is a situation difficult to reconcile with real life. First, one may wonder why the technologically advanced country's managers would be such a devalued commodity. The only plausible explanation would be that the rate of technological development has slowed down considerably in that country and the number of managers available is in excess of current needs, but this would not, then, be a true case of different factor endowments. One may also wonder why the first country's managers would ever go to work in the second country if they are paid less there in absolute terms. This would only be likely to happen if the prices of the goods and nontradeable services they buy in the second country are all so much lower that their real income would rise as a result of migrating. Such a situation could arise, and it would fit the assumption that real autarchy prices for management services are lower in the first country to start with. But it would not fit the common-sense presumption that the type of high-technology goods which managers of the first country are likely to demand as consumers will be more expensive in the technologically poor country. Indeed, one of the problems with Deardorff's example is that it completely separates out services and goods as if efficient services had no impact on the technological content, quality, mode of production (economies of scale, etc.), and price of goods.

In other words, if it is true that there is likely to be trade in management services between the technologically advanced and the technologically poor countries, it is more likely to be because managers exporting their services have an *absolute* advantage for which users in the second country would probably be ready to pay almost any price, and in any case a higher price than in the first country. When dealing with trade in services in the form of factor movements, therefore, it is not necessary, and it may be even totally irrelevant, to refer to the principle of comparative advantage to explain such flows. In Deardorff's example, the managing skills available in the first country may simply not exist in the second country, and it may well be that the second country has to go into debt to acquire them because it may simply not have enough goods in which it is internationally competitive to sell in exchange for those skills. Indeed, the problems faced by many developing countries, as pointed out earlier, is not that they do not have enough of either labor or capital (in the sense of money to pay for imports of equipment) but that they do not have the technology to put these factors to work in an efficient manner. The example of the oil countries is a good case in point. The trade of these countries has been taking place on the basis of what one might call "mutual absolute advantage" between countries purchasing their oil resources (developed with imported technology) and themselves importing management and labor skills as well as finished products from all over the world.

Another interesting attempt to reconcile the traditional theory of comparative advantage with trade in services is that by Brian Hindley and Alasdair Smith [1984]. Hindley and Smith begin their exposition by stating "that services are different from goods—whatever that means in a particular context—does not in itself provide any basis for a supposition that the theory of comparative advantage (which is also referred to as the theory of comparative costs) does not apply to services. For that, it is necessary to point to differences which make the *logic* of the theory inapplicable to services, a much more stringent requirement than mere 'differences.'" The authors go on to distinguish two aspects of the theory of comparative costs, the "positive" aspect which explains why the production of particular goods is cheaper in one location than in another, and the "normative" aspect which asks whether the pattern of production and specialization resulting from international cost differences is economically efficient and socially desirable. They point to the fact that economists concerned with testing theories of trade flows have found it necessary to extend the basic Hekscher-Ohlin-Samuelson model to take account of additional factors of production such as skilled labor, but also to develop new theories which turn on such variables as technological differences, economies of scale, and market imperfection. They do not explain the sources of comparative advantage in terms of the traditional Hekscher-Ohlin model or of these additional factors, but they do consider whether there are policies available to governments which will enable them to change the comparative advantage of their countries in an advantageous way. In their view, unless an affirmative answer can be given to this question (which is, of course, conditional not only on the availability of relevant data but also on the possibility of identifying clearly the factors that determine comparative advantage), the theory must be accepted as valid, since "difficulties in empirical testing of theories do not provide intellectual justification for ignoring the normative component of the theory of comparative costs."

Having thus evacuated the task of giving an articulate answer to the basic question posed in the first lines of their article—namely "Does the theory of comparative advantage, developed over two centuries to clarify thought about trade in goods, apply to trade in services?,"—they go on to develop arguments why from a national standpoint it pays to allow free competition among service industries rather than to maintain protectionist policies in this area. They conclude that "...one of the most important features of services is their role as an intermediate good. Services purchased by other producers will typically be complementary to their production and trade. To raise the price of such services, or to reduce

their quality, by inappropriate policies is therefore to tax production and
trade in service-using industries as well as to tax final consumers of
services...Such taxation of consumers and users of services requires
strong justification." Therefore, they argue that "...from a *conceptual*
point of view there is no difficulty about applying the standard tool-kit of
the international economist to the problems of trade and investment in
services. Services are different from goods in ways that are significant and
that deserve careful attention, but the powerful logic of the theory of
comparative advantage transcends these differences."

Now, it is probably *intuitively* correct to say that the arguments in favor
of free trade and free competition among service industries on the one
hand, and goods industries on the other, are good things from a normative
point of view, but economists should have learned to be wary of their intui-
tions. Much intuitive reasoning about the demand elasticity for particular
goods and services has foundered on the realities of inflation or depression.
Hindley and Smith assume that the free trade theories developed in the
field of goods are applicable to all fields of economic activity, and they infer
from this that free trade policies based on these theories are equally
applicable to services. But this reasoning begs the question of what the
concrete factors are that lead to such normatively defined results and,
therefore, what the appropriate prescriptions are for action to reach
these results.

In other words, it is necessary first to answer the question of whether
free trade in services on the one hand, and free international competition
between services and goods on the other, would be governed by the same
factors that determine the flows of trade in goods (i.e., natural factor
endowments, unit price equalization through the interplay of market
forces, economies of scale, income and price elasticities of demand, etc., as
well as the other more knowledge-based factors referred to by Hindley and
Smith as complementing the classical theory of comparative advantage)
before concluding that the relative availability of these factors is a sufficient
condition for some countries to specialize in the production of skill and
knowledge-intensive services and for other countries to specialize in unskilled and labor-intensive services, and for governments to conduct trade
policies in services which are modelled on their trade policies in the field
of goods.

Hindley and Smith are probably right in saying that "...none of the
potential difficulties in applying the normative theory of comparative cost
to trade and investment in service industries appears to yield any a priori
reason to suppose that the theory does not apply." They are also right in
saying that the question of what determines comparative advantage in

service industries ultimately requires answers based on empirical analysis. Very little such analysis has been possible to date due to the paucity of statistical data, and therefore this is not a ground on which hypotheses such as those advanced by Hindley and Smith can be criticized. Indeed, the classical economists had very little statistical data at their disposal, but they were nonetheless able to put forward very stimulating ideas which later statistical analysis did not disprove (though it has sometimes pointed to the need for expanding the basic hypothetical framework).

A first attempt to assess the relative importance of various factors shaping comparative advantage in services in quantitative terms has been made by André Sapir and Ernest Lutz [1981]. Using a simple econometric model, they found that the main factors were the availability of physical and human capital, and they explained the relative position of developing and developed countries in international markets for main categories of services on the basis of their relative endowments in such forms of capitals. There may be problems with the definition of the variables used by these two authors and with the specification of their linear regression equations, but their model has at least the virtue of bringing out the important role of human capital in international services trade. Leaving aside the question of whether accumulated human capital can be considered as a factor with which countries are naturally endowed, as well as the question of whether the use of human capital embodied in expatriate factors can be considered as a form of trade, for purposes of comparative analysis it is important that Sapir and Lutz have been able, even with a very simple set of linear equations, to identify this form of capital as one of the main determinants of market shares in the world market for services. Hindley and Smith's comments on the Sapir and Lutz study imply that the development of new knowledge and techniques (in particular, informatics) may lead to the appearance of new comparative advantages based through the "disembodiment" of certain services. This would entail that certain tasks which are more or less standardized and labor-intensive in character would be performed in labor-rich countries, while more high-skill-intensive and differentiated tasks, which are not transferable abroad without at the same time transferring the factors possessing the required skills, would continue to be performed in capital-rich countries.

In his analysis of the sources of comparative advantage, Edward Leamer [1984] also has addressed the problem of differences in technology and knowledge and their relation to the static theory of comparative advantage. Referring to Ricardo, he began by stating that "...the technological differences in the Ricardian model can be thought to arise from different endowments in knowledge capital (p. 1)." In discussing the basic assumptions of the Hekscher-Ohlin model, however, he pointed out that in this model, the same technological knowledge applicable to the production of goods is assumed to be available without cost to all countries. This assumption of free access to knowledge gave rise to the following comment by Leamer (when comparing Indian and United States agriculture): "It seems more likely that Indians chose a labour-intensive technique because of low wages than that they were unaware of the capital-intensive technique used in the United States. . . . [But] by assuming that all countries have exactly the same technology, the Hekscher-Ohlin model goes too far, since it assumes that knowledge is free. A more satisfying viewpoint is that knowledge and the dissemination of knowledge are uncertain consequences of economic investment." Although Leamer did not comment further on the role of knowledge as a source of comparative advantage, his contribution is a useful reminder of the way in which this role has been largely ignored in economic theory. Either it has not been taken into consideration in the theory of international trade on the ground that knowledge is a dynamic factor whereas the classical model of comparative advantage is by definition static, or in models of economic growth like those developed by Abramowitz [1957], Kuznets [1960], and Denison [1967], the specifications do not include knowledge or technology among the independent variables. Instead, technology and knowledge are used to explain the relative size of the "residual" or "error" terms in equations estimated for different countries.

Regarding the classical model of comparative advantage, Leamer [pp. 41–44] quite consistently pointed out that ". . . capital is listed as one of the inputs into a production process in an elliptical reference to the fact that production takes time. . . . A second reason for writing "capital" instead of "machines" as the input is that there may be many alternative kinds of "machines" (also buildings, human capital, improvements to land, inventories) that under a special assumption can be aggregated into a single input, called capital. The special assumption is that the relative prices of all these inputs are constant. . . . But time is not an essential element in the static trade theorems, and the very difficult problems of defining and modeling capital in a dynamic world can therefore be avoided. Any study of dynamical changes would surely require a deeper treatment of capital than is evidenced by the traditional model that lists capital as an input along with other factors."

In the static comparative advantage model, human capital and machinery can be treated as fixed inputs or factor endowments because they are not fungible in the short run, and at any given point in time they are, as Leamer observed, the current result of past saving decisions. This obviously applies to static comparisons of the capital endowment of different countries. But what if capital can be transferred from one country to another? Can the Hekscher-Ohlin model still hold when the fundamental assumption of complete immobility of factors between countries is released? Leamer addressed this question and found it possible to integrate the assumption of mobility of factors into the traditional model in such a way that the latter indirectly takes into account factor mobility: "The model with mobile factors therefore expresses outputs and trade as a function of immobile factors only and includes auxiliary relations between the mobile and immobile factors. It is equivalent to the even model [where the number of goods and the number of productive factors are equal, a basic assumption of the Hekscher-Ohlin model] if the number of immobile factors is equal to the number of traded goods" [p. 23].[10]

Another question addressed by Leamer is the possibility of the existence of specialized factors, either because of natural physical endowments or of the availability of specialized knowledge.[11] Leamer also found ways of dealing with such factors in the context of the traditional Hekscher-Ohlin model. He pointed out, for example, that "... although land is not used to produce industrial goods, the level of output of industrial goods depends on both the endowment of labour and the endowment of land.... This relation suggests that resources such as agricultural land will have negative impacts on the comparative advantage of, say, chemicals and will be primary determinants of agricultural outputs. This type of relation will explain, in part, results such as those obtained by Keesing and Shirk [1971], who found that "large" less-developed countries have a comparative disadvantage in manufactures, where large is defined as low population density [p. 32]." The approach is the same as in the previous case, namely to derive the indirect impact of specialized factors on all types of production including those for which the factors are not used. Thus any extraneous elements, including dynamic elements in the production process, are brought into the basic framework of assumptions underlying the Hekscher-Ohlin model. As far as the identification of specialized factors is concerned, "... an explanation of trade in terms of exceedingly fine measures of capital would be too close to a tautology to be very satisfying but simple distinctions between human capital and physical capital are appealing" [p. 3].[12] Hence, if one remains within the four corners of the Hekscher-Ohlin model, it is possible to integrate, both theoretically and econometrically, certain changes in the basic assumption of the model. Leamer's conclusion is that no single alternative model of international trade has the same explanatory power as the Hekscher-Ohlin model, since "... the only credible theory entertained by economists is a

vague amalgam of the many models we use to illustrate distinct features of
the workings of the economy;...the present state of economic theory does
not allow us to articulate fully and precisely even simple alternative models
of trade...[p. 45]."

From Leamer's analysis, we can draw the conclusion that the main
reason why it is intuitively difficult to use the Hekscher-Ohlin theory to
explain international trade in services is precisely that the fastest developing sectors of this trade are those where the most dynamic changes in
production methods and consumption patterns are taking place, which the
static Hekscher-Ohlin theory of comparative advantage is ill-adapted to
deal with. The fundamental question, therefore, is perhaps not whether
in the dynamic world of services the Hekscher-Ohlin theory can provide useful insights into the determinants of trade but rather what elements of that theory retain their explanatory power for services, and in
what circumstances.

H-O and Services

The answer to this question, in fact, depends on how the services
concerned are produced. It should be noted in this connection that even in
the field of goods, the traditional theory of comparative advantage has
been found difficult to apply when dealing with very technologically
advanced goods produced only in certain countries. For this reason
technology and knowledge have been introduced as specific factors into the
basic theoretical framework in an attempt to extend its applicability.
Alternatively, different theories of international trade based on availability
of specialized factors (or what could otherwise be called absolute
advantage) have been advanced, in particular, the "technological gap" or
"product cycle" theories according to which trade develops following a
certain sequence, beginning with exports from the country that possesses
the specialized knowledge or technique for producing certain goods,
followed by the learning process of the initially importing countries, and in
the end with these countries exporting in their turn either to the market of
the original producer (when the latter has shifted to new products and has
become a net importer of the products that have undergone the learning
process) or as a competitor in third markets. Among the authors who have
dealt with this alternative explanation of trade are Kravis [1956], Hufbauer
[1966, and in Vernon, 1970], Keesing [1967], Vernon [1970], Machlup
[1984], Rada [1984], and Edvinsson [1985]. In this connection, it is
interesting to note that breaking down factors of production to identify

"endowments" which can then be referred to as an explanation of trade in accordance with the Hekscher-Ohlin theory can lead to exactly the opposite result, i.e., to denying one of the basic assumptions of the model, namely the essential similarity of factors. (The variability of factor endowment ratios among countries is less than the variability of factor input intensities across industries [Leamer, 1984, p. 2]). Thus, evidence is provided of the specificity or nonhomogeneity of production functions, a characteristic which is at the root of the theory of absolute advantage and intraindustry specialization.

There are two ways of dealing with the determinants of international trade in services. On the one hand, one could consider that because of the differentiated character of services and of the fact that different service functions require specialized knowledge, *all* services are exchanged on the basis of absolute advantage, not comparative advantage. Alternatively, a selective approach can be followed. Certain services are differentiated and require specialized knowledge in order to cater to the specific needs of intermediate users or final consumers;[13] *other* services can be more readily standardized in terms of their knowledge input and the identification of separate units.[14] Trade in the first category of services would be determined more by the absolute advantage conferred by specialized knowledge than in the second category; conversely, trade in the second category of services would be determined more by the comparative advantage conferred by primary factor endowments than in the first category. Indeed, in the case of standardized products (and assuming that the services in question can be internationally traded without any direct involvement of the factors producing them, i.e., traded on a cross-border basis), one can only speak of absolute advantage in the Ricardian sense of static differences in the general level of acquired technology between exporting and importing countries. There are two further questions that suggest themselves. The first is whether services fall more frequently in the first than in the second category. The second is, what does one mean by "specialized knowledge"? The first question will be addressed below; the second, in chapter 8.

If *most* services require specialized knowledge, are differentiated according to the specific needs of users and consumers, and cannot easily be sold internationally without the direct involvement of production factors as carriers of the specialized knowledge, then there is a good case for arguing that trade in services is essentially governed by absolute advantage, by analogy with intraindustry competition in traded goods.[15]

In a field such as services, where trade performance is not readily quantifiable, it is necessary to rely on business experience of market competition rather than on statistical calculations to assess the relative competitiveness of different producers. The services rendered by an automobile can in large part be readily measured, by referring to technical indicators like top speed, petrol consumption, roominess of the interior, etc. But how does one measure the performance of an engineer until one knows whether the dam that he has built holds fast for 50 years, and how does one know whether this particular engineer has performed a better job than that which an equally well-trained engineer from another country would have done? There may exist ex-ante market indicators of performance for certain service providers based on qualifications, experience, or other reference material. However, these indicators are not necessarily related to the prices which the producers concerned can obtain for their services, especially when cultural biases come into play. An engineer with a diploma from the Massachusetts Institute of Technology and no work experience may command a higher price than an experienced engineer holding an equivalent diploma from an equally well-known university in another country. Leaving aside such biases, in the absence of actual work experience, the work of graduated engineers from schools with standardized curricula can be considered as standardized products. But total equivalence of qualifications is difficult to establish between different schools, let alone different countries. Thus, it is only when they have had an opportunity to express their particular talents and have, as a result, become individualized products, that a fairly reliable relationship can be established between price and performance. Their price then depends primarily on their individual *past* performance, that is, on the absolute advantage they have acquired. International business reviews are full of examples of the high demand that exists for managers and technical staff with specific work experience. The price to be paid for their services is usually indicated as "negotiable."

Nonetheless, the natural inclination to categorize makes analysts alert to common characteristics of service providers, in terms both of the content of the services they provide and of the quality of services provided. This, as indicated earlier, may lead to the common recognition of conventional measures of performance based on the characteristics of the knowledge or information contained in individual performance units. As a result, transparency of markets for services would be increased, and eventually it may be possible to identify unit-cost functions for certain services to which the concept of comparative advantage could not otherwise be applied.

In the meantime, the one and perhaps only basis on which comparative advantage in services can be analysed is the so-called revealed comparative advantage index developed by Bela Balassa [1979] and further elaborated, inter alia, by Alexander Yeats [1985]. This index combines the advantage of simplicity with that of looking at actual trade flows. Basically, the index compares the share of a country's exports of an individual good or service in its total exports with the share of world exports of the same good or service in total world exports. If the ratio of these shares is positive (greater than one), the country has a revealed comparative advantage in the good or service in question; if the ratio is negative (less than one), the country has a revealed comparative disadvantage. An analysis of the comparative advantage of major trading countries in a number of service sectors has been done on a similar basis by Anton Brender [1984]. The results correspond to economists' intuitive knowledge of the relative competitive strengths of the countries concerned in the services sector as a whole, based not only on available trade data but also on qualitative judgments of business performance drawn from information about innovations, company profits, takeovers, etc., supplied on a regular basis by specialized and less-specialized news media. Brender's findings are summarized in table 3–2 and figure 3–1.

A discussion of comparative advantage in services would not be complete without a reference to the increasing complementarity between services and goods in production and of the impact of this phenomenon on the competitiveness of individual firms, as well as of whole countries, in the production of services on the one hand, and the production of goods on the other. As Albert Bressand [1985] has pointed out, in advanced production systems it is increasingly difficult to disentangle the service element from the material element in goods. For this reason, Bressand has introduced the notion of *compacks*, or "combined packages" of services and goods giving rise to new types of products, which are themselves the result of new marketing strategies made possible by the technological developments on the basis of which compacks are generated. New forms of comparative advantage are thus developed, where the relationships between different comparative costs per unit of output are very diffused if not totally irrelevant. The production of services and the production of goods, in Bressand's model, are no longer two distinct forms of economic activity, but this does not mean that the traditional theory of international trade applies to services. In practice, we know, of course, that services can be exchanged for goods, so that whether or not the theory of comparative advantage applies to services, there are possible tradeoffs between services and goods at that level. In the case of compacks such tradeoffs would affect the location of production by directing production to those countries which can most efficiently produce the major component of each given compack,

Table 3–2A. Net invisible transactions, 1969–71 and 1980–82, by main trading areas¹ (billion U.S. dollars)

	Major industrial countries		Other industrial countries		OPEC		Non-OPEC developing countries		Other		World exports	
	1969–71	1980–82	1969–71	1980–82	1969–71	1980–82	1969–71	1980–82	1969–71	1980–82	1969–71	1980–82
Nonfactor services²												
Official transactions	-4.2	1.6	0.2	5.2	-0.1	-25.0	3.5	14.7	0.2	1.2	20.4	120.3
Travel	-1.6	-7.0	1.2	6.0	-0.3	-5.8	0.5	5.1	0	0.2	18.6	95.8
Transport	1.3	11.6	1.3	7.5	-0.6	-10.6	-1.9	-6.3	0	0	28.3	142.3
Other services	1.3	17.7	-0.7	-2.5	-0.8	-19.6	-0.6	4.1	0	-0.8	13.9	126.2
Factor services												
Workers' remittances	-3.0	-13.6	3.0	10.2	-0.2	-8.4	0.3	8.4	0	0.4	9.8	40.9
Dividends, licence fees, royalties, etc.	7.5	27.7	-1.1	-3.1	-4.0	-17.8	-1.5	-5.0	—	0	12.4	51.4
Interest	2.5	40.0	-1.8	-22.0	0.1	19.4	-1.1	-30.9	0.6	-6.1	17.3	250.7

Source: Brender [1984].
Notes:
1. Major industrial countries include the United States, Japan, the European community, Austria and Switzerland. Other industrial countries are the countries members of OECD less the former group; "other" includes Eastern European countries and international organizations.
2. Based on IMF definitions: "Official transactions" includes part of IMF category "Other goods, services and income" and part of category "unrequited transfers"; "transport" combines IMF categories "shipment" and "other transportation"; "other services" excludes official transactions.

62

Table 3–2B. Trade trends compared

I. General

1. World exports (1980) (billion U.S. dollars)	World exports (1980) (billion U.S. dollars)	Growth (1970–1980) (percent)
Nonfactor services	*364*	*19.6*
of which:		
Travel	96	17.6
Transportation	142	25.6
Other	136	
Factor services	*343*	*24.0*
of which:		
Labor income	41	15.3
Patents, dividends	51	15.3
Interest	251	31.1
Merchandise	*1,650*	*20.4*

II. Nonfactor services indications

	Net flows (SDR's bil.) 1970	Net flows (SDR's bil.) 1983	Average annual growth (%) 1976–1983
United States			
Communications	.67	1.19	8.5
Construction/engineering	1.07	1.57	5.7
Nonmerchandise insurance	.17	.19	1.6
Other	1.19	.77	−6.4
France			
Construction	1.04	2.3	12.0
Merchanting	.34	.17	−10.4
Nonmerchandise insurance	.57	1.44	14.2
Surveys and technical cooperation	1.17	3.10	14.9
Other	5.13	10.55	10.9
Japan			
Agents' fees	.15	.40	15.1
Management fees	.27	.84	17.6
Nonmerchandise insurance	.58	−.23	−4.8
Other	1.12	4.29	21.5

Source: See table 4–1A.

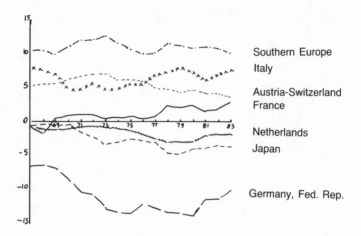

a. Travel[2];

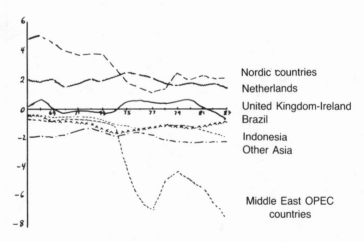

b. Shipment and other transportation[2];

Source: Brender (1984)
Notes: 1. Estimated on the basis of the ratio of payments surplus or deficit to total world
transactions in each item. Only main countries or regions with largest surpluses or
deficits are shown.
2. IMF definitions

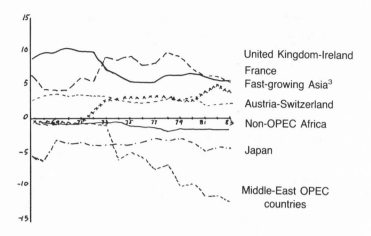

United Kingdom-Ireland
France
Fast-growing Asia[3]
Austria-Switzerland
Non-OPEC Africa
Japan
Middle-East OPEC
countries

c. Other goods, services and income[2].

3. South Korea, Hong-kong, Singapore and Taiwan

Figure 3–1.   Apparent comparative advantage in services, main countries and regions,[1] 1967–1983.

be it a good or a service. Tradeoffs are also likely to affect national trade policies in different ways depending on whether the countries concerned are more interested in protecting domestic production of the goods or services components of compacks. However, it should not be inferred from the existence of tradeoffs that services can be assimilated to goods in terms of either production or marketing methods: complementarity in compacks or substitutability in trade do not mean that services are interchangeable with goods from a functional point of view, with the exception of some consumer goods or services which perform simple standardized tasks, e.g., washing machines and domestic laundry services.

One characteristic of services that is increasingly being recognized is the leverage they provide to the goods-producing sector. Recent evidence has pointed to the fact that services play a particularly important role in national economies as intermediate rather than as final products. For example, in a recent study on data services, Bruno Lanvin [1986] has documented the extraordinary multiplier effect of these services on the rest of the economy. The role of these services in raising the level of integration and internationalization of the "worldeconomy" has also been shown by Bressand [1985]. Similar leverage can also be identified in qualitative terms for other services.[16] Statistics on knowledge content of various service activities, when they become available, may help to quantify these effects as is done for goods.

Notes

1. See, for example, Corden [1971], already quoted. Recent authors like Shelp [1981] and Riddle [1986] emphasize the place of services in total world trade, but there is still much to be done to develop a coherent theory for such trade.

2. Repairs, however, are not necessarily to be viewed as services, since they modify the physical structure of goods and are therefore a form of manufacture or re-manufacture.

3. Various classifications of services are discussed in Riddle [1986]. Classifications by activity or by "industry" are the most obvious because they correspond to the existing organizational structure of output. This structure is rapidly evolving, however, and activity classification may be more reliable in the long run. An interesting alternative is to classify services by commodity, e.g., services related to buildings, to land, to information, to people, etc. On this, see Canada [1984, section E–7].

4. The two most widely used classifications of goods for trade purposes are SITC (Standard International Trade Classification) and CCCN (Customs Cooperation Council Nomenclature for the Classification of Goods in Customs Tariffs). Negotiations are currently under way to develop a so-called Harmonized System of classification, elaborating on the CCCN. Regarding industries (including services), the only available classification at international level is the United Nations International Standard Industrial Classification of all Economic Activities (ISIC).

5. Thus Hindley and Smith [1984] argue that "...countries with a relatively large skilled labor force will have a comparative advantage in the production of services." Sapir and Lutz [1981] state, "...the fact that differences in trade patterns among economies reflect differences in factor endowments lends support to the 'stages approach' to comparative advantage recently put forward by Balassa (1979) for manufactured goods. Indeed, it would suggest that, as developing countries accumulate human and physical capital, they will gain comparative advantage in certain types of services. However, one suspects that industrialized economies will generally retain their prominence in services trade thanks to their technological lead and their abundance of physical and human capital" [p. 21].

6. This is in the sense of being man-made, not merely extracted from the soil in raw form. Note, in this connection, that raw metallic ores have long been transported in rock form to developed consuming countries for metal extraction and processing, and this continues to be done unless transport costs are prohibitive. Similarly, there is still a considerable amount of log trade going on, despite the rapid development of wood industries in many developing countries rich in forestry resources.

7. Strictly speaking, this is only true for "foot-loose" knowledge but not, or much less so, for "locked-in" knowledge. See chapter 8 for an explanation of the difference between these two categories.

8. Leamer only deals with trade in goods; therefore, to the extent that his views converge with those presented above, the argument about the role of knowledge in trade gains in generality. However, the argument maintains a special relevance to sources since they depend more on knowledge and work experience as indicators of value.

9. Both Deardorff and Jones are arguing that the highly paid managers of the first country are, in fact, underpaid compared to the less skilled managers of the second country. This argument may be tenable in autarchy, but it does not suffice to explain trade (see *infra*).

10. This approach can be formalized by the use of an econometric device known as "impact multipliers" which "express that part of the response of endogenous variables to changes of predetermined variables which occurs in the first year" [Goldberger, 1959, p. 16].

11. In this connection, see the discussion of "locked-in" knowledge in chapter 8.

12. This statement would argue against following the approach suggested by Deardorff (see above), where the only way to rescue the traditional Hekscher-Ohlin theory is to distinguish between "good" managers and "bad" managers, and to compare countries in terms of their availability of either or both types.

13. Such services sometimes involve the participation of the user or consumer in the production of the service, as in the case of software services where the user or consumer must learn to use software in order for the service provided to be fully operational.

14. Each contains a given amount of knowledge-input corresponding to a given portion of a total service function, in which case it is possible to reap economies of scale in their production, to calculate unit input and output prices, and to compete through the price mechanism in the same way that producers compete in the goods markets by supplying comparable goods in terms of quality and quantity at different unit prices. Systematic research into the "standardization of software" with a view to permitting economies of scale in the use of human thought processes is one of the tasks of Japan's Institute for New Generation Computer Technology [ICOT, 1984].

15. It is the specificity of otherwise comparable goods, in terms of their technological content and design, that determines that acceptability by users and consumers. Acceptability in turn depends on the degree of correspondence between the specific characteristics of the goods and the specific needs of the users and consumers. And it is the response of the producer of the goods to those needs that determines ability to compete with other suppliers of similar goods.

16. For example, telephone answering services which involve middle-level skills in the devising and manufacturing of the relevant equipment and relatively low-level skills in the actual performance of basic communication and information functions by the staff of answering service firms, imply a certain level of information needs of producers using these services as well as a certain income level and scale of preferences of consumers.

4 DEFINITIONS, FUNCTIONS, AND REGULATIONS

The discussion in chapters 2 and 3 on value creation and comparative advantage in services now needs to be completed by a description of the actual coverage of the concept of services as well as of the actual trade flows that take place, to the extent that available statistics make the identification of such flows possible. This will be done in the next two chapters.

Services are acts of production which result in nonmaterial or intangible products of varying degrees of complexity, the latter being determined by the knowledge content of the production acts concerned. The requisite that the product resulting from service acts should be intangible is a necessary and sufficient condition for defining as services all the activities which, in modern societies, are not directly the result of the processing of physical materials, of the extraction of such materials, or of cultivation of land or water resources. From the point of view of the international economy, however, it is not sufficient to define services in terms of how they are produced; it is also necessary to take into account how they are traded. We have seen that although there are services that can be traded across borders like goods, either directly or through their incorporation in supporting physical materials such as books, one of the essential characteristics of many services is that, in order to be sold or marketed, they require the simultaneous presence of the producer and consumer or user of the service at the point of sale.

A broad categorization of services that fits the description of nonphysical output appears in the International Standard Industrial Classification (ISIC) but it typically lacks any recognizable criteria for differentiating between services activities that are clearly treated as residual from the point of view of the classification as a whole. Similarly, the classification of services in accordance with various types of international transactions to which they give rise, appears in the statistics of the International Monetary Fund (IMF), but again no attempt has been made to combine data on the basis of clear criteria, as evidenced particularly by the fact that the category "other income and non-factor services" includes many different types of services activities either as to their knowledge content or their function in the economy. Tables 4–1 and 4–2 present ISIC and IMF classifications, respectively, with the most recent data on world production and world trade in the services concerned.

A discussion of the various service typologies that can be invented to suit various conceptual approaches to services production or trade is not likely to lead to very intelligible results for a casual observer. Many classifications have been attempted, including one by the present author. Three main approaches have been followed. First, distinctions among services are based on the functional characteristics of physical goods, thus assuming that the pattern of interindustry relationships that exist for goods also applies to services; second, distinctions are based on the functional characteristics of the services themselves; third, they are based on the technical characteristics of services production and trade (table 4–3). All these approaches are essentially heuristic and do not rest on any hard data. While it is true that the discussion of various service typologies does not require a detailed knowledge of the scale of operations within each service sector and subsector, one major difficulty with these approaches is that in the absence of relevant statistics, they are not able to provide reliable information on input/output relationships within the service sector or between this sector and other economic activities. There may be various types of input-output relationships that are relevant for different purposes, but each should be based on economic realities and agreed statistical conventions in order to permit a systematic analysis of the different characteristics of services. It should therefore be kept in mind that any typologies that are attempted at present necessarily rely on impressionistic assessments of the quality and amount of factors entering into the production of service products, as well as of the quality and amount of the products themselves.

Table 4–1.   ISIC classification of services[1]

Division	Major group	Group	
61	610	6100	*Wholesale Trade* The re-sale (sale without transformation) of new and used goods to retailers; to industrial, commercial, institutional, or professional users; or to other wholesalers; or acting as agents in buying merchandise for, or selling merchandise to, such persons or companies. The leasing and rental of industrial machinery and equipment is classified in group 8330 (Machinery rental and leasing). The bottling of natural mineral waters at springs and wells is classified in group 3134 (Soft drinks and carbonated water industries).
62	620	6200	*Retail Trade* The re-sale (sale without transformation) of new and used goods to the general public, for personal or household consumption or utilization, by shops, department stores, stalls, mail-order houses, gasoline (petrol) filling stations, retail motor vehicle dealers, hawkers and peddlers, consumer cooperative, auction houses, etc. Also classified in Retail trade are establishments primarily engaged in renting goods to the general public for personal or household use, except amusement and recreational goods such as boats and canoes, motorcycles and bicycles, and saddle horses. The renting to the general public of the amusement and recreational goods is classified in group 9490 (Amusement and recreational services n.e.c.). Repair and installation services rendered by establishments mainly engaged in retail trade are included in this group. The sale of food and drinks for consumption on the premises is classified in group 6310 (Restaurants, cafés, and other eating and drinking places).
63			*Restaurants and Hotels*
	631	6310	Restaurants, cafés, and other eating and drinking places. Retail establishments selling prepared foods and

Division	*Major group*	*Group*	
			drinks for immediate consumption, such as restaurants, cafés, lunch counters, and refreshment stands. Catering is included in this group. Restaurant facilities operated in connection with the provision of lodging are classified in group 6320 (Hotels, rooming houses, camps, and other lodging places).
	632	6320	Hotels, rooming houses, camps, and other lodging places
71			*Transport and Storage*
	711		Land transport
			Companies furnishing transportation by interurban and suburban railroads; and services allied to railway transportation, such as sleeping-car services, railway express, and switching and other terminal services. Excluded from this group are units operated by railroad companies which are primarily engaged in providing telegraph services (classified in group 7200); in operating hotels (classified in group 6320); and in providing water transport (classified in the appropriate group 712).
		7112	Urban, suburban, and interurban highway passenger transport
			Interurban and suburban bus and coach lines; and urban passenger transportation whether by electric railway, trolley coach, bus, tramways, or subway. The operation of associated terminal, maintenance, and service facilities is included.
		7113	Other passenger land transport
			Passenger transportation services, not elsewhere classified, such as sight-seeing buses, limousines to airports or stations, school buses, taxicabs; and animal-drawn vehicles for the transport of passenger or freight. The rental of automobiles with drivers is also included. The provision of ambulance services is classified in group 9331 (Medical, dental, and other health services).
		7114	Freight transport by road
			Local and long-distance trucking, transfer, and draying services. The operation of terminal

Division	Major group	Group	
			facilities and the rental of trucks, with drivers, are also included. This group does not include delivery departments or warehouses operated by business concerns for their own use.
		7115	Pipeline transport
		7116	Supporting services to land transport Services in support of land transport, such as the operation of toll roads, highway bridges, vehicular tunnels, and parking lots and structures; the rental of railroad cars and of automobiles and trucks without drivers. Storage or warehousing of motor vehicles (dead storage) is classified in group 7192; and the rental of automobiles or trucks with drivers, is classified in groups 7113 or 7114, respectively.
	712		Water transport
		7121	Ocean and coastal water transport
		7122	Inland water transport
		7123	Supporting services to water transport The provision of supporting services to all kinds of water transport, ship leasing and rental
	713		Air transport
		7131	Air transport carriers
		7132	Supporting services to air transport
	719		Services allied to transport
		7191	Services incidental to transport Services incidental to transport, such as forwarding; packing and crating; arrangement of transport (including travel agencies); inspection, sampling and weighting; ship and aircraft brokers. The operation of stockyards which provide pens, feed, and selling areas for livestock temporarily held, either pending sale or in transit to or from the market, is also included.
		7192	Storage and warehousing The operation of storage facilities and warehouses (including bonded and refrigerated warehouses) for hire by the general public when such storage is offered as an independent service.
72	720	7200	*Communication* Communication services rendered to the public

Division	Major group	Group	
			whether by post, wire, or radio and whether intended to be received audibly or visually. Services for the exchange or recording of messages are also included. Radio and television broadcasting studios and stations are classified in group 9413.
81	810		*Financial Institutions*
		8101	Monetary institutions The central banks, commercial banks, and other banks which have deposits transferable by check, otherwise used in making payments, or available on demand.
		8102	Other financial institutions Savings banks; credit institutions other than banks such as saving and loan associations, agricultural credit institutions, industrial development banks, rediscount and financing institutions, personal credit institutions, loan correspondents and brokers; trust companies; investment companies and trusts; security and commodity brokers, dealers and underwriters.
		8103	Financial services Foreign exchange dealers; units primarily engaged in check cashing and exchange or rental of safe deposits; security, commodity, and bullion exchanges; investment research and counselling; stock quotation services; lease and patent brokers and licensing.
82	820	8200	*Insurance* Insurance carriers of all kinds; insurance agents and brokers; organizations servicing insurance carriers; consultants for policy-holders; adjusting agencies; independently organized pension (superannuation) funds.
83			*Real Estate and Business Services*
	831	8310	Real estate This group does not include operators of hotels, rooming houses, camps, trailer camps, and other lodging places, who are classified in group 6320.

Division	Major group	Group	
	832		Business services except machinery and equipment rental and leasing
		8321	Legal services
		8322	Accounting, auditing, and bookkeeping services
		8323	Data-processing and tabulating services
		8324	Engineering, architectural, and technical services. Medical and dental laboratories are classified in group 9331 (Medical, dental, and other health services); and research and scientific institutes). Engineering and technical services carried on in association with manufacturing, construction, or other activities are classified the group appropriate to the activity with which the developmental or testing work is associated.
		8325	Advertising services Market research services provided to others on a fee or contract basis are included in this group.
		8329	Business services, except machinery and equipment rental and leasing not elsewhere classified Establishments primarily engaged in furnishing business services not elsewhere classified to others on a fee or contract basis, such as credit rating agencies; adjustment and collection agencies; duplicating, addressing, blueprinting, photocopying, mailing list and stenographic services; employment agencies; news gathering and reporting agencies; business management and consulting services; fashion designers; bondsmen; fingerprint service; detective agencies and protective services.
	833	8330	Machinery and equipment rental and leasing The leasing of agricultural or construction equipment with drivers is classified in group 1120 or 5000, respectively. The renting of leasing of transport equipment is classified in the appropriate group of division 71 (Transport and storage); renting clothing, furniture, pillows, lockers, and most other personal and household goods is classified in group 6200 (Retail trade); and the renting of pleasure boats and canoes,

Division	Major group	Group	
			motorcycles and bicycles, saddle horses, and similar recreational goods is included in group 9490 (Amusement and recreation services not elsewhere classified).
91	910	9100	*Public Administration and Defense* This group does not include governmental activities other than general administration and regulation in respect of such fields as transport, communication, education, health, production, marketing, and the operation of financial institutions, each of which is classified in an appropriate group, in accordance with the given kind of activity.
92	920	9200	Sanitary and similar services
93			*Social and Related Community Services*
	931	9310	Education services Governmental and private education institutions of all types. Governesses and tutors employed in a private household are classified in group 9591 (Domestic services). Schools that are primarily concerned with recreation, such as bridge and golf schools, are classified in group 9490 (Amusement and recreation services not elsewhere classified).
	932	9320	Research and scientific institutes Institutes primarily engaged in basic and general research in the biological, physical, and social sciences. Meteorological institutes and medical research organizations are included. Organizations engaged in engineering research, product or process development and design, or testing, are classified in group 8324 (Engineering, architectural, and technical services). Laboratories rendering testing, diagnostic, and other services to the medical and dental professions are classified in group 9331 (Medical, dental, and other health services). Research carried on in association with teaching is classified in group 9310 (Education services). Research departments, whether at a separate

Division	Major group	Group	

			address or not, attached to establishments or groups of establishments the activities of which can be classified under a single group of the ISIC are excluded; and are classified in that group.
	933		Medical, dental, other health and veterinary services
		9331	Medical, dental, and other health services The fabrication of dentures and artificial teeth other than to order is classified in group 3851.
		9332	Veterinary services
	934	9340	Welfare institutions
	935	9350	Business, professional, and labor associations Business associations and labor unions and similar labor organizations
	939		Other social and related community services
		9391	Religious organizations Establishments maintained by religious organizations primarily for purposes of furnishing educational, health, or welfare services or for publishing are classified in the appropriate group in accordance with their main kind of activity.
		9399	Social and related community services not elsewhere classified, such as political organizations; civic, social, and fraternal organizations; historical clubs; and poetry associations.
94			*Recreational and Cultural Services*
	941		Motion picture and other entertainment services
		9411	Motion picture production The production of theatrical and nontheatrical motion pictures for exhibition including the production of still and slide films. Services independent of motion picture production, such as casting bureaus, film developing and printing, and film editing and titling are also included.
		9412	Motion picture distribution and projection The renting of motion picture film or tape; and operating motion picture theatres. Services to motion picture distribution, such as film delivery

Division	Major group	Group	
			service and film booking agencies, are included.
		9413	Radio and television broadcasting Radio and television stations and studios primarily engaged in the production and dissemination to the public of aural and visual programs. Included are closed-circuit television services and television and radio relay stations.
		9414	Theatrical producers and entertainment services Theatres providing "live" theatrical presentations. This group also includes services allied with those presentations such as casting agencies and booking agencies for plays, artists and concerts; scenery, lighting, and other equipment services; and theatrical ticket agencies.
		9415	Authors, music composers, and other independent artists not elsewhere classified
	942	9420	Libraries, museums, botanical and zoological gardens, and other cultural services not elsewhere classified
	949	9490	Amusement and recreational services not elsewhere classified
95			*Personal and Household Services*
	951		Repair services not elsewhere classified Establishments specializing in the repair of household appliances equipment and furnishings; motor cars and other consumer goods which are not classified elsewhere. The reconstruction or substantial alteration or renovation of these goods constitutes manufacturing, and not repair services. Repair services in respect of consumer goods which are usually associated with the fabrication of the goods on a custom basis are classified in the appropriate group of Manufacturing. Repair services rendered by establishments engaged in retail trade are covered in Retail trade. The repair of clothing, bedspreads, blankets, curtains, and other personal and household made-up textiles is classified in group 9520 (Laundries, laundry

Division	Major group	Group	

			services, and cleaning and dyeing plants).
		9511	Repair of footwear and other leather goods
			The repair of footwear by establishments manufacturing shoes on a custom basis, is classified in group 3240 (Manufacture of footwear except vulcanized or moulded rubber or plastic footwear).
		9512	Electrical repair shops
		9513	Repair of motor vehicles and motorcycles
			The motor vehicle repair shops of petrol (gasoline) filling stations and the motor vehicle or motorcycle repair shops of establishments engaged in the sale of these vehicles to the general public, are classified in division 62 (Retail trade).
		9514	Watch, clock and jewelry repair
			These repair services when rendered by retailers of watches, clocks or jewellery are covered in division 62 (Retail trade).
		9519	Other repair shops not elsewhere classified
	952	9520	Laundries, laundry services, and cleaning and dyeing plants
	953	9530	Domestic services
			Maids, cooks, laundresses, babysitters, butlers, personal secretaries, gardeners, caretakers, and other maintenance workers for households, whether provided by individuals who are employed by these households or by business units primarily engaged in furnishing these services.
	959		Miscellaneous personal services
		9591	Barber and beauty shops
			This group also includes barber colleges and schools for the instruction of beauty parlor operators.
		9592	Photographic studies, including commercial photography
			Processing motion picture film for the motion picture and television industries is classified in group 9411 (Motion picture production).
		9599	Personal services not elsewhere classified

Division	Major group	Group	
			Personal services not elsewhere classified, such as shoeshine parlors or stands, turkish baths, massage parlors, morticians, crematories, cemetery upkeep, porter services, social escort services, and shopping services.
96	960	9600	*International and Other Extraterritorial Bodies* Establishments of the United Nations, the specialized agencies, the Organization of American States, the Organization of African States, the Organization for Economic Cooperation and Development, the European Economic Community, the Council for Mutual Economic Cooperation, the Council for Mutual Economic Cooperation and other international bodies; and of foreign embassies and other extraterritorial units.
[*Pro Memoria*			
41	410		Electricity, gas, and steam
	420		Water works and supply
50			Construction]

Source: United Nations. 1968. *International Standard Industrial Classification of All Economic Activities.* New York: United Nations.
Note: 1. Detailed descriptions of items are not reproduced in full.

With all these caveats, it is nevertheless useful, for the sake of consistency, to rank services by knowledge or skill content on the basis of available qualitative information as was done in chapter 3 (table 3–1), and, at the same time, to rank so-called high-technology goods according to their service or knowledge content in order to be able, at a later stage, to identify various types of international transactions in services and the leverage effect they are likely to have on the growth of the world economy. Among the long list of different service activities found in the literature, those presented by Herman and van Holst [1984] and, in regard to professional services, the detailed list elaborated by the services of the Commission of the European Communities (reproduced in table 4–4) provide a basis for such a heuristic classification. In the case of services, there is evidently no firm basis on which to rank individual items within each broad category, but the categories themselves are fairly

Table 4–2.   IMF classification of invisible transactions and services[1]

1. *Shipment*—includes:

    1.1 freight, insurance and other distribution services performed on merchandise, i.e., storage and warehousing, packing, forwarding, haulage, etc.

    1.2 transit trade

    1.3 coastal shipping or other shipping of goods between points within a country

2. *Other transportation*—operation of carriers and similar equipment, except labor services performed by carrier crews and insurance on the carriers themselves.

    2.1 passenger services, including services covered by fares and any other services on board carriers paid to the carriers, e.g., for the transport of excess baggage or personal effects such as automobiles

    2.2 port services, including lighterage, stevedoring, airport and harbor dues and fees, tugboat services, pilotage, towage, and maintenance and repair

    2.3 charter (leases) of carriers

    2.4 miscellaneous transportation, other than the transport of goods and persons, i.e., salvage operations, carriage of letter mail

3. *Travel*[2]—goods and services, other than passenger services, acquired by travellers, i.e., persons staying for less than one year in an economy of which they are not residents.

4. *Other goods, services, and income*[2,3]—includes:

    1.1 official transactions, i.e., local expenditures of embassies and consulates abroad for goods or services, including wage and salary payments to local staff; expenditures of military units and agencies and of other official entities abroad.

    1.2 private transactions, including:

    [1.2.1 labor income, i.e., earnings by nonresidents who remain in the country of work for less than one year, including border workers.]

    1.2.2 property income, i.e., nonfinancial property income not recorded elsewhere, in particular from patents, copyrights, etc. (royalties and licence fees).

    1.2.3 other goods and services:

        1.2.3.1 nonmerchandise insurance and reinsurance, including life insurance.

        1.2.3.2 communications, including postal services, cable, telephone, and telecommunications services.

        1.2.3.3 advertising, including by direct mail.

        1.2.3.4 brokerage, including agents' fees and financial

Table 4–2.   (cont'd)

		services performed by banks, underwriters and finance houses (as measured by the amounts of their charges).
	1.2.3.5	management.
	1.2.3.6	operational leasing (rental) other than charters of transportation equipment.
	1.2.3.7	periodicals bought through subscription.
	1.2.3.8	processing and repair.
	1.2.3.9	merchanting and commodity arbitrage.
	1.2.3.10	professional and technical services, including surveys, research, and provision of instruction and technical know-how.

[5.   *Investment income*]

6.   *Unrequited transfers*—including:

[workers' remittances (labor income by migrants who stay, or are expected to stay, more than one year abroad).]

contributions to religious, scientific, cultural, and charitable organizations, and membership fees to nonprofit associations.

scholarship and similar grants for on-the-job training, and grants for technical assistance.

fees for courier registrations

membership fees to nongovernmental organizations.

Source: IMF. 1977.
Notes:
1. Transactions that can clearly not be considered as services are in square brackets.
2. Sales of goods contain an element of retail services but are recorded at the full retail value of the goods. Payments of salaries to local staff (in item 1.1) are not services according to this author's definition.
3. Property income from patents and copyrights (item 1.2.2) may or may not be considered as services, depending on whether the items giving rise to payments are themselves services. Generally speaking, such payments are made for use of intellectual property, which may be considered as a service product rather than as a physical asset.

Table 4–3. Typologies of services, with examples

I. Traditional functional groupings	II. Traditional groupings by factor-content	III. Functional classifications			IV. Classifications based on functions/characteristics	
		(1) Browning and Singlemann	(2) Gadrey	(1) Barcet and Bonamy	(2) McKellar	(3) Plausibly tradeable: Herman and van Holst
A. *Basic or Primary*	A. *Labor-intensive*	A. *Transformational*	A. *Related to the production and marketing of goods*	A. *Related to the production and marketing of goods*	A. Services directly related to people	Park, gardening and agrarian services
Domestic help	Domestic help	Public utilities	1. Transport (goods)	Repairs and maintenance	B. Services for the propagation and care of plants and animals	Gas and water distribution
Porters, guards	Retail trade	Construction	Repairs and maintenance	Cleaning		Building contractors and public engineering
Sanitation services	Recreational services	B. *Distribution*	Restaurants and catering	Surveillance	C. Services related to land, water, air, and minerals	Wholesale and retail trade, including hotels and restaurants
B. *Intermediate*	Hospitals	Transport and storage	Hotels	Trade and storage		Transport (goods and passengers)
Transport (goods)	Accountancy	Communications	2. Retail trade	Rental	D. Services related to buildings and other fixed assets	Travel agencies
Nonlife insurance	Legal services	Wholesale and retail trade	Rental (including real estate)	Restaurants, hotels		Brokers
Wholesale trade	Public administration	C. *Commercial*	Retail banking and insurance	Scrap collection	E. Services related to the manufacture and marketing of goods	Communications, information and news services
Databases	B. *Capital-intensive*	Financial services	3. Passenger transport	B. *Nonmaterial services*		Banking and insurance
Business services	Transport	Insurance	Personal care	Information		Real estate operation
Management	Computer services	Real estate	B. *Nonmaterial support services*	Financial services		
C. *Final*	Wholesale trade	Engineering	Engineering	Cultural services		
Recreational services	Engineering	Accounting		Consulting		
Retail trade	Life insurance	Management		Advertising		
Rental	Financial services	Other business services				
Public	Telecommunications	D. *Collective*				
		Health care				
		Social welfare				

83

Table 4-3. (cont'd)

I. Traditional functional groupings	II. Traditional groupings by factor-content	III. Functional classifications		IV. Classifications based on functions/characteristics		
		(1) Browning and Singlemann	(2) Gadrey	(1) Barcet and Bonamy	(2) McKellar	(3) Plausibly tradeable: Herman and van Holst
administration Life insurance Passenger transport	Real estate	Public administration E. Personal Domestic help Hotel, restaurants Repairs Recreational services	Consulting Business finance Software R&D C. Final consumer services Education Health care Recreational services Social welfare services D. Organization and management Administration (private and public) Management Information services	C. Affecting individuals and their living conditions Health Education Personal care Social welfare	(except transportation) F. Transportation G. Services related to records and information H. Services of general application	Legal and auditing services Computer services Advertising Consultancy and employment services Rental Education Health services Recreational services Cleaning Personal care Auctions Photographic services

Sources: I and II: Nusbaumer [1987]; III. Browning and Singleman, as quoted in Bulthuis et al. [1985]; Gadrey [1986b]; IV: Barcet and Bonamy [1986]; Canada [1984]; Herman and van Holst [1981].

Table 4–4.   Indicative list of liberal and intellectual professions

Actuary	Doctor, general	Pharmacist
Agronomist	practitioner or	Photographer
Analyst	specialist	Physicist
Animated cartoonist	Document researcher	Physiotherapist
Architect		Practitioner of dentistry
Archivist	Economist	Process-server
Artist	Engineer (various	Psychologist
Auctioneer and valuer	disciplines)	Publicist
Auditor	Estate agent	
Author	Estate manager	Sales representative
	Estimator	Sculptor
Biologist		Social worker
Broker	Geologist	Sociologist
	Graphologist	Sports instructor
Chemist	Guide	Stage manager
Chiropractor		Statistician
Composer	Interior designer	Stockbroker
Computer scientist		Surveyor
Conference interpreter	Journalist	
Consultants of various	Judicial officer	Teacher
kinds		Topographer
Industrial property	Landscape gardener	Town planner
consultant	Lawyer	
Marriage guidance		Various consultants
counselor	Masseur	Chartered accountant
Organization and	Midwife	Legal consultant
methods consultant		Property consultant
Tax consultant	Notary public	Veterinary surgeon
Consulting engineer	Nurse	
Criminologist		Window-dresser
	Optometrist	Writer
Decorator	Osteopath	
Dentist		
Designer	Painter	
Dispensing optician		

Source: Commission of the European Communities. 1982. *The Professions in the European Community.* Brussels: EEC.

Note: This list is not confined to the traditionally limited number of professions in the strict sense of the term, such as advocates, notaries, judges, doctors, or architects. It has been drawn up by the EC Commission for indicative purposes to represent the collectivity of liberal and intellectual professions in the present state of development of science, technology, and social institutions; they are occupations which, irrespective of the legal status (salaried, self-employed) of those who pursue them, are characterized by independence and personal responsibility, and are not primarily economic in their content.

straightforward: they correspond with the man-on-the-street's understanding of the workings of modern society. A possible ranking of goods by service content is shown in table 4–5. In the case of goods, there is a considerable amount of statistical data available in the form of input-output tables for most major industrial countries. There may exist differences among countries as to the ranking of individual goods, but broad categories follow the same pattern.

As with any other typology of services, the one suggested in table 4–5 raises fundamental questions to which current practice does not provide a ready answer. First, there is the question of the level of skill content at which one begins to designate a productive activity as a service; second, there is the question of the proportion of nonmaterial content of goods at which one begins to designate the good as a service product. The first problem arises in connection with the treatment of labor services, particularly in the context of international trade. The second arises in connection with certain activities often referred to as service activities, but which involve a relatively large content of material output such as construction, public works and utilities, and art work, as well as with some high-technology products commonly called goods such as integrated circuits, computer tapes or disks containing software or stored data, and other similar physical supports where the value of the support is quasi-nil compared with the value of the contained knowledge.

What Is 'Labor'?

Labor services consume in varying proportions a combination of physical force and intellectual ability. It could therefore be argued that all human work consists of labor services. Distinctions between different types of labor can be made either on the basis of what is commonly called skill, or on the basis of the end-product of the laborer's effort. In the latter case, for example, one can distinguish between a carpenter and a lawyer; the end-product of the first worker is tangible and the second, intangible. Such a distinction does not lead to intuitively satisfactory results, however. Within the same sector of activity, a low-skilled laborer and a highly-skilled laborer can both contribute to the production of a tangible good such as a machine tool. Differences in knowledge-content are the only basis on which a distinction can be made between the two types of labor, which is consistent with the respective contributions of the laborers to the total final value of the machine tool. But there is a further question that arises: whether differences in knowledge-content between the two types of labor call for a distinction which is not only of degree but also of *nature*. If so,

Table 4–5.   Indicative list of goods with a high service component, ranked in ascending order of R&D intensity[1]

SITC number	Description
512, 53, 55, 59 less 599.2	Industrial chemicals: radioactive and associated chemicals, synthetic organic dyestuffs, products of polymerization and copolymerization
719	Machinery and appliances, and parts thereof
718	Machines for special industries
717.1	Textile machinery
715	Metalworking machinery
722, 723, 729	Electrical power machinery; apparatus for electrical circuits; electrical measuring and controlling instruments; electromagnetic appliances, etc.
711	Nonelectrical machinery
391, 724	Tape recorders; radio and television equipment
711 less 711.9	Engines and turbines, except aircraft
661.9	Measuring and control instruments
513, 514, 515	Industrial chemicals
561	Fertilizers
599.2	Agricultural chemicals
58	Plastics and synthetics
54	Pharmaceuticals: vitamins and provitamins; antibiotics; vegetable alkaloids; hormones; glycocides, sera, vaccines, etc.
861	Photographic equipment and apparatus; scientific and optical instruments
ex. 714	Office equipment; photocopiers, etc.; *less* computers
711.4	Aircraft engines
734	Aircraft
726	Electromedical equipment
727, 729.3, ex. 714	Communications equipment, including satellites; transistors, semiconductors and other electronic components; computers.

Source: Adapted from R. Bulthuis, B. van Holst, and G. R. de Wit [1985].
Note: 1. The list being purely illustrative, the amount of R&D separating any two items is indeterminate.

the difficulty is, where does one draw the line between ordinary work effort, such as that performed by the unskilled laborer, and work defined as a service activity such as that of the engineer? There should be some point at which an additional quantity of contained knowledge gives rise to a "mutation" in the work; but the cutoff point is likely to be arbitrary since there is no objective criterion available to define "skill." It would appear, therefore, that unless such an additional distinction can be made, there may be no sound basis for distinguishing services from goods from the point of view of labor input. The same reasoning, in fact, would apply to physical capital used in the production of goods, on the one hand, and in the production of services (e.g., law services), on the other. All goods and services would be perfectly homogeneous in terms of their constituent elements, hence there would be no need to distinguish between them for purposes of analyzing economic structures and trade patterns.

The fact of the matter is that the distinction between labor services which are inputs into the production of goods and labor services which are inputs into the production of services considered as intangible products depends on the particular organization of production in a given country or region to which statistics of output refer. In a given economic setting, some services are sold on the market by independent service-producing enterprises (*externalized* services), while in other economic settings the same services are produced within manufacturing or other goods-producing enterprises (*internalized* services). These differences account for the different shares of services in national output between countries which in all other respects have reached similar levels of economic and technological development. For example, Japan and West Germany have relatively low shares of services in their gross domestic products compared with the United States and Sweden (see table 4–6). The classification of certain types of work as service work on the basis of the accumulated knowledge embodied in the workers does not overcome the problem posed by the existence of different economic structures and thus may be analytically inadequate, though intellectually satisfying if one is interested in comparing certain productive activities leading to the marketing of intangible products with other activities that lead to the marketing of tangible products. Thus, although the accumulated knowledge and technology content of work may on average be equal in two given economies, it may be correct to say that one such economy is more of a "service" or "postindustrial"[1] economy than the other. From this standpoint, the conclusion is therefore that a proper distinction between labor services classified as service activities and labor services classified as goods-producing activities should be based on the type of product issued by the

Table 4–6. Share of services in gross domestic product, 1965 and 1984, selected countries (percentages)

Country and GDP per capita in 1984		1965	1984
Indonesia	(540)	29	34
Philippines	(660)	46	41
Morocco	(670)	49	*51*
Thailand	(860)	42	52
Jamaica	(1,150)	53	56
Turkey	(1,160)	41	47
Colombia	(1,390)	46	50
Brazil	(1,720)	48	*52*
Italy	(6,420)	48	55
Singapore	(7,260)	73	60
New Zealand	(7,730)	n.a.	*60*
United Kingdom	(8,570)	56	62
Netherlands	(9,520)	n.a.	*64*
France	(9,760)	n.a.	62
Japan	(10,630)	48	56
Finland	(10,770)	52	59
Germany, Fed. Rep.'	(11,130)	n.a.	52
Denmark	(11,170)	60	70
Sweden	(11,860)	53	*66*
Canada	(13,280)	61	72
Norway	(13,940)	59	54
United States	(15,390)	59	*66*

Source: World Bank, 1986. *World Development Report 1986.* Washington, D.C.: IBRD.
Note: Figures in italics are for 1983, not 1984.

particular *enterprises* (as opposed to the laborers themselves) in which such labor services are employed. Consequently, high technology goods like those listed in table 4–4 involve the use of services inputs to the extent that they are produced with service products purchased on the market, and involve the use of ordinary labor of different levels of skill to the extent that they are wholly produced within single enterprises. In practice, the emergence of the service economy as evidenced by statistics of gross national product is a phrase that depicts the increasingly independent mode of production of services and their marketing as specific products to be used as intermediate inputs in production processes. The relationship of this structural phenomenon to the accumulation of knowledge is that the handling and treatment of accumulated knowledge itself requires increasingly specialized skills which, on the one hand, stimulate enterprises to divest themselves of knowledge-intensive work departments that require closer attention and management than can be given to them in the complex organizational structure of a manufacturing firm. On the other hand, they stimulate the creation of independent service firms to compete, first, with the knowledge-intensive work departments of manufacturing firms, and second, among themselves.

From the point of view of international trade, the distinction between labor services (skilled or unskilled) embodied in goods and labor services traded directly as products is very clear, because trade in goods has traditionally been subjected to different policies than factor movements and, for that matter, capital movements. However, when services are traded in their own right—that is, as products sold across borders—the nature of the transactions is exactly the same as when goods are sold from one country to another, and the only distinction that logically remains between the two types of products is that one is tangible and the other, intangible. This is the same as to say that, except for this physical characteristic, services are no different from goods to the extent that the services are marketed just like goods, i.e., as value-added packages. The similarity would be total if units of such value-added packages could be as easily delineated in the case of services as they can in the case of goods and, especially, if such units were sufficiently homogeneous to command a common market price as do goods of similar physical description and performance (quality). Labor services, of course, are embodied in the laborer, and it is not the laborer himself who is sold internationally, but what he does. Hence, the traditional notion of trade, as being the exchange of products at a distance and in particular between different countries, does not apply to this type of transaction in services.

There is, however, a risk of logical inconsistency in describing services as intangible products and requiring that the notion of international trade in such products conform to that which applies to goods. In effect, the intangibility requires, as already mentioned, that the traditional notion of trade be extended to cover transactions not only between residents of different countries but also between nationals of different countries whenever the sale of services abroad involves a temporary as well as permanent presence of the owner of the service on foreign territory. This extension, it should be noted, does not impair the distinction made earlier between services produced independently and sold on the market as service products, and services produced within the organizational structure of manufacturing, agricultural, or other enterprises. Thus, the labor services of foreigners employed in steel plants are pure *factor* imports, whereas foreign labor services employed in a law firm are imported service *products*.

Tradeability

Returning now to services embodied in goods, the main problem of definition relates to certain types of activities which have sometimes been classified in the service sector and sometimes not, depending on which of their characteristics are considered dominant. In the first place, these activities give rise to a type of goods that have the characteristic of nontransportability; the other activities concerned are an inseparable mix of production and distribution of goods whose utility rests largely in their being transported in a continuous flow to users and consumers. The activities in question are the construction of buildings and public works on the one hand and the provision of so-called "public utilities" on the other.

In the case of construction, it is clear that the end-products are goods. These goods are immovable and cannot, therefore, be traded at a distance, whether across borders or within the boundaries of a national territory. When considering the tradeability of services, therefore, it seems totally irrelevant to include construction activities. In most analyses of services output carried out up to now, it has been customary to combine pure construction work with the engineering work (including the work of architects) which is a necessary input into it or which, at least, enters into the preparation of the elements used in it (for example, in do-it-yourself construction kits). The reason for considering construction activities as services is, in many instances, more institutional than analytical. It is difficult in practice to separate the work of building contractors into its constituent elements, since such contractors deal both with the planning, conceptualizing, and even esthetic and/or artistic content of the products they sell and with the practical execution of their projects. They draw the plans and mix the cement. On the other hand, it does not seem logical to consider buildings or public works as products essentially made up of engineers' and architects' applied knowledge. First, as in the case of high-technology goods, the distinction between goods and services output in this area depends on the particular organizational structure of construction firms. Second, there is usually a much more important proportion of physical output, whether calculated in weight, volume, density, or raw material content, in the final product than in other similar products, notably in many high-technology products of the electronics industry, e.g., semi-conductors. Thus, it is justifiable conceptually to separate out the actual erection of buildings or the construction of roads and bridges from the conceptualization of such projects. However, available production and trade statistics may not allow such a distinction to be made, in which case it is preferable to include the total value of construction output among services in order not to "lose" the engineering content which makes an important contribution to the national product and to the international trade of many countries.[2]

With regard to so-called public utilities, namely electricity, gas, and water supply, it is much more difficult to distinguish between the physical and the nonmaterial elements of final output because the physical products yielded by the production processes are not so readily identifiable as in the case of construction work. Electricity and gas are invisible, and water, a visible natural product, undergoes only a minor degree of processing in relation to its mass, except where it is recovered and recycled. Apart from producing electricity and gas and purifying water, public utilities transport these goods over distribution networks which are the products of the construction industry. Among the three constituent elements of output, production (or processing), transportation, and construction, it appears that the transportation uses up the smallest amount of resources and usually exhibits decreasing marginal costs over the relevant production range (unless network capacity is smaller than peak demand). Whatever the scale of output, therefore, public utilities are overwhelmingly goods-producing activities, and for this reason they should be excluded from the service sector.[3]

Having dealt with these particular cases, we may now turn once more to the general notion of tradeability as it applies to services, in order to see whether and how this notion is affected by certain characteristics of services such as intangibility and nonstoreability. To begin with, we have seen that the latter characteristics make it essential in certain cases for factor movements to substitute for service-product movements, even to the extent of factors establishing resident status in foreign countries in order to be in a position to supply their services on a continuing basis. Thus, a construction firm can send a whole team of engineers, skilled service workers (surveyors, draftsmen, and the like) and primary labor (brick-layers, cement mixers, etc.) to a foreign country to execute a specific construction project, and repatriate them once the project is completed. But a construction firm can also, if a commission to undertake more than a single project in that country is likely, wish to establish a presence there in order to carry out on a more systematic basis the related project planning and execution work. In such cases we would say that intangibility and non-storeability make engineering and skilled service workers nontradeable. Nevertheless, we should note that there are particular market circumstances that increase or decrease the degree of tradeability of individual services. Thus, if the construction firm in question had already a solid international reputation which had crossed the borders, it could probably bypass the confidence-building step of establishing a local presence and reduce factor movements to a minimum by carrying out most engineering work in its home office.

Other influences on the tradeability of services have little or nothing to do with the relative degree of embodiment or disembodiment of services in particular production factors. Examples are geographical location and topographical characteristics of particular countries or areas. A case in point is the location of a particular country, area, or city in a given time zone which permits it to perform a linkup function between financial markets in different parts of the world. Another case is that of island economies where the absence of rail or road links with neighboring countries makes rail and road services nontradeable compared with countries situated next to each other on a continuous land surface. There are also certain regions of the earth where the frequency of atmospheric disturbances reduces the effectiveness of telecommunication connections and others where the contrary is true.

Tradeability of services may also be dependent on the availability of what Leif Edvinsson [1985] calls "thoughtware." Thoughtware may be considered as a natural advantage to the extent that certain natural conditions facilitate the development of intellectual activities in some regions more than in others. It is generally accepted that human beings have the same basic intellectual capacity in all regions of the world, but even among the most sincere advocates of Third World development, there are those who attribute the economic difficulties of underdeveloped countries to the effects of the physical environment on human beings [Kamarck, 1976]. The present author does not, however, subscribe to this view.

Functions

Besides examining alternative typologies of services in relevant theoretical terms, it is useful to consider their practical implications. As indicated earlier, one approach is to classify services in terms of the main functions they perform in the economy. All services have in common a number of functions which they fulfill in different degrees. If classified according to the function that dominates individual activities, services lend themselves to a systematic analysis of their characteristics, just as the hierarchy of goods among raw materials, producer goods, and consumer goods permits a rationalization of production and marketing processes that helps one understand the overall functioning of the economy.[4]

While the various functional forms of services permit fairly clear distinctions among broad categories of activities, for detailed breakdowns it may sometimes be more difficult to decide which of the various functional forms represented is the most important.

The main functional forms that seem relevant to a coherent set of definitions are: (1) the knowledge-carrying function; (2) the communication function; (3) the linkage function; (4) the information function. Functions (2) and (3), linkage and communication, of course have very much in common. For purposes of analysis, it is useful further to distinguish between linkages that are market-creating—i.e., that establish *channels* of communication between producers and consumers and among producers, and pure communication functions which provide the means for carrying information. Again, there is a certain relationship between the information function and the knowledge-carrying function; the first consists of the collection and processing of raw data, and the second in the dissemination and transfer of accumulated knowledge and know-how. Table 4–7 shows a tentative classification of major sectors of service activities according to these four criteria. Under the knowledge-carrying function, we find general knowledge-disseminating functions such as education and training, as well as a number of important producer or business services such as engineering, architecture, law, accounting, etc., and other professional services catering to the general public, such as medical care, justice, crime prevention, and, generally, public administration. Public administration fits into this category to the extent that it performs educational tasks and/or protects economic agents, sometimes against their will, thanks to the broader and more objective knowledge that government officials are supposed to have of the economic and social environment in which private firms and individuals carry out their activities. In the linkage category we find the obvious distance-reducing services such as transport of various kinds including transport of voice and image over telecommunication or satellite networks, as well as a number of services that support the market system by creating a favorable environment for the development of market relations. This includes public services like civil law and diplomatic services, and activities more directly related to

Table 4–7.   A tentative classification of services by functions

A. Knowledge-carrying function	B. Linkage function	C. Communication function	D. Information function
Education (all levels)	Transport (goods)	Telephone and telegraph	Databases
Training (including military)	Wholesale and retail trade	Mail services	Data processing
Museum management R&D	Brokerage	Performing arts	Marketing
Painters, sculptors, composers	Rentals and leasing	Radio and TV broadcasting and	Cultural services
Consultancy	Real estate	publishing	News services
Engineering	Banking and other financial	Advertising	Business management
Religious services	services	Franchising	Library services
Medical services	Insurance, reinsurance		
Defense services	Diplomatic services		
Legal services			
Sports instruction			
Supervisory services			
Computer software and data-			
processing services			
Laboratory services			
Architecture and design			
Administration, including police			
Accountancy and audit			
Justice			

95

the creation and maintenance of business links between producers and between producers and consumers, such as financial services (particularly trade finance, mortgage finance, consumer finance, etc.) and all forms of insurance and reinsurance. Communication services are those characterized by information-carrier functions such as broadcasting, data transmission, and more specifically business-related services like advertising and franchising. Finally, information services are all those relating to data, like databases, computer data processing, libraries, editing, press, statistical, and research services. Evidently, the classification of certain services in one or the other category is sometimes moot, and the reasonableness of the scheme adopted must be left to the appreciation of the reader.

The important thing about any classification of services is that it is difficult to find a service activity which is not in one way or another devoted essentially to developing or maintaining a complex network of interrelationships between economic agents either in city, region, country, or internationally. Examples of services not specifically devoted to this task are found mainly at the consumer level: for example, personal and domestic services, entertainment services (although these sometimes carry a considerable amount of information between the entertainer and the consumer), and some particular types of services that one finds both in the private and in the public sector, such as gardeners, game wardens, etc.[5]

It is interesting to compare the classification of services in table 4–8 with the various classifications that exist for goods. We have spoken before of a classification of services for trade purposes which could be based on their knowledge content as an indication of their level of "processing," just as goods are classified by degree of industrial processing in the Standard International Trade Classification (SITC) of the United Nations. For other purposes, goods are classified according to the material they contain. This is the basis for the tariff classification adopted by the Customs Cooperation Council (CCC). There are also functional classifications of goods such as investment goods, consumer goods, and within the latter category durable and nondurable consumer goods, and also classifications based on the type of benefit or "service" that can be derived from different goods, such as food, toys, houses, etc. It should not be surprising, therefore, that in the field of services many different classifications can coexist based on the purpose at hand. Moreover, because of the absence of classifying conventions for most purposes, the coverage of similar categories of services may differ from one author to another. The difficulty rests with the fact that only a few types of services have been subjected to close analytical scrutiny, while for most others, it is still difficult to discern which characteristics (among many) are to be deemed essential, all the more so as some services evolve rapidly in character and content with the advent of new technologies and creative innovation. For example, the character of retail banking has been radically transformed as a result of financial deregulation in a country like the United States; whereas some years ago the essential characteristic of retail banking may still have been the taking of current account deposits from consumers and the making of personal and mortgage loans to them, nowadays it may be portfolio management, billing, tax accounting, and the like.

The temptation to fit services into categories which have been created for goods should generally be resisted, unless there is clear evidence that similar natural differences or similar economic hierarchies exist between them. Obviously, classifications based on physical materials are ruled out. As we have just seen, the borderline between intermediate and consumer services is sometimes blurred and changing. Moreover, due to the interaction between producer and consumer which exists for many services, e.g., in consumer self-service or in civil law suits, hierarchies based on analogies with goods-production patterns may not hold. For example, it has been suggested (including by the present author [Nusbaumer, 1984]) that services can be classified as primary, intermediate, and final products. Although this may be correct in descriptive terms, it does not necessarily mean that input-output relationships which such a categorization implies for goods also applies to services. As discussed in chapter 7, the notion of network may be a more relevant guide to understanding, how services interact than the notion of linear processing chains implied by the very use of the expression "input-output."

Because services can be classified in many different ways and can be seen to perform many different functions, some observers have concluded that one of their main features is heterogeneity and, indeed, that heterogeneity among services is greater than among goods. If it were true that services are so different from each other that only a few activities can be compared and that each set of comparable activities constitutes a distinct facet of economic life, then of course it would become difficult if not impossible to speak of services generally and also to consider them as economic products comparable to goods. As it were, banking and entertainment could not be lumped together as services because their functions are so fundamentally different, and their only common characteristic is intangibility. In truth, on the basis of this reasoning one could also say that there is no such thing as "goods." After all, the only thing machine tools and spoons have in common is that they are made of metal. As such, they are classified in the same chapter of the Customs Cooperation Council Nomenclature (CCCN) for tariff purposes. The real problem is not that services differ among themselves, or that goods differ among themselves, it is that economic activities do not really fit the three-sector classification which, following Fischer [1939] and Clark [1960], all national and balance-of-payments accountants still use.

On the other hand, if goods were differentiated only on the basis of the functions they perform or of the services they provide, many statistical conventions that play a useful role would have to be abandoned. The fact that goods can be classified in this way does not in reality exclude their being classified according to the material of which they are made or to some other physical characteristic, or according to the way in which they are produced (e.g., agriculture against industry). Similarly, the fact that many services are produced in different ways, perform different functions, contain different elements of information and knowledge, and are traded differently, does not constitute a plausible reason for denying them common characteristics which, at least for certain analytical purposes, take precedence over their heterogeneity.

Regulations

These considerations are important when looking at the way in which various activities in the field of services are regulated by national governments or at the international level. The regulatory environment in which service activities take place is another possible basis for differentiating among them. From this standpoint there are different classifications possible, depending on the purposes of the regulations, or on their generic or specific character. Some observers go one step further and argue that one major source of difference between services and goods is that the regulations to which service activities are subjected at the national level are of a totally different character than the regulations affecting the production and marketing of goods. It is therefore interesting to see whether services can be classified according to the types of regulations most commonly found at national and international levels and to compare such a classification with a similar one for goods. If the regulations affecting services were found to be systematically different from those affecting goods, this would provide one new way of defining services that may deserve particular attention not only in economic analysis but also in international economic relations. If, in addition, it was found that services are significantly different from goods in the sense of their production and distribution being much more regulated in most countries, it may justify a presumption that their role in national economies is to produce externalities which have a higher social than private value, since it is generally on such grounds that the intervention of the state is justified, either to sustain the activities of private producers or to substitute for deficiencies of the market. Services, like goods, may be subject to quality standards, prohibitions, locational requirements, etc. However, in most instances, it is the processes of production and distribution which are being regulated rather than the characteristics of the products, because in the case of services it is often difficult if not impossible to distinguish between the act of production and the product. Nevertheless, whenever that distinction can be made, it should be reflected in any classification used to compare services with goods from the point of view of the number, variety, and types of regulations affecting them. Table 4–8 presents a classification of major categories of services according to the most current types of government regulations applied to them and indicates in each case whether goods are subjected to the same or to comparable regulations.

The information presented in table 4–8 lends some support to the view that services are more regulated than goods. The table does not, of course, give any idea of the content of the regulations nor of their effect on the activities concerned. A much more detailed, case-by-case analysis would be necessary in order to compare, over the whole range of services and goods-producing activities, the real impact of regulations which on the face of it may look particularly punctilious. Unfortunately, no such analysis has been carried out to date.[6]

In the absence of concrete evidence on the impact of regulations on the allocation of resources within the private sector and in the national economy as a whole, the assumption that regulations create welfare-reducing distortions can only be made if there are a priori reasons to expect that the market mechanism is the optimum regulator for services as it is for most goods. This is precisely the point that causes the most serious disagreements among policy-makers and private sector operators. Those who maintain that the central linkages provided by services in national economies and their role in the process of economic development justify the intervention of the state in the allocative mechanisms, see such intervention as a means of reducing or eliminating distortions caused by the free interplay of market forces. If, on the contrary, services are thought to be governed by the same laws of supply and demand as goods, then state intervention is justified only to correct market imperfections. The same divergencies of views arise with regard to regulations affecting international transactions in services. We shall return to this problem when discussing the proposed establishment of international disciplines to govern these transactions in chapter 8. In that context we shall also have to

Table 4–8. Regulation of service activities: examples of measures and activities covered

1. Internal market regulation	2. International service transactions affected			3. Noneconomically motivated regulation	4. Corresponding regulation of the goods sector
	(a) Cross-border trade	(b) Establishment trade	(c) Factor migrating		
1. Public procurement	Data processing; Shipping; Engineering; Other professional services; Education and training.	Insurance; Banking; Construction-engineering.	Consultancy	Defense services	Yes
2. Quantitative restrictions	Advertising; Franchising; Broadcasting; Data services.	Banking; Leasing; Retail trade; Transport; Accounting.	Business services; Medical and legal services; Performing arts.	—	Yes
3. Public monopolies	Telecommunications; Data processing; Broadcasting;	Telecommunications; Banking; Insurance.	—	Transport (air, sea, rail); Education; Broadcasting)	Rare
4. Local content	Transport (air and sea)	Insurance; Education; Management	—	—	Yes
5. Fees and dues	Air transport; Shipping; Data processing; Tourism; Broadcasting	Telecommunications (leased lines)	—	—	Yes
6. Standards	Tourism services; Transport (road and sea)	Insurance; Banking; Telecommunications	Professional services	Insurance, Banking; Professional services	Yes
7. Special taxation of income	—	Banking; Insurance; Air transport; Accounting; Hotel-motel services	—	—	Rare

examine how the fact that certain services are nonmarketable public goods or are produced under natural monopoly conditions impinges upon the possible scope of international disciplines.

Data Problems

In presenting various classification schemes either proposed or in use, Dorothy Riddle [1986, p. 13] rightly observes that "systems that cannot be used for data collection are of only academic interest." It would be a mistake, however, to exaggerate the practical difficulty of collecting data on production and trade in services. If experience in the field of goods is any guide, many apparently insuperable problems can be solved either through improved data-collection methods or through the use of relevant indicators. At the same time, it would be wrong to lose sight of the inconsistencies of the existing statistical apparatus which sometimes make qualitative analysis preferable to deductions based on unreliable data. Brian Ames [1986] has pointed out the various pitfalls in existing statistics on production, trade, and employment in services. One of the main problems is that these statistics lump together activities with a multiplicity of functions or create overlapping categories covering different aspects of a single service activity.

In fact, difficulties of data collection are so great that the problem of overlapping exists not only for narrowly defined service activities but also for broad categories. With regard to statistics on national production of services, Ames points out the inconsistencies among the United Nations System of National Accounting, the Courcier System of National Accounting used by the majority of French-speaking developing countries, and the Material Product System (MPS) used by centrally planned economies. The United Nations System (SNA) is the most commonly used. Based on the United Nations International Standard Industrial Classification of all economic activities (ISIC), this system defines five broad categories of services activities: wholesale and retail trade, restaurants, and hotels; transport, storage, and communication; financing, insurance, real estate, and business services; public administration and defense; and community, social, and personal services ("other services"). The MPS distinguishes between wholesale and retail trade, transport and communication, and other material services. Material services are directly related to the production and distribution of goods, including repairs and transportation. All services not so related are treated as nonmaterial.

It is clear that the broad categories retained by any system of national accounts cover activities which do not necessarily fit together from an analytical point of view. Thus, in the SNA the sector of "transport, storage, and communication" includes telecommunication, telematics, satellite transmission, broadcasting, etc., which have little to do with road transport, shipping, etc. In "financing, insurance, real estate, and business services" are lumped together a whole series of activities, particularly in the subcategory of business services, which perform different linkage, knowledge-carrying, communication, and information functions and which fit in different sections of the functional classification presented in table 4–8 above. Again, the whole range of "public administration and defense" services covers different governmental activities with different functions, while the category "community, social, and personal services" includes activities which are marketed and others more properly classified in the "informal economy."

In addition to the lack of a clear basis for the distinctions made between different categories of services in the national accounting systems in current use, Ames [1986] has pointed to a number of other conceptual problems with those systems. First, there is the problem that many service activities are internalized in manufacturing enterprises and therefore are not recorded separately in national accounts, and other service activities are carried out inside households or in the informal economy and are not recorded at all. The extent to which domestic service activities which are carried out inside a household in traditional societies appear in national account statistics depends on the rate of female participation in the labor force, which varies considerably from country to country and within the same country over time. Finally, services perform important linkage functions which produce externalities of which no record appears in national accounting, although they often constitute a sizeable portion of the value added in service activities. This portion of value added not only goes unrecorded but it is often not directly measurable because economic agents responsible for it and those benefiting from it are not aware of its existence.

With regard to statistics on employment in services, the major sources identified by Brian Ames are the *Yearbook of Labor Statistics* published by the International Labor Organization of the United Nations (ILO), and the *ILO Capital Labor Force Estimates and Projections, 1950–2000*. With the exception of public administration and defense, the broad categories of service activities used by ILO are the same as those appearing in SNA production statistics. The conceptual limitations of ILO data, apart from the fact that the statistics are not comparable from country to country except in the Capital Labor Force Estimates and Projections, are the underreporting of service employment, which results from the existence of an informal economy, and the distortions arising in the recording of household work.

In both the United Nations production statistics and the ILO employment statistics, construction and utilities are excluded from the service sector. As argued above, this is a priori a reasonable decision for utilities but not for construction. On the other hand, both of these classifications include repairs among service activities, whereas it can be argued that repairs are a form of physical production and therefore should be excluded from services in the same way as public utilities.

In addition to the conceptual problems pointed out by Ames, current statistical systems are also incomplete in failing to provide a basis for distinguishing clearly between domestic production and exports of services. This relates to the distinction between intermediate and final products, which is much less easy to make for services than for goods. Thus, it is unlikely that aluminium ingots or cement reinforcing bars would find much of a market with private consumers. By contrast, a lawyer can render his/her services both to an enterprise and to an individual, and there is no clear external sign distinguishing these two types of services either from the point of view of their physical characteristics, or of the inputs entering into their production. Most statistical systems ignore the destination of services sales and even the nationality of the buyers. If the latter are business enterprises located abroad, all sales to them will be recorded as intermediate transactions and will be deducted from GNP, whereas in fact they are exports. An example of the difference which a clearer distinction between the destination of intermediate services can make is that of Luxembourg, where a complete overhaul of the accounting system applied to banking services undertaken in 1977 resulted in a increase in the recorded exports and GNP of that country [Arndt, 1984].

The question of statistical definitions of service transactions is thus important for a clearer understanding of the role of services not only in national economies but also in the international economy.

This brings us to an examination of the third set of statistics on services, namely those on trade, and the definitions on which they are based. The definitions used by most balance-of-payments statisticians around the world are those of the International Monetary Fund (IMF). The IMF provides an analytical framework for determining the tradeability or nontradeability of services. In its *Balance-of-Payments Manual* [1977], the IMF does not, however, make use of the notion of *trade* but rather speaks of international *transactions* and international *payments*. In normal parlance, trade, of course, refers to the sale of goods across borders, and this type of transaction is included in the IMF definition. However, the IMF bases its concepts of an international transaction on two factors: (1) a change of ownership of a real resource, which can be a good or a service as compared to a simple transfer of wealth (paragraph 203); and (2) a change of ownership taking place between a resident of a country and a nonresident enterprise or individual. This definition means that for an international transaction to take place, there does not need to be a movement of goods or services across borders. Thus, sales of goods or services to foreign tourists temporarily present in the country are international transactions according to the IMF definition. The converse of this type of transaction, namely the delivery of labor services abroad in the context of a special project or more generally, if the workers do not reside abroad for more than one year, is equally an international transaction.[7] It is only because little attention has been paid to the development of international transactions in services that the effects of applying the IMF definition to international trade theory have so far been disregarded. The facts that consumers do move in great numbers to foreign countries and that a considerable amount of international service transactions takes place through movements of factors have been ignored because they did not fit the accepted framework of analysis of movements of real resources between countries. In effect, further extensions of the notion of *trade* in services may be required to deal with the special characteristics of services. These also involve movements of factors for the simultaneous production and delivery of service products, but the reference in this case is to foreign direct investment. Foreign investments in service activities are often a sine qua non condition of their delivery, whereas in the field of goods they are more often than not an alternative to cross-border trade. For analytical purposes, therefore, it is useful to consider applying an *IMF plus* definition of international transactions, covering the permanent establishment of firms abroad as a means of ensuring continuous access to foreign markets whenever service production and distribution are inseparable facets of the same activity.

It is relevant in this connection to examine the distinction between so-called "factor" and "nonfactor" services as it arises from IMF *Balance-of-Payments Manual* definitions and as it is used in traditional economic theory. Obviously, nonfactor services are those which we have called up to now "service products," i.e., activities that produce economic effects abroad from the movement of *compacted* results of productive activities (e.g., an insurance contract, an engineering blueprint, etc.) across borders. In addition, the IMF includes in nonfactor services transactions carried out abroad by nonresident producers who remain in a foreign country for less than one calendar year. Contrasting with these so-called nonfactor transactions are factor returns which are based on the production activities of labor and capital exported to foreign countries and remaining in these countries for more than one year (residents). The definition of service-related factor movements is conceptually easy, but the corresponding financial flows are almost impossible to identify. Returns on investments and income from labor operating abroad are usually recorded gross irrespective of whether they originate in the services or goods sector. Theoretically, it would be possible to distinguish between these factor returns; if only because of the fact that there is an increasing intermingling between the production of services and the production of goods in modern economies, such distinctions are bound to be very difficult, and the data based on them open to doubt. The question arises, therefore, whether one should at all concern oneself with returns to factors from abroad for purposes of studying international trade or transactions in services, unless there is some hope of one day being able to separate those that are service-related from the totals. The conclusion to be reached at the present time is that it is confusing to refer to "invisible" transactions as the equivalent of international transactions in services, since such invisible transactions in the IMF definitions include returns on factors used abroad in the production of goods.

We have already referred to the fact, also noted by Ames [1986], that trade in services is understated in the balance of payments because many services are aggregated into merchandise export and import data. This problem is linked to the definition of services or, for that matter, of goods. Its implication is that, while for services embodied in goods, available statistics provide adequate information on the *direction* of trade, this is not true of services traded in their own right. Naturally, this difficulty does not arise with regard to services sold to or purchased from abroad through the temporary displacement of factors. Cross-border services transactions, on the other hand, are recorded on a payments basis, and very often payments are classified by currency of settlement. Thus, a large number of payments for services may be made in U.S. dollars which in fact originate in or are destined to countries other than the United States. The consequence of this recording system is that exports of services originating in nonhard currency areas or destined to such areas may completely disappear from the books of the relevant trading countries' central banks, as well as from world service trade statistics. Finally, the very fact that many services transactions are recorded on a payments basis results in only *net* flows appearing in balance-of-payments accounts, which may be useful for financial purposes but are not at all informative about shifts of real resources among the producing and consuming countries involved in the exchange. Any examination of comparative advantage based on net inflows and outflows is questionable since the data do not offer the possibility of studying intrasectoral trade in areas where the differentiation of products (e.g., specialized insurance/reinsurance services) in accordance with their specialized knowledge-content is a major source of international competitiveness.

Concluding Remarks

In chapter IV of his book, *The Theory of Protection*, W.M. Corden [1971] has a section dealing with nontraded goods, whose title is "Limitations of the Orthodox Analysis."[8] Corden's comments in this section illustrate the dangers of trying to extend traditional trade theory to services without first trying to clarify the notion of tradeability. At the same time, it is necessary to go one step further than Corden. Tradeability cannot be defined in static terms, i.e., without taking into account technological developments that affect the degree to which services are traded. This point has been brought clearly into light by Bhagwati [1986] in a recent article in which he deals with "increased tradeability of services: long-distancing phenomenon and innovations in provider mobility." Bhagwati speaks of "services becoming, not goods but long-distance services so that the physical presence of the provider of the services is no longer necessary for the transaction with the user," and he gives the following example: ". . . instead of Pavarotti singing on the gramophone record, he sings over satellite TV." Increased tradeability of services, in the form of "disembodied" products or of service acts performed by nonresident productive factors, is bound to affect traditional thinking about protection of national service markets. The orthodox analysis of the effects of trade taxes and subsidies faces limitations not only on account of the existence of "nontraded goods" but also on account of the total irrelevance of trade taxes and subsidies as instruments of protection.

With regard to the definition of services, it should be clear by now that any common characteristics found among them are relevant only to the purpose at hand, just as in the case of goods. All services are intangible, but this hardly contributes anything to our understanding of their role in the economy. It is no more instructive than knowing that goods are made of materials extracted from the earth's crust or grown on the earth's surface. Perhaps the only usefulness of drawing attention to the intangibility of services is to stress that they are an almost pure product of human intervention, with little or no assistance from the physical environment. To define services thus requires a detailed analysis of production, trade, and consumption patterns at the sectoral level. Such sectoral analysis should show in particular to what extent services are complementary to goods in international trade or may substitute for traded goods thanks to such processes as "unbundling" [Bhagwati, 1986; Findlay, 1985]. Complementarity and substitutability with goods evolve rapidly with new technological developments but also as a result of changes in regulatory environments. Similarly, the boundaries between different types of services evolve with new technology and deregulation or re-regulation. These developments are described in the next chapter.

Notes

1. The expressions *service* and *postindustrial* economy are used here interchangeably and without specific connotation. Many similar expressions have been used to describe the emerging economic structures of advanced industrialized countries and of certain countries still classified as developing. The meaning of some of them has been analyzed, e.g., by Dorothy Riddle [1986]; their interpretation remains, however, largely subjective. In this book, no specific interpretation is offered of any of these expressions, but their general meaning should emerge from the contents of the book.

2. This is also the opinion of Dorothy Riddle [1986, p. 20] and of the UNCTAD secretariat [1983]. D. Riddle adds that "the 'nonservice' portion [of construction] can be viewed as a stand-in, or 'shadow price,' for all the service activities presently reported in the manufacturing account." This argument is less convincing, inasmuch as two statistical errors do not make a statistical truth.

3. This opinion is not shared by Dorothy Riddle [1986, p. 21] on the ground that utilities have the primary function of providing time, place, and form utility for the user. Apart from leaving these variants of utility undefined, Riddle states, "In any case...the average GDP contribution from utilities is minimal; hence classification differences will have little effect on overall analyses." This argument is hardly more convincing than the similar one made by Riddle about construction (see preceding footnote).

4. The distinction between linkage, communication, and information functions is well documented in the literature. See, among others, UNCTAD [1985], Lanvin [1986], and Nusbaumer [1986].

5. One particular type of service activity which does not seem to fall in any of the above categories is art. Art is at one and the same time an activity that processes and communicates information, carries knowledge, and provides satisfaction to consumers. Because it deserves special attention due to its specificity, it will be discussed further in chapter 9.

6. Regulations on services have been extensively described, but rarely analyzed. (See, for example, Griffiths [1975], OECD [1983, 1984], and Tempest [1986].

7. In his discussion of international statistics on trade in services, Brian Ames gives a different interpretation of the IMF definition of a transaction. He speaks of the IMF criteria as if they were applied to a definition of trade, but, as we have seen, the IMF does not use this terminology. On the other hand, while Ames concedes that sales of services to foreign tourists

can be considered as traded services, he does not include in this notion the logical counterpart of such sales, namely the sale of services to residents by nonresidents temporarily operating in the purchasing country. This is a logical nonsequitur which is justified by Ames on the ground that in the latter case one is dealing with factor movements. While it may be true that trade theory uses immobility of factors as one of its central assumptions, this assumption is not made by the IMF, and, if temporary factor movements are excluded from the notion of international transactions, so then should movements of consumers to the place of residence of producers. Indeed, movements of consumers are equally assumed away by traditional trade theory. These comments can be extended to Lanvin and Prieto [1986] who follow much the same approach as Ames.

8. The full text of the relevant passage, of which parts were quoted in a preceding chapter, is as follows: "... the analysis does not refer to non-traded goods or services, that is, to goods (and, above all, services) the prices of which are not determined in the world market. This is a profound limitation with important implications. The line between traded and non-traded goods is not always a clear one since world market conditions certainly *influence* the prices of non-traded goods, but there is little doubt that in most economies a large part of domestic production consists of goods that can more reasonably be described as non-traded than as traded goods. This category would normally include services, distribution, building, and often parts of the production of power. In addition, many goods which are potentially tradeable are, because of their weight or their particular appropriateness to local tastes, not in fact traded."

5 FACTS AND FIGURES

It may seem contradictory to treat services as a homogenous sector of activity and at the same time to speak of various groups of service activities as service "sectors" in their own right. We have already argued the reasons why there is no reason to reject the notion that services have enough common characteristics to be considered as generally distinguishable from goods, and we have also pointed out the close intermingling of service production with goods production. This does not mean, however, that services cannot be grouped in different sectors corresponding to sets and subsets of functions performed by them in the economy at either the national or the international level. Among those, the activities that represent the greatest interest from the point of view of their impact on the international economy are banking, insurance, telecommunications, data services, professional and business services, transport, and what may be called the two "hybrid" categories of tourism and labor services. Table 5-1 shows the relative importance of these service sectors in international trade.[1]

Banking

Banking is sometimes considered as part of financial services together with insurance, and sometimes as a separate sector.[2] For our purposes, we

Table 5–1.   Relative importance of main services in international trade[1] (million U.S. dollars)

	Number of countries covered	Year	Credits	Debits
Insurance (all types)	13^2	1977	5,337	5,443
	16^2	1984	$7,076^3$	$8,102^3$
Commissions and	10^4	1977	4,874	7,824
brokerage	13^4	1984	7,458	12,520
Films and television	8	1977	374	467
	11	1984	983	1,039
Construction/	7	1977	5,941	3,885
engineering	10	1984	9,552	5,154
Communications	7	1977	1,389	1,513
	9	1984	2,947	4,310
Overhead expenses and	6	1977	2,041	2,854
management services	7	1984	5,746	4,927
Advertising	5	1977	234	644
	6	1984	450	1,336
Merchanting	6^4	1977	$13,484^5$	$10,952^5$
	6^4	1983	$23,124^5$	$n.a.^7$
Consultancy and	3^4	1977	3,007	1,302
technical cooperation	5^4	1984	5,516	3,027
Banking	$1^{4,6}$	1977	543	n.a.
	3^4	1984	1,312	55
Rentals	2	1977	70	103
	3	1984	91	307
Pro memoria:				
Intellectual property	13	1977	7,174	5,363
income	16	1984	12,563	8,823

Notes:
1. OECD countries only. Based on preliminary and incomplete data from various sources.
2. No debits statistics are available for the United Kingdom, except for loss/damage to U.K. importers.
3. Data concerning Japan appear inconsistent.
4. No debits statistics are available for the United Kingdom.
5. Mostly France.
6. Mostly United Kingdom.
7. Insufficient coverage.

define banking as a separate sector of activity because the financial intermediation function performed by banks is at one and the same time more varied and based on a different form of funding than insurance. Banks acquire funds from the public not in the form of premiums paid in exchange of a promise to compensate losses incurred under well-defined circumstances, but in the form of deposits made either as a matter of convenience, i.e., in exchange of financial services delivered on a day-to-day basis, or in expectation of a profit, i.e., in exchange for intermediation performed by the bank in the medium-term or long-term financial markets. The functions of banks and insurance companies converge at the long end of the market, where both place funds in mobile or fixed assets in the expectation of capital gains or returns extending over a long period.

This being said, the definition of a bank differs considerably from one national legislation to another, generally depending on the range of financial services that a bank may provide in different countries. Moreover, the trend of deregulation of financial services which began in many countries in the early 1980s tends to modify traditional concepts of banking and other financial services, thus blurring the boundaries among these service sectors [Koulen, 1985]. One of the difficulties in analyzing banking services is that there is, in many cases, no meaningful distinction between the provision of a service in the sense in which this activity has been defined above, and the movement of capital which includes both funding and the investment of available funds. Further, the concept of financial innovation to which frequent reference is made in technical journals covers the ability of financial experts to diversify not only the source of supply of funds, which involves making expected returns attractive to different fund providers, but also the destination of funds, which involves making available funds attractive to would-be users of capital in various productive activities, whether goods-producing or services-producing. No statistical record or descriptive analysis of banking operations gives a true account of the amount of innovation that enters the intermediation function of banks in today's interdependent world. At the same time, it is obvious that national banking regulations very often confuse the fund-raising and fund-allocating functions of banks with their role as providers of financial expertise. In effect, most national regulations appear to be geared to the control of movements of savings and investments without paying much attention to the innovative role of banks, whose contribution to intermediation often takes the form of circumventing the very same regulations, thus allowing the real needs for returns to capital or access to finance to be satisfactorily fulfilled. For example, the expansion abroad of banks through foreign establishment often represents a way of circumventing national exchange regulations and/or domestic restrictions on lending. On the other hand, such foreign expansion is often closely related to the development of the foreign operations of nonbank firms and, therefore, it has usually been considered that financial services, like other services, accompany or follow the international activities of goods-producing firms, rather than developing their foreign activities on their own account [Grubel, 1977].

By establishing themselves abroad, banks can capture local savings but can also channel savings from their home countries to multinational enterprises. In addition, having established a presence in foreign markets and acquired the necessary knowledge and work experience in those markets to advise home-based enterprises whose business commitments they back, banks are increasingly entering pure counseling work and intermediation for Third Country enterprises which may be direct competitors to the firms whose activities they initially nurtured. This in turn is used as a springboard for the expansion of local counseling in countries where the capacity for apprehending global market problems is limited or constrained by national regulations. In the latter case, government regulations may act as an incentive to foreign banking business if restrictions in areas such as exchange control, taxation, and prudential requirements are less stringently applied to foreign-based financial intermediaries benefiting from the strong financial backing of their home office in a hard-currency country. Nevertheless, it is a general characteristic of foreign banks that their operations in foreign currencies are more important than in local currency, reflecting the foreign orientation of the business of their main customers [Koulen, 1985]. For the same reason, foreign banking establishments often have a very modest rate of participation in local retail markets, though confidence factors may also play a role. Indeed, all evidence points to the difficulty for banks to do business in foreign markets in areas that involve generating confidence in the public at large, compared with more selective banking activities such as securities handling or bond underwriting where the financial risks are clearly identifiable and the services offered address themselves to knowledgeable customers.

Many observers of the activities of transnational banking corporations (TNCs) have been struck by the geographical concentration of assets and by the limited range of operations of such corporations. However, both these aspects of banking TNC's are normal phenomena, in the sense that the main source of capital funds for the activities of these firms is by nature in capital-rich countries and, given the links of bank with major transnational enterprises in other sectors, the "best" risks they handle rest with private enterprises which made their mark in their home market. In other words, both banks and their main customers must establish their credit worthiness in the eyes of local investors. Lack of confidence in local subsidiaries and affiliates of foreign banking institutions would therefore not necessarily be overcome by the expansion of local lending activities of such subsidiaries and affiliates; conversely, banking subsidiaries with no international market standing whose home offices are located in weak currency countries are not likely to attract business from fund-holders.

This being said, and leaving aside the technicalities of modern banking which surpass in complexity anything a student of monetary policy would have imagined some decades ago, one of the forces behind financial innovation in modern days is clearly the very high degree of sophistication of financial customers themselves. Owners of investible funds are no longer ready to settle for traditional, low-risk, but basically unrewarding financial products when they see that, in other countries and under other regulatory systems, investors are able to "play" with diverse and rapidly changing financial opportunities for a profit. This more demanding attitude stimulates competition among financial institutions, and confers an absolute advantage onto those institutions that apply their acquired knowledge and work experience of market operations more systematically than others. This absolute advantage is at the root of their expansion, in national and international markets. In effect, all analysts of the evolving structure of national financial systems and institutions draw attention to innovative factors, new technologies associated with innovations, competitive spirit, and strategic interventions in markets in response to new demands, all of which exert a forward push on deregulation trends, either emerging or already operating, in national legislations.[3]

A basic element of this innovative process is the constitution of financial conglomerates and the merging of previously narrowly defined subsectors of financial activities, leading to the widespread establishment of "universal" banking rights in many countries. In addition to this expansion and diversification of the intermediation function of banks, pressures for deregulation lead to parallel pressures for the dismantlement of national barriers to foreign participation in banking markets, except in those economic territories or entities where considerations of infant industry development or variously defined national security concerns restrain the process. Naturally, it cannot be expected that the ideal conditions for the development of global markets for goods and services will ever be fulfilled in a multicultural, multipolitical, and multidimensional world. As we shall see later, there is considerable dispute over the influence of transnational corporations in both goods and services markets and on the policy options of countries, particularly where the share, scope, and quality of their intervention in production and distribution processes stifle local capacities to emulate them, not to mention the capacity of local governmental authorities to resist political and other pressures which they may try to exert.

Among the various activities performed by bankers are: investment services, underwriting, advisory and trust services, insurance brokerage, pension fund management, administration of estates, leasing, factoring, hire purchase, credit card, billing, value storage (vaults), commodity trading, etc. For the casual observer, it may be difficult to reconcile this large group of heterogeneous services with the notion of *banking*. However, the two defining criteria given above, mainly the intermediation role and the financial advisory role, are common features of all the various service functions, and it may be considered that the apportioning of resources among these functions is a matter that is internal to the individual banking enterprises. Thus, the structure of the banking sector may be modified as a result of new technology, new market opportunities, or competitive pressures which challenge traditional demarcation lines between financial institutions and the kinds of business they are conducting [Llewyllyn, 1985]. Special subsectors of banking only deserve attention as they branch off from the main "universal" body of banking transactions into characteristic functions, either as a result of market factors or regulatory constraints. When state regulations determine sharp demarcation lines between different types of institutions and the business they conduct, it is, of course, necessary to analyze them separately in order to have an overall view of the workings of the financial system of a given country. On the other hand, if deregulation sets in, the demarcation lines tend to become blurred as each type of institution attempts to expand into what were previously the exclusive lines of business of other types.

Among the most noteworthy influences of technology on the structure of commercial banking is the development of electronic fund transfers.[4] The essence of payment systems based on electronic fund transfers is "the passing of messages representing transactions or information between customers and bank computers" [OECD, 1983b, p. 37]. The application of electronic techniques for payments purposes is an alternative to traditional paperwork and only replaces the latter when justified by economies of scale. It so happens that beyond a certain scale of operations, the cost of a marginal message flowing through the economic transfer system is nearly constant and effectively near zero. In a certain sense, therefore, electronic payment systems have all the attributes of natural monopolies, that is, unless they can be expanded beyond a point where average cost is still declining; if priced at marginal cost they will result in losses for the operating unit. On the other hand, it is clear that there are externalities involved in the operation of such mechanisms given the benefits to society of quick and secure means of transferring real resources at least cost, as well as the advantages of establishing wide-ranging networks thanks to which output (returns) per unit of input (capital) can be maximized. Given the complexities of international financial relations, and the seignorage involved in the management and manipulation of funds, where fund managers operate like central credit authorities in their particular market fields of influence, it is unlikely that a scale of operations can be reached by any one operating unit so that marginal cost pricing represents a viable market strategy. Therefore, pure competitive behavior may not be expected in the area of electronic fund transfer.

In practice, the question does not really arise to this day since much of the transferring business takes place on monopolized national telecommunications networks which do not operate under competitive market conditions. The existence of such monopolies has sometimes been questioned (see next section) but they at least have the advantage of absorbing the decreasing cost element of value-added financial services, thus allowing a sort of "carefree" competition on the part of financial service suppliers in the world market. When the international interbank network called SWIFT (Society for World-Wide Interbank Financial Telecommunication) was established in the late 1960s by a group of European banks with a view to countering the competitive advantage of large U.S. banks having their own private international telecommunications systems, it was expected that the high volumes of traffic generated over the SWIFT system would be carried at considerable savings over leased lines for which national PTT's would make standard charges [OECD, 1983b, p. 149]. State monopolies such as the PTT's are usually considered to set prices for their services at levels higher than marginal cost, but lower than their monopoly position in the market might permit in the absence of consideration of the social benefits of access to telecommunications services for the wider public. In effect, PTT's have been aware of the potentially profitable nature of the traffic involved in SWIFT operations and have, initially at least, imposed charges for leased lines which took into account the loss of profitable telex traffic resulting from the substitution of direct interbank linkages for this traffic.

From the point of view of the productivity of financial services, the shift from labor-intensive paperwork to electronic fund transfer is one instance in which service industries have exploited the possibilities of standardization of their service transactions (figure 5–1).[5] The categories of banking messages which are or will be included in SWIFT operations are: customer transfers, bank transfers, foreign exchange confirmations, special

SERVICES IN THE GLOBAL MARKET

Figure 5-1.   Staff numbers and clearing activity in London banks, 1972-1984.

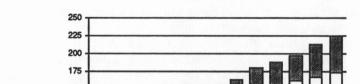

Automated clearing   ☐ Voucher clearing   ◆- Staff numbers

Source: Rajan and Cooke (1986)
Notes: —Indices of the London clearing banks' staff numbers and clearing activity.
        1972 = 100
       —Number of staff employed in the London clearing banks—parent banks only—as
        at 31 December.
       —Number of items cleared through Bankers' Clearing House and Bankers'
        Automated Clearing Services.
       —The figures therefore include some items cleared by institutions other than the
        London clearing banks.

reconciliation messages, collections, documentary credit, and securities [OECD, 1983b, p. 150].

Interestingly, there is at present no evidence that the standardization and industrialization of day-to-day banking transactions on the basis of computer-communications systems have led to a reduction of bank branching either at the national or at the international level. Although the evidence is scant, there are contrary indications that increasing competition between banks as a result of both deregulation and technological developments acts as a stimulus to the expansion of networks of bank offices in key market locations. This phenomenon is apparently related to the development of a more innovative part of banking business which consists in catering to specific needs of borrowers and to the provision of an increasing array of investment opportunities to lenders. Additionally, the growing financing requirements of complex modern economies precipitate banking institutions into a worldwide competition for loanable funds, and this in itself makes it necessary for them to establish in new locations in order to capture local savings. This corporate behavior is fully consistent with the characteristics of knowledge-intensive service activities which require close interaction between the producer and the consumer and result in the supply of nonstandardized service products. There is no contradiction in the fact that banking institutions seek to reap economies of scale in some aspects of their activities as a means of financing the expansion of more skilled-labor-intensive operations in distant markets.

It may be argued that the establishment of branches in distant locations is itself a capital-intensive type of production, due to the high cost of buildings and telecommunications infrastructures that need to be acquired or established, and that there is therefore no reason to distinguish between branching activities and technological improvements in the home office from the point of view of the structure of resource use. However, this is where it is appropriate to distinguish between the funding functions of banks and their role as providers of financial services involving specialized knowledge and experience on the part of the economic agents concerned. Sophisticated and customized financial services can be rendered through the movements of skilled factors, but funding operations generally require a presence in the market. The funds collected locally through this presence then enter into the mainstream of standardized and internationalized banking transactions on which economies of scale are made. Consequently, the pure services function and the funding function are complementary aspects of the branching-out process, and in many cases it is not certain which of the two is the prime mover.

The statistics available on international banking operations are generally not sufficiently detailed to permit a quantitative ranking of the relative importance of the different categories of services discussed above in qualitative terms. The data presented in table 5–1 can nevertheless be supplemented in certain respects and, for a number of major trading countries, this is done in tables 5–2 and 5–3.

National account statistics on banking services are in many cases equally uninstructive. There are basically three ways of calculating the contribution of these services to gross national product,[6] which correspond to the three main functions of banks, i.e., the creation of money, the provision of a payments mechanism and related services, and financial intermediation. The first approach was that proposed by H. P. Brown [1949] and used in the Australian national accounts from 1947 to 1972. It consisted in calculating the contribution of banks to national income on the basis of

Table 5–2.   Indicators of international trade in banking services, 1970 and 1981

	Foreign assets of "deposit" banks (billion U.S. dollars)		Foreign liabilities of "deposit" banks (billion U.S. dollars)	
Country	*1970*	*1981*	*1970*	*1981*
Australia	..	0.4	..	0.7
Austria	1.0	22.5	1.0	25.5
Belgium	4.9	70.0	5.7	83.1
Canada	7.6	37.8	5.5	61.0
Denmark	0.4	5.3	0.4	5.3
Finland	0.2	3.2	0.3	4.9
France	10.1	141.8	10.8	135.7
Germany, Fed. Rep.	14.4	84.5	9.1	66.8
Greece	0.1	1.7	0.1	4.7
Iceland	—	—	—	0.2
Ireland	1.3	8.6	1.3	10.4
Italy	11.5	39.7	11.6	51.3
Japan	6.6	84.6	5.5	100.4
Luxembourg	3.6	114.5	2.5	106.1
Netherlands	5.3	66.1	5.1	65.2
New Zealand	0.1	0.4	—	0.1
Norway	0.4	1.9	0.3	6.4
Portugal	0.3	1.5	—	6.3
Spain	1.0	14.8	1.2	27.9
Sweden	1.0	7.5	0.8	14.1
Switzerland	14.1	162.4	12.1	135.0
Turkey	..	0.8	..	—
United Kingdom	37.4	430.9	40.4	446.8
United States	12.8	306.3	31.3	229.2
Total OECD	114.1	1,607.2	145.0	1,587.4
Other countries	35.3	496.0	17.8	542.2
of which:				
Bahamas and	7.2	192.4	7.4	192.4
Caymans				
Bahrain	0.1	42.7	—	41.4
Hong Kong	1.2	49.8	0.4	45.3
Panama	0.3	41.1	0.4	41.3
Singapore	0.5	70.2	0.5	69.6
All countries	149.4	2,103.2	162.8	2,129.6

Source: IMF, International Financial Statistics Yearbook as reported in OECD [1983]. *The Internationalization of Banking: The Policy Issues.* Paris: OECD.

Note: Claims on, and liabilities to, nonresidents by deposit money banks, other deposit-taking financial institutions, and international license banks operating in the countries covered in IMF statistical records.

.. = not significant

— = not recorded

Table 5–3. Selected data on foreign banking operations, major financial centers

Country[1]	Interbank accounts (percent of total liabilities, 1981)		Foreign-currency transactions (percent of total liabilities, 1981)		Nonresident accounts (percent of total liabilities, 1981)	
	Foreign banks	Domestic banks	Foreign banks	Domestic banks	Foreign banks	Doemstic banks
Belgium	80.6	40.5	80.1	41.5	77.4	43.8
France	78.4	51.2	70.0	27.7	59.1	18.2
Germany, Fed. Rep.	73.2	23.0	n.a.	n.a.	45.4	4.5
Luxembourg	74.0	39.1	93.8	45.9	88.7	56.0
Switzerland	49.6	19.4	53.5	20.6	57.9	26.6
United Kingdom	22.0	19.4	88.9	36.5	56.2	25.6
United States[2]	75.5	17.7	..	..	47.7	12.9

Source: OECD, 1983. *The Internationalization of Banking: The Policy Issues.* Paris: OECD.

Notes:

1. Data partly estimated. Due to differences in definitions, the data are not fully comparable across countries.

2. Economic Consulting Services [1981] provides the following data for 1980 (in billion U.S. dollars): net overseas interest income, 4.8; interest income of domestic offices from nonresidents, 2.6; noninterest income attributable to international business, 1.7; total foreign revenue of U.S. banks: 9.1 billion U.S. dollars.

.. = not significant.

wages and salaries paid by banks. This involved including in national income the whole output of banks without any deductions in other parts of the economy, and because it led to double-counting it has not been widely used.

The second approach was that of the U.S. Department of Commerce [1947], later adopted by the *first* United Nations System of National Accounts (SNA); it consisted of calculating an income imputed to bank depositors for the use of their money, equal to the excess of interest and dividends received by banks over interest paid out, this income being assumed to be used in paying for uncharged banking services. Thus, "...depositors will regard it as receiving, in turn for depositing their money with banks, an income in kind in the form of payments mechanism and other services, in much the same way as factory workers may receive, in addition to their cash wages, free canteen meals" [Arndt, 1984, p. 200]. The allocation of the imputed bank service charge between households and enterprises, which corresponds to its allocation between final and intermediate expenditure, was based on deposit ownership. In the revised United Nations System of National Accounts it was recognized that inadequate statistics of deposit ownership made the procedure difficult to apply in many countries, with the result that national income may be artificially increased to the extent that imputation is made to deposits of households instead of business enterprises other than banks. For a variety of reasons, this second approach has also come under serious criticism [Arndt, 1984, p. 201] due to different interpretations being given to the functions of banks, particularly regarding their function of creating purchasing power through the lending process.

The third approach placed the emphasis on the financial intermediation function of banks. This approach was incorporated in the 1968 revision of the SNA. As reported by Arndt, one explanation of this approach was that "...interest received is viewed as consisting of a pure interest component and a service charge for organizing funds."[7] Thus, most of the output of banks was considered as intermediate products, which are excluded from GNP, "...the only exception being services to household depositors for which banks make explicit charges and of services to household borrowers for which banks receive interest on consumer loans" [Arndt, 1984, p. 202].

Regarding these various approaches to national accounting of services rendered by banks, Arndt commented that "all of the net investment function of non-bank financial intermediaries and a large and increasing proportion of the net investment income of deposit banks is appropriately regarded as payment for financial intermediation rather than for payments-mechanism services, in order words, for services to borrowers rather than to depositors." However, as he pointed out, in the discussion of the treatment of financial enterprises in national accounts, international aspects of the problem were ignored. He then went on to show that while it may be correct to conclude that most services of banks and other financial intermediaries are to be treated as intermediate products because they are rendered to business enterprises, this is not valid for an open economy. "Services rendered to non-residents represent final products whether the customers are business enterprises or not" [Arndt, 1984, p. 205]. The problems for countries with a large international financial business is to find a statistical method whereby the financial services rendered to foreign customers may be included into their gross domestic product. Such a method, which has been applied by Luxembourg since 1977, involves transferring, in the balance-of-payments accounts, factor service receipts to the nonfactor service receipts account, as well as consequential adjustments to avoid double-counting. The results can be quite striking. In the case of Luxembourg, the imputed bank service charge as a percentage of gross domestic product was 26.7% in 1977, which means that about a quarter of GDP was counted as intermediate product, whereas this figure would be only 12.4% if exports were counted out. Thus, the SNA treatment of financial services previously applied by Luxembourg lead to the exclusion of more than half of these services from the GDP of this country. Similar adjustments made for other countries which are large exporters of financial services might have some interesting consequences on the ranking of countries by per capita income levels, particularly some Asian financial centers.

Telecommunication and Data Services

Telecommunication and data services are often dealt with together because it is the existence and rapid development of telecommunication services that has made the recent explosion of data services possible and significant, while it is the tremendous amount of technological innovation in data services that has enhanced the economic value of telecommunication services. Pure telecommunication of the traditional type consists of carrying voice and image over long distances. Pure data services of the traditional kind consist of methods of analyzing, classifying, and presenting data in a given location, which is either the same as that of the data sources or some distance away. New technologies have transformed both processes simultaneously by integrating methods of transferring information messages (voice, image, or text) from one information terminal to another, and methods of information processing. On the one hand, there has been the development of new telecommunication relays or carrying media such as telecommunication satellites and fiber optics; on the other, the development of computer techniques for the handling of large amounts of data in so-called "real time," a notion that covers an infinite array of manipulations of basic information in a minimum of time, the volume of information treated and the time needed for treatment being a function of the capacity of the computer and the degree of refinement of electronic processes.

The application of computer technology to data processing and to the transmittal of data over long distances has lead to the "digitalization" of telecommunication networks, with the revolutionary consequence that the notion of *data* which is usually associated with figures, words, graphical representation, pictures, etc., that is, with various traditional forms of expression of human ideas, has given way to the notion of *information* which is not associated with any particular form of expression. The merging of telecommunication and data-processing technologies has lead to these two types of activities being considered in combination under the descriptive of "telematics" or "computer-communication" services. Apart from the specific technological developments that have lead to this emergence of a totally new "sector" of service activities, the development of new methods of treatment of basic facts and of application of acquired knowledge of relationships between those facts has exerted considerable leverage on the development of new methods of production and distribution of both services and goods, and has spurred inventions of new products in both areas. One particular consequence of the expansion and constant refinement of telematics services has been the de facto reduction of distances among market operators, not only nationally and regionally but also internationally. Thus, the significance of both time and geography as barriers to economic intercourse has been considerably reduced, and a global market has emerged for telematics and "associated services," i.e., services using the telematics infrastructure. In the area of international trade, the whole field of activity dealing with the transfer and processing of information over long distances is subsumed under the expression of "transborder data flows" or TDF.

The transmission and processing of data through telecommunication networks requires the establishment of terminal infrastructures, including data-processing capabilities, at both ends of the telecommunication line. The exchange of data, either raw or processed, across borders is a form of trade directly comparable to trade in goods, the only difference between the two being the medium of transport used. Terminals can be compared to seaports and transmission lines to shipping routes, although it may be argued with Bressand and Distler [1985] that information technology brings about a qualitative change in the relationships between economic agents which is best described in terms of *networks* (see *infra*). Because TDF's are related to the broader concept of information, they can be considered as including image and sound broadcasting. In these cases also, there are two aspects to international exchange, namely the facilities on which the transmission of information depends, and the trade—in the traditional sense of the term—in information proper. It may be noted in this connection that the use of telematics and other forms of advanced telecommunication technology has reduced to a considerable extent— though not in all service areas—reliance on physical supports for such transmission such as magnetic tapes, sound recordings, and printed text. At the same time, through the separation made possible between the content of the information and its processing in different locations, the new technologies have permitted a certain standardization of certain comparatively routine functions as well as a displacement of the locus of production of these functions to countries comparatively well endowed with low-skilled labor factors.[8]

Due to the complex relationships between telecommunication and data services, it is difficult to find consistent and comparable figures on production and trade in this combined field of activities. The fact of the matter is that information and the associated services enter as what might be called "new raw materials" in many production processes. There exist no conventional units of measurement for these services, and their economic impact has more often than not been assessed mainly in qualitative terms. Methods of work, organization, and corporate structures have all been influenced by the introduction of information technology, not only in production but also in distribution and consumption, and the benefits, if any, of such changes are mostly in the form of external economies or X-efficiencies.[9]

In international discussions of the impact of telematics on national economies, much attention has been devoted to the influence of different patterns of ownership of telecommunication networks on the growth of these services, as well as on the ability of different economic operators to "capture" the benefits inherent in the external economies created. In particular, the question has arisen as to what extent national telecommunication monopolies maintained in a number of countries (PTT's) may or may not be acting as a brake on innovation both in the production and delivery of telematics services and in enterprises using those services. This might occur when PTT's attempt to extend their "natural" monopoly powers to cover the provision of so-called "enhanced" or "value-added network" services (VAN's) which include information storage, retrieval and processing, and computer software, as well as the various types of equipment needed to supply and consume such services.[10]

Public monopolies can extend their powers not only through the fixing of mandatory standards for equipment and services but also by directly restricting access to the telecommunication networks they control. Private companies, in order to be able to use telematics on an intrafirm or commercial basis, must rely on the leasing of communication lines from public telecommunication monopolies ("private leased lines"). The conditions on which such leasing takes place, regarding both price and volume of transmission allowed, determine the competitiveness of private firms operating in this field, not just among themselves but, more importantly, vis-a-vis the PTT's. From an economic standpoint, the issue is one of efficiency of public intervention. In a stable economic and technological environment, and in the absence of the abuse of fiscal power by the state, it may be assumed that the pricing of services produced under conditions of natural monopoly is at a level that just covers marginal costs, and is therefore lower than it would be under private operation. Substantial social benefits for the general public may result in terms of ease of access to communication and information.[11] However, if this practice is applied to new service products which do not, at least at this stage, correspond to basic consumer wants, it may stifle private-sector initiative as a source of technological development in the country concerned, unless the monopoly itself is at the forefront of research and innovation in the field in question. In reality, irrespective of the sociopolitical philosophies that dictate the behavior of states in this respect, the problem of the scope of PTT activities must now be seen in its international dimension, i.e., taking into account the competitive pressures that firms operating abroad in open telematics markets are able to exert on the PTT's. Such pressures can take various forms, including the provision of "off-shore" value-added network services to producers of services and goods located in countries where telecommunication monopolies remain in operation. Undoubtedly, therefore, the fact that telematics services operate in different regulatory frameworks in different countries is also likely to considerably influence the type and content of multilateral disciplines that can be devised to govern international transactions in these services.

The new wave of economic literature on services abounds with commentaries on the pervasive effects of the development of telecommunication and data technologies on the competitivity of firms in all fields of activity, and consequently on the structure and efficiency of production on the economy as a whole.[12] The importance of understanding and dealing

with the economic issues raised by these services cannot be underestimated. In fact, the extensive literature on telecommunication and data
services, which outstrips by far the amount of writing done on any other
category of services activities, bears witness to the widespread fascination
with technological developments in these fields, as with their potential
effect on the future evolution of the world economy. At the same time, the
very rapidity of technological developments and the pervasiveness of their
effects raise a number of controversial policy, legal, and technical issues
both at national and international levels which have become the subject of
intensive debate.

The problem of state intervention in national telecommunication
markets is only one aspect of the question. For one thing, state intervention in telecommunications is not confined to national boundaries. At
the international level, satellite transmission is, at least for the moment,
largely controlled by an intergovernmental agency called INTELSAT. This
body, set up in 1964, has about 110 member countries and carries about
two-thirds of all international telephone traffic and almost all international
television broadcasts. "The private sector is not free to compete directly
with this system, but can use it for customised business services" [LOTIS,
1986]. Issues in the area of competition policy also arise in connection
with the definition of technical standards for telecommunication and
data-processing equipment and services, both nationally where telecommunication monopolies tend to impose their own standards, thus limiting
private sector entry into the market for equipment and related services,
and internationally where major transnational corporations which play a
dominant role in the markets for equipment and services are thereby able
to impose their own technical standards on competing firms.[13]

Among the legal issues raised by the widespread use of information
technology, many are of universal concern, though they may be approached
differently in different countries, and some may be more specifically
related to macroeconomic policies or to specific aspects of international
relations. Among the latter are: (1) fiscal policies, where the difficulty of
defining an adequate tax base for information services may result not only
in tax evasion but also in tax inequities; (2) the legal right to access, store,
process, and transmit data which may be "sensitive" from the point of view
of national security; and (3) the extraterritorial application of national
legislation restricting or prohibiting the collection or use of data or, on
the contrary, establishing "information-free zones" which may impair the
effective implementation of other countries' legislation, e.g., for the protection of property rights in a patent, copyright, trademark, and trade
secret. The other more universal legal issues relate to human rights,

consumer protection, personal privacy protection, liability for faulty information, criminal fraud prevention, and issues related to social and cultural integrity and ideological and political identity. All these also have the attributes of purely political issues.

It is perhaps in the legal area that the most difficult problems are posed by the rapid development of telematics. Most of these problems revolve around the protection of the creative rights of producers on the one hand and the protection of the liberties of consumers on the other. In the first case, the technical ease with which data can be accessed, stored, and processed facilitates evasion or outright infringement of patent and copyright legislation, in particular in areas where such legislation does not cover new types of intellectual property such as computer software. The importance of software grows both with the increased versatility of advanced telecommunication and data-processing equipment for the long-distance transmission of digital messages, and with the considerable expansion of markets for this equipment, in particular the extraordinary explosion in the use of telematics by individual office workers and private consumers. Generically, the lack or the inadequacy of protection of intellectual property may hinder the spread of innovative technology by inducing its owners to confine their activities to countries where they feel that existing legislation provides them with sufficient protection to be able to reap the benefits of their inventions. Specifically, services and other productive activities which make intensive use of telematics—for example, financial services of all kinds or manufacturers of high-technology products—may find that the risks of piracy of proprietory information are too great to justify major investments in new computer-communications equipment.

From the point of view of consumers, one major concern is the possible loss of control over access to and use of information on their private life and social and economic situations. The problem is technically similar to that of access and use of proprietory information of a private enterprise, but it is of a different nature since it affects the civil rights of individuals and not only their economic rights. The protection of individual privacy may induce governments to adopt restrictive regulations on the use and transfer of personal data within national boundaries and across national borders. The result may be to seriously restrain the activities of enterprises that rely on the availability and analysis of such data for the effective performance of their operations, such as banks and insurance companies. A large number of governments have already adopted data-protection legislation that sometimes extends restrictions on the transmission of data across borders and beyond individuals, to cover industrial firms or financial institutions (table 5–4).[14]

Table 5–4.   Status of data protection/privacy legislation—January 1986

Country	National	Subnational	Reports
Australia	(P)	L	R
Austria (Rev)	CL		
Belgium	P		R
Brazil	P		
Canada	L	L	
Colombia	P		
Denmark (Rev)	L		
Finland	P		R
France	L		
Germany (Rev)	L(P)	L	R
Greece			RP
Hong Kong			RP
Hungary	L		
Iceland (Rev)	L		
Ireland			RP
Israel	L		
Italy	P		R
Japan			R
Luxembourg	L		
Netherlands	CP		R
New Zealand	L		
Norway (Rev)	L		R
Portugal	CP		
Spain	CP		R
Sweden	L		R
Switzerland	(P)	L	R
Turkey			RP
UK	L		R
US	LP	L	R
Yugoslavia			RP

Source: Transnational Data Report, January 1986.
Notes:
L   Law adopted
R   Government report/bill prepared
C   Constitutional provision
P   Parliament (Congress) consideration
(P)   Draft legislation prepared
RP   Government report in preparation
Rev   Law being revised

In Europe, the Council of Ministers of the Council of Europe has adopted, on 18 September 1980, a "Convention for the protection of individuals with regard to automatic processing of personal data" which lays down basic principles and special rules on transborder data flows, and establishes mechanisms for mutual assistance and consultations among the contracting parties to the Convention. The aim of the Convention is not to hinder such flows, since it states in its Article 12 that "...a party shall not for the sole purpose of the protection of privacy, prohibit or subject to special autorization transborder flows of personal data going to the territory of another party." However, it allows parties to the Convention to derogate from this provision insofar as its own legislation provides a greater protection than that of a party to which the data would be destined, and when transfers of data to the territory of another party are really designed as a means of circumventing national legislation for purposes of transferring data to a third, noncontracting state.

The Organization for Economic Cooperation and Development (OECD) has also adopted, on 23 September 1980, "Guidelines Governing the Protection of Privacy and Transborder Flows of Personal Data," which set minimum standards to be observed in the handling of issues, such as limitations on the collection of data, data quality, specification of purpose, limitation of use, security safeguards, openness of procedures, participation of individuals, and accountability of the data-collecting authorities. Whereas the Guidelines apply to the privacy of personal data irrespective of the manner in which these data are handled, the Council of Europe Convention focuses on automatic processing of data.

One important aspect of the development of telematics is the rapid expansion of intracorporate data flows carried on privately managed computer-communication systems, which operate on the basis of leased lines in countries where telecommunications networks are nationalized. There is an abundant literature on the impact of transborder data flows on the structure and competitiveness of transnational corporations.[15] As pointed out by the United Nations Centre on Transnational Corporations [1982, p. 35], "...transborder data flows give transnational corporations a greater capacity to maintain the coherence of the corporate system as a whole and to allocate corporate resources more efficiently and effectively." Transnational corporations also appear to be the main producers, vendors, carriers, and users in the so-called "international on-line database market", that is, the segment of the information-service industry where the operators are organizations that compile information and make it available in computer readable form (database producers) on a commercial basis through telecommunication networks [UNCTC, 1983].

The important role played by transnational corporations in the transborder data flow area raises the question of whether these new technologies are likely to accentuate the perceived dependency of less-developed countries on the industrialized world in general, and on these corporations in particular, or on the contrary provide new development opportunities for these countries. At the present time, the views expressed on this issue seem mainly to be based on inarticulate fears and political prejudice, but the matter would clearly deserve close attention in the context of any effort to develop multilateral disciplines for the liberalization of international transactions in services.[16]

Insurance and Reinsurance

Insurance services perform a function of facilitation of trade and a function of financial intermediation whereby they channel private savings into long-term investment. The facilitation function consists of providing a hedge against risks of various kinds attendant upon the sale of goods and services in distant markets. The intermediation function is similar to the funding function of banks, except insofar as insurance companies specialized in the long end of the market; that is, they collect funds on the basis of long-term contracts, e.g., life insurance policies rather than deposits. Other forms of "pure" risk insurance such as automobile accident insurance, fire insurance, and liability insurance may be considered as performing facilitation functions for investment.

Insurance services tend to increase in sophistication, in terms of both the types of risks covered and the alternative forms of risk coverage offered, as market relationships become more complex as a result of an increased variety of market operations taking place and/or as a result of the multiplication of market operators. At the same time, as the scale of operations of producing and distributing enterprises increases, the size of risks associated with operations also grows, sometimes to the point of overstripping the financial capacity of individual insurance companies. In such cases, insurance companies themselves subscribe policies with so-called reinsurance companies, providing so to speak a second line of defense against primary risks. Reinsurance services may be compared to a wholesale business, since they involve interfirm transactions, as opposed to direct insurance services requiring extensive marketing facilities to reach and assist individual consumers. The bulk of the world's reinsurance operations take place in the nonlife-insurance sector. Moreover, because one of the fundamental principles of insurance is to spread risks as much as possible in time and space, reinsurance is one of the most international insurance operations. Tables 5–5, 5–6, and 5–7 provide basic information on the size of the international insurance and reinsurance markets, based on premiums collected, as well as on the distribution of insurance business among major countries.

Insurance services are sometimes considered as a subset of "financial services" [United Kingdom, 1984] due to the fact that they are engaged in the business of collecting and investing funds for the public. Clearly, however, these services perform very specific functions in the area of management of uncertainty and risk [Giarini, 1985a], and for this reason, the activities of insurance companies are more closely bound up with the life of enterprises and individuals. Insurance services do not substitute for banking and other financial services concerned with the handling of monetary transactions, but are complementary to them and may even in some cases be a precondition for such financial transactions to take place, e.g., in the case of house mortgages or export credit financing. As the scale and diversity of international trade operations expanded, particularly since World War II, the relative importance of international insurance and reinsurance operations in total world insurance activities has expanded correspondingly. At the same time, the accumulation of private wealth generated by a long period of economic prosperity has permitted a rapid growth of life insurance operations which are most closely associated with the placing of private savings. However, apart from reinsurance operations, the degree to which insurance transactions take place internationally is still relatively limited (see next chapter), due to government regulations aimed at the protection of such savings and/or at the retention within national boundaries of the financial resources they represent. Indeed, in many countries, particularly developing countries, governments have made a special effort to mobilize domestic capital through the establishment of national insurance companies and the imposition of restrictions to the contracting of insurance policies abroad as well as to the placement of insured risks with foreign reinsurers. There may sometimes be a contradiction between these two objectives in view of the fact that the need for consumer protection of policy-holders argues against allowing insurance companies to invest their disposable capital where the funds are most needed, i.e., in fledgling domestic enterprises whose products substitute for imports or are destined for export to the world market. In many cases this has lead to the contraction of insurance offered in the countries concerned, as local investors were reluctant to channel their capital into insurance in view of the comparative lack of opportunities for profitable investment by insurance companies in the domestic market and the consequent unpredictability of their financial results.[17]

Table 5–5. World[1] insurance and reinsurance premiums, 1970–1983 (billion U.S. dollars)

Year	Total life	Total nonlife	Total reinsurance	Western Europe				United States				Rest of the world			
				Total	life	nonlife	reinsurance	Total	life	nonlife	reinsurance	Total	life	nonlife	reinsurance
1970	39.5	68.3	9.4	29.0	5.8	17.4	5.8	71.9	27.2	42.5	2.2	16.4	6.6	8.4	1.4
1980	145.9	250.9	40.5	142.6	30.8	86.0	25.8	201.9	68.3	124.9	8.7	92.7	46.7	40.1	5.9
1983	180.1[2]	263.3	40.0	129.1	33.5	72.4	23.2	244.7	87.2	147.3	10.2	109.6	59.4	43.7	6.5

Source: Compagnie Suisse de Réassurances. *Sigma*, October 1985 and May 1986.

Notes:

1. Less Eastern Europe and China.
2. Average 1980–1983.

Table 5–6. Nonlife insurance business by major branches and regions, 1970–1983[1] (billion U.S. dollars)

		Motor	Accident	Fire	Marine	General liability	Other branches	Total
Europe	1970	5.4	1.2	1.6	0.7	0.8	2.7	12.3
	1980	24.2	5.6	7.4	3.0	4.5	16.6	61.2
	1983	25.5	5.9	7.5	3.0	4.5	20.1	66.1
North America	1970	14.8	5.8	2.6	0.5	2.2	18.8	44.7
	1980	42.2	19.1	5.2	1.1	8.1	56.6	132.3
	1983	51.0	20.5	5.6	1.2	7.7	69.9	155.9
Other countries	1970	2.4	0.4	1.2	0.5	0.1	0.4	4.9
	1980	12.5	3.8	6.6	2.3	0.6	2.7	28.5
	1983	14.9	6.9	7.6	2.5	0.8	3.8	26.4
Total	1970	22.6	7.4	5.4	1.7	3.1	21.8	61.9
	1980	78.8	28.5	19.2	6.4	13.2	75.8	222.0
	1983	91.4	33.3	20.7	6.7	13.0	93.8	258.4

Source: Compagnie Suisse de Réassurances. *Sigma*, March 1986.
Notes: Sums may not add to totals due to rounding.
1. For 1983, average 1980–1983.

Table 5–7. Per capita insurance premiums (1983) and number of insurance companies operating (1985) in selected countries

Country	Per capita premium (US dollars)	Total no. of companies	of which: domestic	of which: foreign
Switzerland	976	104	78	26
United States	972	6,093	5,791	302
Japan	586	86	44	42
Germany, Fed, Rep. of	584	516	404	112
Australia	548	168	69	99
United Kingdom	495	712	634	78
Netherlands	475	439	285	154
Sweden	407	267	253	14
France	351	482	318	164
Singapore	163	64	23	41
Korea, Rep. of	97	20	18	2
Argentina	24	257	238	19
Brazil	8	97	95	2
Thailand	8	74	69	5

Source: Compagnie Suisse de Réassurances. *Sigma*, April and November/December 1985.

One result of growing restrictions on the participation of foreign insurance companies in domestic markets is that international reinsurance is gaining in relative importance compared to direct insurance in the international market. Paradoxically, the trend toward protection of national insurance markets may increase the need for access to the international reinsurance market due to the limited capital resources of fledgling domestic insurance companies which would otherwise leave many risks without cover.[18] Because reinsurance is so international in character, the world reinsurance market tends to be more competitive and less regulated than direct insurance, while at the same time, due to the size of the risks involved in reinsuring business, the market tends to be dominated by a few large firms operating on a global scale (table 5–8). On the other hand, one particular feature of reinsurance business is that much of it can be carried out from the home office of the insurance companies, and this possibility of course increases with the development of telematics. A company like Lloyds of London is said to attract business to the United Kingdom in the sense that it does not need to establish offices abroad to seek customers; it plays in the insurance field a role comparable to that of a

Table 5–8.   The 15 largest reinsurance companies in the world, 1983

Company	Country	Net premiums collected (million U.S. dollars)
Münchener Rück	Germany, Fed. Rep.	3,239
Groupe Suisse de Réassurances	Switzerland	2,701
General Re-Group	United States	1,416
Gerling Konzern	Germany, Fed. Rep.	648
Mercantile & General Re-Group	United Kingdom	631
Employers Re-Group	United States	612
Prudential Re-Group	United States	443
Kölnische Rück	Germany, Fed. Rep.	436
American Re	United States	382
Frankona Rück	Germany, Fed. Rep.	368
SCOR (Société Commerciale de Réassurance)	France	355
Toa Fire & Marine Re	Japan	350
Hannover Rück	Germany, Fed. Rep.	275
INA Re	United States	252
Unione Italiana di Riassicurazione	Italy	246
Total		12,354

(*Pro memoria:* in percent of total world reinsurance business: 30.1%)

lender of last resort in the banking sector. It might be noted, however, that the rapid development of communication as well as financial links across countries may make it increasingly possible to set up underwriting syndicates that are less dependent than in the past on the reinsurance services of major companies, thus at one and the same time increasing the scope for developing new reinsurance capacities in countries which have so far relied exclusively on foreign markets, and introducing greater diversification and competition in the world reinsurance market.

One traditional form of insurance that deserves special mention is transport insurance associated with international trade in goods as well as with the international transport of passengers. Transport insurance is the most obvious example of the complementary role of insurance services in the process of expansion and diversification of markets. These activities can be divided into two parts, those related to the insurance of means of transport such as ships and airplanes, and those related to the insurance of goods and persons transported. The level of transactions in both categories has tended to increase, in the first case due to the increase in the unit price of transport equipment, in the second case due to the tendency for the value-weight ratio of goods transported internationally to rise over time (Table 5–9). The historical dominance of international trade channels by present-day developed countries has tended to concentrate transport insurance in those countries, but in recent years an increasing number of developing countries have taken measures to extend domestic control over transport insurance on goods imported into and exported from these countries [UNCTAD, 1981; OECD, 1983].

Transport

Every observer of the service scene feels he/she knows a lot if not enough about transport. This is indeed a service activity whose function in the economy is easy to understand. The various forms of transport of course have their specific characteristics, but apart from porterage which nowadays only plays an important role in very underdeveloped economies, all forms of transport are intensive in physical capital and require considerable investments in infrastructure: roads, ports, telecommunication networks, satellite launching pads, etc. These give rise to what economists call indivisibilities, which translate into high fixed costs, the corollary of which is rapidly diminishing marginal costs of incremental units of transport service. With such production characteristics, the presence of "natural" monopoly situations is only limited by the emergence of congestion in transport networks. Such congestion which makes the commercial exploitation of transport facilities feasible, exist on roads, airports, harbors, and other such forms of infrastructure where there are limitations of space, but not necessarily on telecommunication networks where the limit to carrying capacity is determined more by technological progress than by space limitations. This is one reason why, as we have seen above, telecommunication networks are often the object of state intervention due to the presence of decreasing marginal costs within the range of marketable output.

Limitations of space influence the allocation of transport resources not only through price but also through state regulation designed to counter the social distortions that might result from allocation systems based on pure price rationing. This is an example where the social cost of the operation of transport facilities is higher than its private cost if pricing is left to the free interplay of market forces. Thus, a bridge owner may charge

Table 5–9. Transport insurance data

1. Nominal and real premium growth of marine insurance, 1965–1983

	Premium (U.S. $ million)	Nominal growth (%)	Real growth (%)
1965	1,497	—	—
1970	2,794	13,3	8.8
1975	5,368	14,0	5.2
1980	10,468	14,3	4.9
1983	9,022	-4,8	-11.4

2. Value of freight and insurance on imports (billion U.S. dollars), 1950–1981[1]

World	4.74	7.51	10.15	14.35	23.12	57.64	123.57	127.00
Industrial countries	2.96	4.92	6.98	10.32	16.70	35.32	71.17	69.05
Oil exporting countries	0.21	0.36	0.49	0.58	0.97	5.49	15.28	18.01
Non-oil developing countries	1.55	2.22	2.65	3.42	5.30	16.46	35.67	39.90
of which: Africa	0.29	0.48	0.52	0.74	1.21	3.26	5.46	6.40
Asia	0.31	0.40	0.58	0.76	1.07	4.50	12.80	14.62
Western Hemisphere	0.61	0.92	0.96	1.07	1.67	4.53	9.15	9.58
Other	0.30	0.38	0.54	0.78	1.26	4.13	8.48	9.33

Sources: Sigma, No. 5, May 1986.
IMF, 1982. IFS, Supplement on Trade Statistics. Washington, D.C.: IMF, table, p. xvi.
Notes: 1. Based on estimates of c.i.f./f.o.b. ratios on the basis of premiums paid in 1980, marine insurance represents 0.56% of world exports, that is, 8.5% of freight and insurance combined. The ratios of premiums paid to world exports for preceding years are as follows: 1975: 0.67%; 1970: 0.98%; 1965: 0.89%.

toll prices just covering depreciation of investment plus normal profit but which only certain users would be prepared to pay. At the same time, such a price might not make it worth crossing a natural obstacle over the bridge for less fortunate travellers or transporters, who would continue to use more traditional means of crossing such obstacles, e.g., by boat if the bridge is over a river or around a mountain path if the bridge is over a precipice. Were the bridge owner to charge for each crossing on a marginal cost basis, however, his private cost would be higher than the social cost of operating the bridge, as in the case of telecommunication networks examined above. The criteria on which social cost are calculated will, of course, vary from country to country and within the same country, from place to place. Sometimes, considerations of national prestige or security enter into the calculation of social cost, as in the case of national regulations governing the allocation of the so-called "five freedoms of the air" (figure 5–2).[19] In the field of road transport there are similar regulations that limit the right of carriers to load return cargo after having delivered goods from their place or country of residence, or that limit the right of ships to pick up cargo for ongoing destinations on routes serviced by the liner trade. Such limitations may be written into international liner agreements or "conferences" (see below), or may be imposed unilaterally by individual countries, as in the case of coastal shipping or cabotage. The concept of regulating access to and use of transport networks[20] has been extended to the field of telecommunications by the introduction of the "gateway" system, whereby certain countries control the entry and exit of data flows. This is done either with a view to taxing the value-added contained in these flows (particularly in the case of raw data which have undergone processing abroad) or to controlling the destination and use of basic data, for purposes of fulfilling various national objectives like protecting the personal privacy of citizens or their intellectual property, monitoring access to sensitive information, or protecting domestic data-processing firms against foreign competition.

The tendency of national governments to regulate various forms of transport has led to the establishment at the international level of inter-governmental arrangements for the coordination of national monopoly regulations, or to the establishment of cartels or cartel-like relationships among private transport companies benefiting from the official support of their home governments. An example of the first type of arrangement is the CEPT (European Conference of Post and Telecommunications Administrations), which groups the national telecommunications administrations (PTT's) of 26 countries in Europe members of UPU (Universal Postal Union) or ITU (International Telecommunication Union).

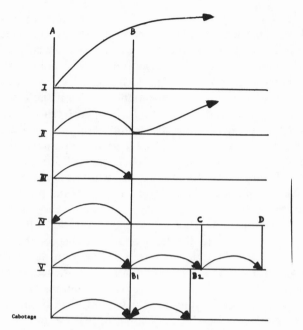

* The movements depected in the chart are those of a hypothetical airplane belonging to country A.
Legend: Freedom I : right of transit without landing
        Freedom II : right of non-traffic stop for refueling, etc., but not for setting down or picking up load
        Freedom III: right to set down traffic from country A in country B
        Freedom IV: right to pick up traffic from country B for country A
        Freedom V : right to carry traffic between foreign territories, e.g. from country B to C and C to D
        Cabotage : right to carry traffic within the territory of a foreign country
Source: I.A.T.A.

Figure 5–2.   The five "freedoms of the air"*

Examples of the second type of arrangement are so-called liner shipping "conferences," which are agreements among private shipping companies providing scheduled shipping services on set routes to fix freight rates and other charges as well as some minimum standards of performance. In an intermediate category are the agreements concluded between airline companies members of IATA [see IATA, 1978], in which both private sector and nationalized airlines participate, and which are subject to the approval of their respective governments. In the field of road transport, the TIR Convention constitutes a third type of arrangement, this time of a more liberalizing character. It is designed to simplify and accelerate customs formalities by providing standard customs declaration forms (the TIR carnet) as well as technical standards for road vehicles operating under the Convention.[21]

As one of the most "visible" items of invisible trade, international transport is well documented from both an analytical and statistical point of view. Fairly detailed data are available on the volume of traffic as well as on international receipts and payments for transport services. Tables 5–10, 5–11, and 5–12 show such receipts and payments for the world as a whole and for the main trading countries, in respect of the principal modes of transport. In addition, the long history of data collection on transport flows has permitted the gradual definition of statistical conventions for the measurement of such flows (e.g., ton miles, passenger miles, etc.) which provide good approximations of basic units of transport service. At least in the area of passenger transport, the notion of class of accommodation also provides a basis for quality distinctions which facilitate the evaluation of cost per unit of output and therefore of the productivity of transport services. This is certainly an advantage over other service activities which, as we have seen, often lack reliable bases for estimating units of production and hence productivity of factor inputs. However, such distinctions of value-added by class of accommodation are likely to become increasingly blurred as a result of the rapidly spreading trend of deregulation of transport services at the national and international levels. In this regard, the effect of deregulation is twofold. First, it enhances competition between privately owned and publicly owned transport operators, as a result of which the standards of service imposed (sometimes as a somewhat artificial means of capturing demand discrimination benefits) by public companies are modified according to different marketing criteria. Second, the pricing structure of transport tends more and more to reflect the private costs of providing the services rather than the social costs that govern the operating strategy of public monopolies.[22]

The evolution of the pure service element in transport, as distinguished from technological progress in transport equipment and supporting physical infrastructure and facilities, has been characterized by a high rate of innovation in areas such as routing, interconnection (multimodal transport), flexible load management, cargo handling and warehousing, etc. In the area of passenger service, the multiplication of arrangements suiting the particular needs of different categories of consumers has lead to a considerable and ever-increasing diversification of service products, epitomized by the explosion of charter air traffic in response to consumer

Table 5–10. International seaborne shipping, volume and payments

Regions and countries[1]	Year	Tanker cargo (million metric tons)		Dry cargo (million metric tons)		Total (million metric tons)		Payments (million SDRs)	
		Loadings	Unloadings	Loadings	Unloadings	Loadings	Unloadings	Credit	Debit
World[2]	1978	1,956	—	1,666	—	3,622	—	28,545	47,889
	1984	1,525	—	1,890	—	3,415	—	47,301	80,020
Industrial countries	1978	137	1,429	1,062	1,429	1,199	2,547	23,975	25,267
	1984	205	1,085	1,230	1,085	1,435	2,315	36,550	41,464
of which:									
United States	1978	2	379	272	167	274	546	2,226	4,660
	1984	16	230	327	157	243	387	4,171	9,072
United Kingdom	1978	50	76	41	77	91	153	3,191	1,913
	1984	92	51	45	85	137	136	2,485	2,848
Japan	1978	—	261	81	297	81	558	3,587	2,486
	1984	—	235	94	368	94	603	7,469	4,095
Developing countries	1978	1,699	474	495	396	2,194	870	4,570	22,622
	1984	1,165	395	540	535	1,705	930	10,751	38,556

of which:

Africa	1978	305	66	87	78	392	144	1,015	4,412
	1984	285	105	85	100	370	205	1,131	5,414
Asia	1978	207	128	167	161	374	289	1,309	5,010
	1984	135	160	185	240	320	400	4,904	11,405
America	1978	280	259	219	82	499	341	908	3,549
	1984	225	100	245	85	470	185	1,989	4,336
Middle East	1978	907	19	14	73	921	92	488	7,807
	1984	520	30	25	110	545	140	958	14,615
USSR	1978	102	6	49	38	151	44	n.a.	n.a.
	1984	118	8	48	68	166	76	n.a.	n.a.

Sources: United Nations, 1986, *Monthly Bulletin of Statistics*, January; IMF, 1985. *Balance-of-Payments Statistics, Volume 36, Yearbook Part 2.* Washington, D.C.: IMF.

Notes:

1. Comparability between volume and payments data may be impaired by differences in the coverage of regions and in the definition of shipping ("shipment" in IMF statistics) between the two sources.

2. Volume data for loadings and unloadings being very close, only loadings are shown. On the other hand, it will be noted that there are major—unexplained—discrepancies between world credits and debits.

n.a. = not available.

Table 5–11.   World railway traffic (billion freight net ton-kilometres)

Region	1970	1984
World	5,020	7,142
Europe	559	605
North America	1,302	1,663
South America	36	94
Asia	501	967
Oceania	28	43
Africa	100	131
USSR	2,495	3,639

Source: United Nations. 1985. Monthly Bulletin of Statistics, November.

demand for cheaper fares than were offered by state-controlled scheduled airlines, and later by the development of à la carte air services by competing private airlines in the wake of deregulation in major countries. Innovations in air services have, in turn, been made possible by rapid advances in telecommunication and air-traffic control technologies. Information technology has also provided the basis for many innovations in other fields of transport, notably road and rail transport. The upshot of these developments is a considerable increase, in this as in other areas of services production, in the human and physical capital content of value-added in transport services, where the possession of the basic physical infrastructure ceases to confer a distinct competitive advantage on government-owned transport companies, at least in countries where the right to use the infrastructure is granted to the private sector on a cost-recovery basis.

Professional, Business, and Scientific Services

A large and increasingly important category of services consists of activities based on the utilization of acquired knowledge and work experience to perform specific functions related to production, distribution, or consumption of other services or goods. Another way to present these services is to describe them as flagbearers of culture, whether the service rendered is disassociated from the economic agent delivering it (e.g., an artbook or an architect's blueprint) or remains embodied in that agent (e.g., a lawyer's speech in court or a surgical operation). One characteristic of many of these services is that they may be rendered at any place and at any time

Table 5–12.   Civil aviation traffic

Region or country	Year	Freight ton-kilometers (millions)	Passenger-kilometers (millions)
World[1]	1984	36,560	1,085,910
Australia	1980	516	25,500
	1984	792	26,124
Brazil	1980	492	10,524
	1985	744	11,400
Canada	1980	768	33,084
	1984	1,044	31,224
France	1980	2,088	34,128
	1985	2,976	39,252
Germany, Fed. Rep.	1980	1,584	21,048
	1985	2,496	24,432
India	1980	396	10,764
	1985	528	14,880
Israel	1980	300	4,596
	1985	600	6,504
Italy	1980	540	12,396
	1985	780	14,580
Japan	1980	1,980	51,216
	1984	2,940	61,416
Netherlands	1980	996	14,196
	1985	1,488	18,240
Singapore	1980	564	14,724
	1985	1,020	21,744
United Kingdom	1980	1,368	50,160
	1984	1,644	45,048
United States	1980	10,236	389,520
	1985	11,520	478,620
USSR	1980	3,084	160,296
	1985	3,192	187,608

Source: United Nations. 1986. Monthly Bulletin of Statistics, July.
Note: 1. Member countries of the International Civil Aviation Organization (ICAO).

without the need for much supporting physical capital, and independently of the particular corporate structure within which the economic agents operate. Thus, a doctor can work in a hospital, in the medical office of a manufacturing firm, or in his own medical office. Another characteristic of these services is that because they are very knowledge-intensive, they exert the most profound influence on production processes and methods as well as, where relevant, on processes of distribution of goods and services and on consumption patterns.

The most versatile services in this category are education and fundamental research. Educational and research institutions can be seen as service enterprises that sell knowledge products to would-be economic agents who thereby acquire and accumulate human capital. The knowledge sold enters into the economy either as raw material or as intermediate or final products depending on the use made of it. As raw material, it serves to produce new and more sophisticated knowledge, say, in preparing students for a teaching or research career. As intermediate products, it services in the production of various goods or services either within or outside corporate boundaries. As final product, it serves to inform consumer wants and enhance the ability of consumers to participate directly in production and distribution processes that rely on a large component of "self-service." Education and research are usually considered to have the greatest amount of economic leverage because of those variegated applications, which all concur to expanding and diversifying production possibilities (i.e., to move production possibility frontiers further from the origin). The very fungibility of these economic resources confers upon them the character of *intrinsic wealth* which is normally associated only with money or gold.[23] Consequently, average levels of education of a country's population are associated with quality of economic performance. (See the example of Finland in figure 2–6; the rise in the average level of education is held to explain, from the supply side, the very dynamic growth of this country during the last quarter century and, especially, its transformation from a raw material-based economy to a high-tech economy.)

Traditionally, education and research services (including such peripheral activities as library services) were subject to very strict physical and regulatory constraints. They could not operate without (1) concentrating their production in fixed locations where customers and users had to travel to procure the services (universities, institutes, etc.); and (2) standardizing as much as possible the service products being supplied to various categories of consumers in the form of academic curricula or preset training programmes. Although the comparison may seem disrespectful to academics, they had much in common with the tourism services supplied by modern tour operators. Nowadays, education is dispensed over television networks, and libraries can be accessed on personal computers [Pauli, 1985; Gershuny and Miles, 1981].

Despite the importance of professional and scientific services both in the context of national economies and in international trade, output data for these services are scant if not nonexistent. In national accounts statistics, educational and research services are usually evaluated on the basis of the expenditures of students or, in the case of nationalized education systems, of budgetary allocations relating to the expenditures incurred by teaching institutions. Similarly, various estimation bases exist for professional services which are not always consistent and which, in any case, rarely provide direct evaluations of the output of the economic agents concerned. For example, data available for advertising refer to total monies spent for purchase of this service (see table 5–13), while data on construction engineering refer to overall size of construction contracts, usually without any breakdown between actual building and services proper. Nevertheless, the available data for major countries (see table 5–14) show the growing importance of this particular category of services, including at international level.[24]

The main feature of professional and scientific services which deserves

Table 5–13. Advertising expenditure in selected countries, 1985

Country	Expenditure[1] (millions of dollars)	Expenditure as percent of GDP (per cent)
Austria	323	0.49
Belgium-Luxembourg	412	0.53
Finland	792	1.54
France	2,413	0.49
Germany, Fed. Rep.	4,704	0.76
Greece	89	0.29
Ireland	89	0.56
Italy	1,790	0.51
Netherlands	1,077	0.89
Norway	685	1.25
Portugal	49	0.25
Spain	1,223	0.76
Sweden	655	0.71
Switzerland	890	0.93
United Kingdom	5,417	1.27
Japan	12,174	1.00
United States	57,686	1.59

Source: European Advertising and Media Forecast, April 1986, quoted in Tempest [1986].
Note: 1. Not including "below-the-line" advertising such as promotions, direct marketing, etc.

Table 5–14.   Disparate data on international transactions in business and professional services

1. *Consulting services, etc.*
Brazil:
    Exports of engineering services, 1976–1981 (million U.S. dollars)[1]

1976	*1978*	*1979*	*1980*	*1981*
186.5	175.2	225.3	61.0	25.9

United States:
    Accounting: Foreign revenues of the "Big Eight" accounting firms, *1977*[2]
        1,374 million U.S. dollars
    Business professional technical services: 1980 foreign revenue estimates[2]
(million U.S. dollars)

Management and consulting	750
Legal services	278
Technical services	47
Total	1,075

Education: Total foreign-derived revenues, 1980[2]
        1,270 million U.S. dollars
Franchising: Total foreign receipts, 1980[2]
        1,257 million U.S. dollars
Employment: Total foreign revenues, 1980[2] (million U.S. dollars)

Temporary employment agencies	422
Executive search firms	125
Permanent placement firms	—
Total	547

Health services: Total foreign receipts, 1980[2] (million U.S. dollars)

From hospitals owned	250
From health consultants and allied services	16
Total	266

2. *Construction-Engineering*
United States: Construction-management and design services exports (Contract awards), 1980[2] (million U.S. dollars)

Construction management	4,280
Design	1,081
Total	5,361
(Feasibility studies, 1979	905)

France: Engineering consulting services, gross export sales, 1979[3]
        550 million U.S. dollars

3. *Leasing*
United States: Foreign revenue of U.S. leasing industry, 1980[2]
  2,347 million U.S. dollars
Europe: Total new assets acquired, 1980–1981[4] (million U.S. dollars)
  1980: 16,931
  1981: 15,947

4. *Information Services*
   (a) *Data processing*
United States: Revenues earned overseas, 1979–1980[2] (million U.S. dollars)
  1979: 430
  1980: 600
   (b) *Computer software and services*
World: Data banks and related services[5] (estimated numbers)

Data banks	2,900
Data bank producers	1,400
Data distributors	500

Japan: Data bank service market: sales[6] (million yen)

1973	1978	1980	1981	1982	1983	1984
7,620	27,069	44,059	60,737	52,342	78,713	96,654

Europe: Marketed computer software and services: domestic sales 1984[7] (billion U.S. dollars)

France	2,410
Germany, Fed. Rep. of	1,734
Italy	1,021
United Kingdom	1,552
Others	3,387
Total	10,104

Notes to sources:
1. International Trade Centre, 1984. *Study of the Development of Foreign Trade in Technical Consulting Services from Developing Countries*, document *ITC/DPMD/84/6*. Geneva: ITC.
2. Economic Consulting Services, Inc. [1981].
3. OECD, unpublished document.
4. *The Banker*, May 1983.
5. *Le Mois Economique et Financier*, 10/86.
6. Suzuki (1986).
7. *Transborder Data Report*, September 1986.
General note: 1. New data, based on revised analytical methods, have recently been published for the United States in a Special Report by the U.S. Office of Technology Assessment: *Trade in Services, Exports and Foreign Revenues* [1986]. For practical reasons, it has not been possible to take this publication into account in the present table.

attention is their inherently ubiquitous character, related both to the nature of their knowledge-content (FLK; see chapter 8) and to the mobility of the economic agents in which they are embodied. Efforts undertaken by private or government authorities to settle and concentrate these essentially mobile factors of production in institutions such as universities, research centers, hospitals, and professional associations of various kinds (lawyers, doctors, engineers, etc.) are a reflection of the concerns of (1) private groups to organize service cartels in order to protect owners of particular knowledge resources against entry in the industry and/or price competition from new suppliers inside or outside the domestic market, or (2) governments to protect acquired knowledge, whether considered as a national[25] resource or as a social asset, against foreign competition.

This tendency to capitalize on or to monopolize acquired resources, seen as accumulated assets, reflects the fact that, whereas some nations can be said to be naturally endowed with better intellectual faculties than other nations, the same cannot be said generally of human beings.

God may not have created all men economically equal, but it would be presumptuous for any man to think that He has not created all men intellectually equal, or at least with the same intellectual potential. Yet, the distribution of men among nations and territories has very little to do with modern economic rationale, and even less with natural human factors. It should be no surprise that some human groups should have better sets of economic opportunities due to their being brought together through the vagaries of history in specific geographical locations called "countries," while other human groups have had to wrestle with more complex physical and cultural factors which may have impaired or slowed down the development of their intellectual faculties, *ergo* of their economic potential. In short, there is no a priori reason to infer from the fact that particular conjunctions of factors confer upon certain countries a greater efficiency in the economic use of knowledge and technical know-how, that the human beings living in these countries are naturally more intelligent than those living in other countries. Absolute economic advantage should not be confused with natural economic advantage.

Knowledge can also be readily transferred to any part of the globe, so that the only way to maintain a "comparative" advantage in knowledge-intensive services is to limit or prohibit access to the information base that constitutes the raw material of these services. This said, however, it remains true that owners of knowledge, whether or not they limit access to information on which they base their operations, also possess *specific* skills which give them a comparative advantage in the accomplishment of certain service functions, lasting for at least the time necessary for the learning process of potential competitors to be completed.[26]

In conclusion, professional and scientific services are among the most elusive, though most important, types of productive activities, which explains the difficulty of quantifying their economic impact on production, distribution, and consumption processes throughout the economy. On the other hand, intuitive reasoning provides an explanation for the rapid development of these service activities in modern economies (see figure 5–3), in that the quest for knowledge and the search for new applications of scientific and technical discoveries precipitate a self-generating process of innovation and entrepreneurship, which develops at an accelerated pace as its information base expands.

Figure 5–3. Share of GDP and share of employment of "finance, insurance, real estate, and business services" at constant prices.

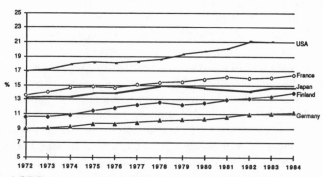

a. Share of GDP at constant prices;

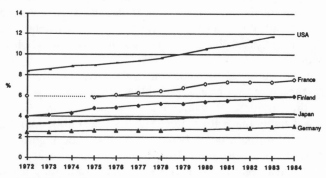

b. Share of employment.

Source: OECD, 1986. National Accounts, Vol II, Paris, Vol II (prices)
Notes: Base years for GDP data are as follows:
    France: 1970; United States: 1975; Finland, Germany and Japan: 1980.

Distribution Services

This category of services covers wholesale and retail trade, but it may also, for certain purposes, include the services of brokers and sales agents, who for other purposes might be classified in financial services, insurance, or transport. Generally speaking, the notion of distribution services covers the services of intermediaries either between different producers or between producers and consumers.[27] They are to be distinguished from "pure" consumer services which are not involved in the transferring of other services or goods along a market chain, linking up a distant and anonymous producer with the buyer of the services or goods (and which consist, on the contrary—see below—in directly producing final products for individual consumption). Thus, the function characterizing wholesale and retail trade is that of creating interlinkages in the marketplace by extending the reach of, and by consolidating, commercial relationships. In traditional economies, this function is associated with the handling of goods, and due to the requirements of storage and transport, with the establishment of a physical infrastructure (warehouses and stores) which has made the activities of the economic agents concerned readily identifiable. For this reason, statistics on wholesale and retail trade have been collected for a considerable amount of time in many countries. In modern economies, however, the use of electronic data transmission and processing reduces the importance of traditional distribution structures; it tends to blur the distinctions between wholesalers and retailers by facilitating the derouting and rerouting of retailers' orders in response to market fluctuations at the initiative of the retailers themselves. At the same time, it is obvious that in the area of services trade, the need for storage and transport of the products traded is minimal or nonexistent; therefore, there exists no physical base to distinguish between wholesale and retail activities.[28]

The available statistical data on wholesale and retail trade (see table 5–15) may, therefore, not be representative of the full range of activities related to the creation of value-added in distribution. In advanced economies it is likely that with better statistics it would be found that this sector of activity, broken down between the two subcategories, is more important than the statistics show. Consequently, and contrary to common perceptions in this regard, wholesale and retail trade may in fact have increased *pari passu* with the expansion and diversification of markets, and in particular with the increase in the share of service activities in total national product.[29]

Country	Year	GNP/capita (1984 U.S. dollars)	Sales (billion U.S. dollars)	Share of GDP (percent)	Population (1984, millions)
India	1984	260	22.6	13.2	749
Indonesia	1984	540	12.5	15.6	159
Côte-d'Ivoire	1979	610	1.8	20.8	10
Thailand	1984	860	3.1	8.4	50
Colombia	1984	1,390	4.7	14.0	28
Chile	1983	1,700	3.0	16.9	12
Brazil	1983	1,720	35.6	15.6	133
Mexico	1984	2,040	17.6	22.8	77
Korea, Rep. of	1984	2,110	11.9	14.6	40
Argentina	1983	2,230	4.9	16.5	30
Hong Kong	1983	6,330	4.9	18.2	5
Italy	1984	6,420	49.2	15.6	57
Singapore	1984	7,260	3.4	18.7	3
United Kingdom	1984	8,570	42.8	11.6	56
Belgium	1984	8,610	14.1	19.8	10
Austria	1984	9,140	21.5	14.0	8
Netherlands	1984	9,520	6.7	12.4	14
France	1984	9,760	52.6	11.8	55
Japan	1984	10,630	170.0	14.3	120
Finland	1984	10,770	4.6	9.9	5
Germany, Fed. Rep.	1983	11,130	66.2	10.8	61
Denmark	1984	11,170	6.3	12.6	6
Australia	1980	11,740	21.5	14.0	16
Sweden	1984	11,860	9.3	10.6	8
Canada	1984	13,280	30.3	9.3	25
United States	1983	15,390	556.0	17.0	237

Sources: United Nations, 1986. *Monthly Bulletin of Statistics*, July and September; World Bank. 1986. *World Development Report 1986.* Washington, D.C.: IBRD.

151

Final Consumer Services

In a society where the manufacture of goods represented a path-breaking achievement over traditional handicraft methods of processing raw materials, any economic activity not connected with the transformation of raw natural resources into consumable products was naturally considered as intrinsically unproductive. At the time, where the fascination of material wealth was an integral part of economic thinking, the ingenuity of thinkers and technicians was not rated as real contribution to output, since the product of their activity remained essentially intangible. Therefore, every service activity which did not involve the transformation of raw materials into visible and tangible consumer goods was not considered part of economic production. The tendency to consider service activities as unproductive corresponded to identifiable patterns of consumer demand which were oriented more toward the possession of new physical goods than toward unmeasurable amenities which could, in any case, be provided by service laborers paid at or below subsistence wages. Service activities whose function is uniquely to satisfy the immediate wants and desires of individual consumers tended to be regarded by Western economists as more sources of hedonistic satisfaction which, in accordance with neo-classical moral standards, could not possibly be associated with the notion of economic value.

An indicative list of consumer services appears in table 5–16; data on consumer expenditure on services, which is the closest one can get to an evaluation of the importance of these services in total product, is shown in table 5–17 for major countries. The information in these two tables calls for two remarks. First, it is noteworthy that the range of consumer services is very wide, and that this category includes a number of services which are much more technology-intensive and complex than is commonly believed. This is because one generally associates consumer services with activities related to basic needs or wants of consumers and which, in traditional societies, tend to be performed by servants. These are the activitie listed at the beginning of table 5–16: laundry, child care, domestic help, and the like. In fact, domestic and personal services nowadays cover a whole range of activities which either have become commercialized or are performed by the consumers themselves with the help of machines. In other words, some of the primitive domestic and personal services have become externalized, that is, have increasingly been supplied from outside the home, while some have become internalized in the sense of involving the direct participation of consumers in their production—the home being, in both cases, taken as the initial locus of output. Examples of services

Table 5–16.   Illustrative list of consumer services

Food retailing, including street vendors
Restaurants, canteens, and other collective food distribution services
Other goods retailing
Goods rental services
Personal care (hairdressers, etc.)
Hotel, motel, camping, etc., services
Taxis and public transport
Goods delivery
Consumer advisory services
Gardening
Architecture services
Interior decorating
Fashion designing
Medical and nursing services (including opticians)
Child care and guardianship
Community and welfare services
Religious services
Sports instruction services
Unemployment services
Education and training (all fields)
Translation
Law services, including notaries
Travel agencies, travel guides, etc.
Real estate agents, insurance agents, etc.
Real estate services (rentals)
Retail banking
Insurance, life and nonlife
Performing art services
Professional sports
Lottery, casino operations
Computer software services
Telephone, telegraph, and mail services

---

externalized in this fashion are transport services (the taxi replacing the private chauffeur), laundry services (the local laundry service, or better still, the local laundromat, replacing the house servant), cooking (the town traiteur replacing the house cook), etc. The same consumer services provide examples of activities becoming internalized, e.g., house cleaning (the vacuum cleaner replacing the cleaning woman), laundry (the washing machine replacing the local laundry service), transport (the private

Table 5–17. Share of consumer services in total domestic expenditure at current prices, selected countries[1] (percentages)

Country	GNP per capita (1984 U.S. dollars)	Year	Total	Rent	Medical care	Transport and communication services	Education	Entertainment[2]	Other[3]
India	260	1973	12.5	2.3	1.4	3.3	2.2	0.6	2.7
		1983	13.9	1.8	1.3	6.2	1.4	0.6	2.6
Korea, Rep. of	2,110	1973	19.6	3.0	1.8	5.0	1.6	2.3	5.9
		1983	24.5	3.7	2.4	6.5	3.6	2.6	5.7
Hong-Kong	6,330	1973	26.1	8.0[4]	3.6	4.8[6]	1.0	4.1	4.6
		1983	28.2	9.5[4]	3.9	5.0[6]	0.7	4.7	4.4
Singapore	7,260	1973	31.4	6.1[4]	1.6	5.9	0.5	6.1	11.2
		1983	30.2	4.7[4]	1.5	6.2	0.4	6.3	11.1
Belgium	8,610	1972	29.8	11.1[4]	4.6	4.5	0.1	2.5	7.0
		1984	35.3	12.4[4]	6.2	6.0	0.1	3.0	7.6
France	9,760	1972	34.2	11.2	6.2	5.4	0.2	3.8	7.4
		1984	39.4	11.6	8.8	6.9	0.2	3.9	8.0
Japan	10,630	1972	30.7	9.0	4.4	4.4[6]	n.a.	5.3[5]	7.6
		1984	38.7	11.3	6.1	5.9[6]	n.a.	5.6[5]	9.8
Finland	10,770	1972	29.3	11.9	1.5	5.8	n.a.	3.8[5]	6.3
		1984	27.8	8.0	1.4	6.4	n.a.	4.7[5]	7.3
Germany, Fed. Rep. of	11,130	1972	18.7	6.9	1.5	0.8	n.a.	6.0[5]	3.5
		1984	21.5	8.8	1.8	1.0	n.a.	5.5[5]	4.4
Australia	11,740	1972	36.8	11.9	4.7	7.5	0.7	3.9	8.1
		1984	34.2	12.4	3.7	6.8	0.8	3.7	6.8
Canada	13,280	1972	32.3	11.1[4]	1.7	5.4	1.7	3.8	8.6
		1984	35.6	13.1[4]	2.1	6.1	1.6	4.1	8.6
United States	15,390	1972	35.6	9.6	6.2	6.5	1.3	4.0	8.0
		1984	36.3	9.8	7.7	6.2	1.2	3.6	7.8

Sources: United Nations, 1986. *National Accounts Statistics, Main Aggregates and Detailed Tables, 1983.* New York: United Nations. OECD. 1986. *National Accounts, Vol. II: Detailed Tables, 1972–1984.* Paris: OECD. World Bank, 1986. *World Development Report 1986.* Washington, D.C.: IBRD.

Notes:
1. Countries selected partly on the basis of availability of statistics.
2. Excluding restaurants and hotels.
3. Including restaurants and hotels, personal care, and other miscellaneous goods and services.
4. Including fuel and power.
5. Including education.

154

automobile replacing the train or bus), etc. The appearance of similar activities among those externalized and those internalized is a reflection either of different stages of economic development and/or of the technological awareness of consumers, or of different consumer preferences, when the consumers have the option of acquiring the capital equipment substituting for house labor or of dispensing with such acquisitions as well as with the house labor and spending the income thus saved on purchasing the services of specialized firms in the marketplace.

The increase in the technological content of consumer services is a result of the cost-saving efforts of service-producing enterprises but also of increased demand for "intelligent" service deliveries by sophisticated consumers. Sometimes, the satisfaction of demand for more intelligent services requires an effort on the part of the consumers themselves, who must understand and adapt to the techniques put at their disposal to fulfill their variegated needs. Thus, a consumer who wants to be able to record television shows on a videocassette machine must learn to make this machine function; a consumer who wants a home telephone-answering service must know how to operate the telephone-answering device; and a consumer who wants to operate a home microcomputer must learn to assimilate the software delivered with the computer. In the words of Orio Giarini, "In the service economy, users increasingly form part of the production systems: they need to understand and operate complex systems' applications, organize maintenance systems, and carry out repairs and recycling. They have become part of the production-utilization system which, in turn, needs their active contribution and participation. No longer are they, or can they be, passive consumers. No longer do they buy products where the utility or value is embodied in the object. Instead they have to make an effort to extract the utilization value from the product" [Giarini, 1986].

A quick glance at table 5–16 shows that many services classified in the "final consumer" category are not currently traded and indeed may not be tradable. That is to say, it is not possible under most circumstances to transport such services over any distance between the producer and the consumer. The classical example of the nontransportability of services is the haircut. In a certain sense, this particular characteristic of final consumer services is no different from the characteristic of some intermediate services like banking, insurance, engineering, etc. However, the fact that the services we are dealing with in this section are final distinguishes them from the services just cited, in that they are not embodied either in goods which are then used in the production of other goods sold to final consun,ers (for example, maritime insurance paid on imported shoes) or in services which are used as inputs into other services sold directly to consumers, like information embodied in travel services or education in medical services.

Final services, therefore, affect the welfare of consumers, and their value is totally embodied in the consumers themselves as part of their well-being, whether obtained in exchange for a portion of their money income or thrust upon them as an unrequited transfer of utility.[30] For the reason that the services rendered to final consumers "disappear" from the marketplace, just like food disappears when it is eaten, such services are usually considered as of a transient nature, in contradistinction, for instance, to durable goods which render their services over time. However, not all final consumer services are of this nature, since some capital-intensive services like insurance and housing as well as cultural services like education and art also belong to this category.

In fact, it is sometimes difficult to distinguish not only among services and goods (like teaching and textbooks) but also among consumer services which are truly final and those which have some characteristics of durable services because they are more capital-intensive to produce and they have more long-term embodiment effects on consumers due to the high degree of "self-service" involved in their acquisition. Many of these problems of identification of the borderline between services and goods appear in the broad category of service activities called "tourism." Leisure travel involves the consumption of both final services and goods by tourists and, while most of it is nonstorable, the advent of photography has permitted a more durable consumption of travel experiences while transforming photographs of sites, landscapes, and tourist accommodations into an intermediate output for sellers of tourist services in distant markets through various pictorial forms of advertising. In addition, services rendered abroad to business travellers are, at least in part, an intermediate input into the production activity of such travellers, whether they are engaged in service or goods-producing enterprises in their home country.

Government Services

There are basically two ways of distinguishing government services from other services: (1) they are rendered by government authorities or agencies as opposed to private sector firms or individuals; (2) they have the characteristic of public goods. In terms of economic classification (and in addition to those which can be classified as public goods) government services can be intermediate, final, human-intensive or physical- capital-intensive, or labor-intensive. In practice, with the exception of government services which have the characteristic of public goods, the distinction between government and private services does not rest on firm economic criteria and tends to depend rather on considerations of a sociopolitical and ideological nature, which vary from country to country and from period to period in the same country. The debate on the activities of public telecommunication monopolies evoked above illustrates the kind of problems that arise in attempting to deal with certain marketable services as a specific type of government activity. Indeed, theoretically, all service activities have a claim to being either in the private sector or in the public sector. The distinction that is effectively made in actual life does, however, exert a considerable influence on the extent to which services can be traded internationally, either across borders or through other forms of transactions.

Generally, governments do not like competition on their own markets. When they have the monopoly of a service activity, they make every effort to keep out competition from private operators, be they nationals or foreigners. This does not necessarily prevent them from competing with private operators or other government suppliers in world markets for the services concerned. Nevertheless, the bigger the markets controlled by government entities, the smaller the total volume of world trade in services. It should be noted that the resulting narrowness of the world market may constitute a considerable hindrance to the development of efficient services internationally, by limiting the potential for reaping economies of scale in activities which are developed on a highly human- and capital-intensive base and are susceptible of a high degree of standardization.

For analytical purposes, the concept of government services should best be limited to those which are in the nature of public goods. Public goods are generally considered as nonmarketable due to the fact that in principle, their volume of production and range of consumption cannot be physically controlled except through complicated rationing systems. Radio and television broadcasting used to be a good example of such goods, but modern message-coding techniques make rationing relatively easy. On the other hand, the maintenance of law and order, though it may be apportioned differently in different parts of the national territory, remains practically impossible to measure both on the output side and on the consumption side of the hypothetical market equation.[31] However diffused, the economic benefits from government services which have the character of public goods are clearly perceived by all economic agents of the private sector in situations where public authority breaks down or threatens to break down. The cost of substituting for the externalities generated by public intervention are often prohibitive, and rather than assume them many private enterprises which have integrated them into their input/output structure at subsidized prices prefer to cease business altogether. This is the reason why in countries, regions, or localities where the security of persons and property is not maintained, there is a rapid loss of economic substance in addition to any other damage that may be created by those who take advantage of this absence of public authority. A case in point is the "urban decay" which has set in in many large cities of industrial countries.

The borderline between what might be called "essential" public services and similar services which are or could be provided by the private sector may, however, fluctuate in accordance with the degree of economic and political development of particular societies. Thus, in some countries hospital service and education are considered as public goods or near-public goods due to the emphasis being placed on the externalities they create in the long run in the form of permitting the development of a healthy and educated population—an asset not only for economic development but also for social well-being, including the maintenance of law and order. In other countries, such service activities as banking and life insurance are considered as performing as much a public good as a private service function, due to the fact that public ownership of the cor-responding means of production is the only known way, given the low state of developmnt of financial markets, of collecting private savings and chanelling them into productive investment.

Notes

1. The reader must be aware that the shifts in coverage of various service groupings in dif-ferent classifications are at least as much the result of the paucity of statistical data as of the different purposes for which services activities are grouped in one way or another. Therefore, for the time being, it is necessary to learn to live with a certain confusion in the definition of services as pointed out in the last chapter, and to concentrate on conceptual aspects until improvements in the statistical base allow a more searching comparison of detailed sets of activities which presently are lumped together.

2. The use of the term *financial services* to cover both banking and insurance is in the British tradition. See, for example, *United Kingdom National Study on Services* [1984].

3. See, for example, David T. Llewellyn [1985]: "The process of structural change in the financial system has recently accelerated perceptibly. This acceleration is associated largely with proposed changes in the stock exchange and securities industry and with the prospect of radical change in the building society sector. In this next phase the dominant pressures are likely to be a yet more intensive competitive environment combined with the impact of new technology in the financial services industry....The traditional money transmission

mechanism, hitherto dominated by banks, is thus being undermined both by new technology and the entry of alternative institutions. The prospect of electronic transfer of funds, home banking and point of sale facilities will likely create new opportunities for building societies and others to challenge the dominance of banks. One of the responses to this potential is that clearing banks have recently made significant change in their funding strategy by giving greater priority to securing personal sector savings deposits. The likely future evolution of the financial system is apparent in existing trends. Traditional demarcations between different financial institutions are being steadily eroded and in the process the financial system is becoming less structured. Banking activity is not now restricted to banks. This process is moreover unlikely to be restricted to financial institutions, as some major retail chains have the branches, opening hours and general standing to make the provision of financing and 'banking' services a viable business proposition."

4. Most of the information in the following paragraphs is drawn from OECD [1983b].

5. Rajan and Cooke [1986] have analyzed the process for the British banking system. While their main focus is on the employment effects of new technology, their observations throw light on other important aspects of automation in banking: "...the extensive application of information technology in financial institutions in the last decade has not caused job displacement: quite the reverse, since the employment level has increased by 40 per cent during this period. In fact, the intuitively simple link between technology and employment looks paradoxical against the background of this historical experience....In spite of substantial improvements in labour productivity achieved through reorganization, improved practices and 25 years' continuous investment in automation, the growth in the banks' business has to date outweighed all these factors. However, the explanation of the apparent paradox of increasing staff numbers is much more complicated than a simple increase in business. It can be explained when analyzed within a systems context. This shows that a modern-day production process relies on a combination of tangible as well as intangible inputs. As the terms imply, the former comprises physical inputs such as labour, materials and machinery: the latter the abstract, but no less important, inputs such as management culture, employee attitudes and customer inertia....In the financial institutions [such] compensatory gains on the demand side specifically associated with new technology have given rise to employment opportunities, and are loosely referred to as the product effect. Thus when analyzing the employment impact of new technology in the economic context, the labour-saving process effect on the supply side has to be set against the compensatory product effect on the demand side, to see which of the two is dominant. So far, in the financial services sector the product effect has been dominant: the cost-effective growth in business volumes has given rise to opportunities that have moderated the process effect."

6. For a detailed comparison of these three approaches, see H.W. Arndt [1984]. Arndt deals also with variants of these approaches. The subject is very technical, and the reader is referred to the basic literature quoted in Arndt and elsewhere for a more precise explanation of the statistical issues involved.

7. The full quotation by Arndt of *Australian National Accounts: Concepts, Sources and Methods* is as follows: "Interest received is viewed as consisting of a pure interest component and a service change for organizing the funds. It is not practicable to allocate all the service charge to customers [i.e., among borrowers by industry]. The part relating to consumer loans (including hire-purchase) is treated as being paid by the customer and included in private consumption expenditure. The remainder, termed the imputed bank service charge, is not allocated to customers but treated as being paid by a "nominal industry" which accordingly has a negative operating surplus of this amount."

8. This phenomenon has been described and analyzed by various authors. See, *Among*

Others Jagdish Bhagwati [1985]; Harry Freeman [1985]; R. Bulthuis, B. van Holst, and G. R. de Wit [1985].

9. Leibenstein [1966], who was apparently first to coin the phrase, specified three elements as significant in determining X-efficiency: (1) intraplant motivation, (2) external motivational efficiency, and (3) nonmarket input efficiency. He also noted, "The data suggest that cost reduction that is essentially a result of improvement in X-efficiency is likely to be an important component of the observed residual in economic growth. In addition, there is no doubt that, in some of the cases of reduced cost, new knowledge was conveyed to the firms involved, and this too is part of the residual. It is of special interest that such new knowledge involves knowledge *dissemination* rather than invention" [emphasis added]. For a discussion of the effect of information technology on the functioning of multinational enterprises, see in particular Rada and Pipe [1983].

10. Examples of services already provided by some PTT's are databases, videotext, teletext, electronic mail, etc.

11. The private cost of producing at marginal cost volume is assumed to be greater than the social cost (= foregone consumers' surplus) because the consumers' surplus is not counted as a benefit to the private producer. This surplus is assumed to be greater than the subsidies needed to produce marginal cost volume, provided that the subsidies do not create otherwise costly distortions in the economy. The net social benefit expected from the natural monopoly is therefore equal to the increase in consumers' surplus *minus* the cost of subsidies. If subsidies give rise to misallocations of resources elsewhere in the economy, the achievement of a net social benefit may involve some discriminatory pricing of the services. For a more detailed exposition of these concepts, see Vickrey [1964, particularly pp. 249 and following].

12. See, among others, F. Warren McFarlan [1984]; Michael E. Porter and Victor E. Mellar [1985]; James I. Cash, Jr. and Benn R. Konsynski [1985]; Hisao Kanamori [1985]; R. Bulthuis, B. van Holst, and G.R. de Wit [1985].

13. In this connection, see Bruno Lanvin [1986]: "In data services, the ability to provide any particular product relies heavily on the availability of (or access to) sophisticated and technology-intensive equipment. For the makers of such equipment, technological innovation and the associated "technological gap" is generally a first protection against would-be competitors. But for the leader, technical norms are another way of raising barriers to the entry of such competitors. The efficiency of such barriers is even considerably strengthened in a deregulated environment." A testimony to the importance of standards is the ongoing war for supremacy in the field of computer technology between International Business Machines (IBM) on the one hand, and other computer manufacturers on the other. IBM has developed its own computer network methodology, the Systems Network Architecture (SNA), which it seeks to impose throughout its commercial operations, thus expanding the captive market for its hardware and software. Other computer companies in the United States, Western Europe, and Japan are supporting the development of another system called Open Systems Interconnection (OSI) developed by international consensus within the framework of the International Standardization Organization (ISO). In 1985, the Commission of European Communities has sued IBM for monopoly behavior and forced the company to accept the application of OSI (which allows interconnections between computers otherwise incompatible) in its European operations.

14. Discussions of the status and impact of transborder data flow restrictions can be found in United States Centre on Transnational Corporations [1982], and in Bigelow [1986]. The issue is closely monitored by TDR, *Transnational Data Report*, a monthly review specializing in the international information economy.

15. See, in addition to the extensive studies prepared by the United Nations Centre on

Transnational Corporations, the work of Bruno Lanvin [1986], and the collection of writings in J.F. Rada and G.R. Pipe [1983], including the article therein by this author.

16. See, for example, E. Gonzalez Manet [1986] and Deepak Nayyar [1986].

17. See United Nations Centre on Transnational Corporations [1980]: "By 1975 the number of insurance companies, domestic and foreign, operating in Africa had declined to 377 as against 552 in 1968. In Asia, this number was 780 in 1975 as against 827 in 1968. In Latin America it was 886 in 1975, as against 1,156 in 1968. Thus for every million people living in the developing world, there were on the average three insurers to serve them in 1975 as opposed to 18 for every million people in the developed countries."

18. The main problem in addition to lack of technical expertise is often that direct premium income is too small relative to the risks to be covered.

19. In the context of international air traffic negotiations conducted within the IATA (International Air Transport Association), the five freedoms of the air are defined as follows for a carrier of nation A: freedom 1, right of transit without landing; freedom 2, right of non-traffic stop for refueling, etc., but not for setting down or picking up load; freedom 3, right to set down traffic from nation A to nation B; freedom 4, right to pick up traffic from nation B for nation A; freedom 5, right to carry traffic between foreign territories, e.g., from nation B to nation C by carriers of nation A. Another very rarely granted sixth freedom consists of the right to carry traffic within the territory of a foreign nation, or right to "cabotage" (see figure 5-2).

20. In the case of air and sea transport, although there are no visible "roads" along which traffic moves, the network is materialized by air traffic and maritime shipping lanes on the one hand and airports and harbors on the other, which correspond to railways and train stations and roads and bus terminals in the case of public surface transports. It is only in private automobile and other forms of road traffic or transport that the need for special infrastructure to receive and service transport equipment is more decentralized, but this is due to the relative lightness and maneuvrability of the transport equipment used rather than to the ownership structure of transport media. Theoretically at least, private railway, airway, and shipping systems could be developed in different fashion by the construction of multiple train stations, airports, and harbors managed by private interest. In reverse, there is no physical need for buses to be parked in central stations other than the convenience of public authorities to allocate specific land sites for this purpose, generally in conjunction with their concern to keep strict control over the capital they have invested in transport equipment.

21. The "Customs Convention on the International Transport of Goods under cover of TIR carnets," concluded in 1959 under the aegis of the United Nations Economic Commission for Europe, operates through associations of goods carriers approved by their respective governments. Its main objective is to facilitate transit trade.

22. In particular, total deregulation of a given transport sector may be accompanied by the elimination of state subsidies resulting in (1) reorganization of transport networks and (2) a redistribution of transport charges among different categories of consumers.

23. As a store of value immediately convertible into money, gold, despite all the efforts of moralists and Friedmanites to turn it into derision, continues to be cherished by individuals and governments alike.

24. Some subsectors such as construction-engineering and accounting are usually deemed to benefit from a broader and more reliable statistical coverage due to the role of major multinational enterprises and/or multinational trade associations in these particular fields.

25. General knowledge being a fungible resource, one cannot speak of "natural" endowments as in the case of factors of production such as primary labor, land, or specialized knowledge (LIK; see chapter 8).

162   SERVICES IN THE GLOBAL MARKET

26. This is the implicit reasoning behind the product cycle theory elaborated by Vernon and others; see Vernon [1966, 1970, 1979].

27. They also cover, and increasingly so, a large element of consumer self-service, due to the fact that distribution and self-service take place in the same locations, e.g., supermarkets. However, from both epistemological and economic standpoints, to call retail consumer self-service a "distribution" service is a misnomer. Such a laxist use of words merely reflects the fact that the role of self-service in modern economies is not yet well understood and, in any case, does not fit any existing classification of economic activities.

28. This may not be the case for services embodied in goods such as books, computer diskettes, phonograph records, etc., but it clearly applies to services such as those of lawyers, architects, construction engineers, consultants, etc.

29. The stability of the share of wholesale and retail trade in total services in economies at different levels of development has been noted by many observers, but so far no attempt has been made to identify separately wholesale transactions in services that do not pass through registered wholesale trade networks.

30. The latter is often the case for community or social services, which are rendered by groups of consumers to individual members of the group or to consumers outside the group on moral, religious, political, or other grounds. Unrequited transfers of certain categories of services also take place vis-a-vis selective groups of consumers through government agencies, but in this case, at least if the government budget is in equilibrium, the transfer consists in a redistribution of income from consumers not entitled to benefit from such transfers to those who are, through the medium of taxation.

31. For a discussion of the role of services classified as public goods in postindustrial societies, see this author [1986, chapters 1 and 3].

6 THE INTERNATIONALIZATION PROCESS

"By contributing to make technical and legal obstacles to trade more and more permeable, data services have undoubtedly been instrumental in the increasing importance of services as a whole in international transactions" [Lanvin, 1986]. Technological developments indeed represent one major factor in the internationalization of service activities, through the modification of marketing modes that they bring about. This has been referred to earlier (chapter 5) for individual service activities. As data services continue to develop and the technological means at their disposal undergo constant transformation, it is difficult at this point in time to perceive the durable changes in production structures that will develop. Moreover, it seems clear that innovations in the field of telematics are not the only source of expansion of service activities internationally. Parallel to the expansion of transborder data flows generated by the rapid evolution of telecommunication technologies, recent decades have witnessed a considerable growth in foreign direct investment by service companies. For example, as table 6–1 shows, outward flows of foreign direct investment in services of three major countries have about tripled between the late 1960s and the early '80s. They represented a share of total foreign direct investment flows from these countries of between 30% and 60% in the

163

Table 6–1. Foreign direct investment (FDI) in services, major home countries

Country, currency and year	FDI in services		Total FDI		Share of services in total FDI (per cent)	
	Stock	Flow	Stock	Flow	Stock	Flow
United States (billion U.S. dollars[1])						
1966	16	n.a.	52	n.a.	31	n.a.
1983	82	n.a.	226	n.a.	36	n.a.
United Kingdom (billion U.S. dollars)						
Average 1970–1971[1]	n.a.	0.6	n.a.	1.4	n.a.	41
Average 1978–1980[1]	n.a.	3.4	n.a.	6.9	n.a.	49
Germany, Fed., Rep. (billion DM)						
1966	1	—	10	—	10	—
1980	17	—	74	—	24	—
Average 1973–1977	—	1.1	—	4.9	—	22
Average 1981–1983	—	2.8	—	9.1	—	31
Japan (billion U.S. dollars)						
1960	—	—	—	—	20	—
1980	13	—	32	—	40	—
1973	—	1.2	—	3.5	—	39
1982	—	4.7	—	7.7	—	44

Source: Sauvant and Zimny [1985].
Notes:
1. Including services related to petroleum industry.
2. Excluding oil.
n.a. = not available.
— = not applicable, or not significant.

164

latter period. While there exist no hard data on foreign direct investment except for certain countries and practically none at all for transborder movements of data, it is possible to assess qualitatively the importance of these flows and to provide an analytical basis for the assessment of trends in this area.

From Trade to Integration

We have already seen that, for services, foreign direct investment is not a substitute for trade. One can go a step further and say that in many circumstances foreign direct investment is complementary to trade in services. In sectors such as banking and insurance, for example, the possibility to communicate internationally through telematics permits closer interlinkages between branches and subsidiaries of companies operating in different markets, as well as between financial and insurance companies worldwide and their client multinational enterprises in the goods-producing sector. In parallel, financial institutions and insurance companies, in order to collect the necessary information base to service their clients and be in a position to expand their activities in new domains and regions, increasingly need to establish a presence in distant markets, each anchor point acting as a relay in a global network of information flows and business connections internal to individual companies or shared by the majority of operators in a given sector of trade. Due to the complementarity between investment and trade in services, the internationalization process requires both guarantees of access for services traded across borders (mainly through telecommunication networks) in given markets, and guarantees for the freedom of establishment and investment of services suppliers to those markets. Thus, the distinction between trade policy and investment policy, which has been an unquestioned dogma in international economic relations to this day, no longer corresponds to economic reality at least as far as services are concerned.[1]

Services are traded internationally on the basis of acquired knowledge and experience in the provision of determined economic functions. Unless services can be standardized and the various steps in their production process can be organized so as to produce uniform results, it is not possible to disassociate the content of the service from the quality of the provider. For example, data processing can be broken down into data entry on computer tapes or diskettes, data communication through telephone lines or satellites, data treatment in computers on the basis of specialized software, retransfer of processed data, and analysis and use of processed data for production or marketing purposes. The mechanical parts of this sequence, namely data entry and data transfer, and to some extent data treatment, are physical-factor intensive, using much labor in the first instance and much capital in the latter two. The other operations, namely elaboration of computer software and analysis and use of process data, are human-capital intensive. The first three operations can also be standard-ized, whereas the latter two produce results which vary not only with the quality of the supplier but also with the difficulty of the problems and the capacity of the individual supplier to solve them in different circumstances. Therefore, the first three operations can be performed more cheaply in different locations depending on the particular physical factor endow-ment of these locations, whereas the latter are not dependent for their satisfactory performance on any particular quantitative distribution of factors between locations. In other words, the efficiency of production of the more sophisticated or knowledge-intensive portions of services production processes is unrelated to the location of these processes, which is the same as saying that competitiveness in advanced service activities is indifferent to factor endowment.

An important corollary to this theorem is that, contrary to what happens in the field of goods, the ownership of the means of production of services cannot be readily separated from the ownership of services production technology.[2] This poses serious problems for transfers of technology from more advanced to less advanced countries in the service sector, inasmuch as such transfers (whether or not they give rise to payments or other forms of compensation) have no direct influence on the choice and use of factors of production in the recipient countries, when the technology cannot be disembodied. This particular relationship between technology and factors of production in the field of services also has implications for the nature of the protection that can be afforded to intellectual property rights in this sector. Whenever technology can be traded as a separate good, it can also be protected from theft or misuse like any other goods. Thus, intellectual property rights for mechanical production technology can be easily circumscribed. On the other hand, when the technology is embodied in the producer, the protection of intellectual property rights is not separable from the protection of the economic agent embodying the technology. In extreme cases, the absence of protection may be equivalent to an obligation for the service provider to work for free. Normally, the protection of his intellectual property rights implies the protection of his right to supply services directly to users and consumers. Hence, in the same way that a relationship of complementarity exists between foreign direct investment and cross-border transactions in services, a relationship of complementarity exists between the protection of intellectual property and transactions in embodied services, whether these take place on a cross-border or an establishment/investment basis.[3]

The process of internationalization of services is not just a quantitative phenomenon described in terms of the autonomous development of services activities worldwide. Of equal importance is the fact that it consists in the development of a global market for economic activities which affect the supply (i.e., the availability) of goods and other services, and their mode of production and distribution. That is to say, the internationalization of services also takes place through their increased incorporation into goods, through the networking of economic relations, and through the increased interaction between international transactions in services and international transactions in goods. We have already discussed earlier the effects of increased incorporation of services into goods. In the field of networking, the relevant phenomenon is the increased diversification of individual firms' activities, using common or complementary technologies and information bases. For example, some railway companies sell as distinct service "packages" the rolling stock and repair-shop management systems which they have developed for their own use; some machinery manufacturers also market separately the after-sales service software which they formerly included in physical sales contracts. There are many other similar examples of joint production activities evolving into separate, though interdependent, sources of income for individual firms. Networking as defined above also takes place among rival firms which exploit common information and technologies to reduce costs and shift the field of competition between them to more differentiated and client-specific products. Relationships are established either among manufacturers, among service firms, or across sectors.[4] The increased interaction between international transactions in services and in goods is the net result, in a global market setting, of the two preceding phenomena, namely the incorporation of services into goods and networking. For example, international transactions in telecommunication and computer equipment, either central or peripheral, are complementary to the growth of internationl sales of information services as well as to the development of educational and training media, designed to make individual consumers and corporate users more responsive to the equipment marketed.

One area where there has been considerable development of system interconnections on a worldwide basis is that of financial services. We have earlier referred to the operation of SWIFT (chapter 5). In addition to telematic linkages among banking institutions worldwide, the internationalization process in this sector has taken two other forms: first, a special type of networking whereby a number of services are being provided through joint ventures, corporate agreements for marketing and distribution, new supply arrangements, and joint participation in the ownership and management of associated firms[5]; second, the establishment of subsidiaries and representative offices in foreign countries.[6] This process has entered a particular dynamic phase in the last 10 to 12 years as evidenced by the data in table 6–2. In this, as in other sectors where internationalization is proceeding rapidly, the first phase of internationalization was generally related to the development of the operations of multinational corporations, but this was quickly followed by an autonomous expansion of business related either to the development of offshore currency markets, or of what bankers call "sovereign lending," namely lending by private commercial banks to foreign governments. A factor in the development of such lending has been the recycling of petrodollars following the first oil shock of 1973. With the development of new telecommunication techniques and of financial innovations originating mainly in countries where a large-scale deregulation process was under way, financial institutions have become increasingly interdependent worldwide, not only for the collection and placement of funds and exchanges of currencies but also, as in the case of airlines, for access to a common information base as well as the treatment of data.[7] Thus the common use of information and information-processing tools transforms the role of information itself. Instead of being a source of competitive power by remaining exclusively in the hands of a small number of commercial firms or of a single commercial firm, it becomes a source of competitive power by being commonly accessible, just like a raw material freely traded on the world market, to all firms participating in the internatioalization process. Participation in this process is, however, a sine qua non condition for benefiting from this new competitive power, precisely because the establishment and use of common information networks can only be shared among firms that render services to one another across networks and therefore do not derive any exclusive profit from being part of the network.

On the other hand, firms not involved in the internationalization process do not render similar services to firms that are; hence, they cannot expect to have access to the common resource, since they do not have a comparable stake in the interdependence of operations of the members of the network. The common information and data-processing bases are therefore only public goods as between the participants in a given "society" of commercial operators, just like other public goods can exist solely for given social and economic entities usually contained within

Table 6–2. World network of overseas bank branches and agencies, 1961 and 1978

Host countries	Home countries	United States	United Kingdom	France	Germany, F.R.	Switzerland	Japan	Middle East
United States	1961	—	n.a.	n.a.	n.a.	2	8	2
	1978	—	19	11	13	8	49	17
United Kingdom	1961	11	—	2	..	..	3	..
	1978	56	—	13	6	8	23	20
France	1961	3	24	—	..	..	..	1
	1978	21	21	—	2	..	1	6
Germany, F.R.	1961	3	2	5	—	..	2	..
	1978	22	8	16	—	..	12	8
Switzerland	1961	n.a.	1	1	..	—	..	..
	1978	8	8	10	1	—	..	..
Other Europe	1961	4	30	44	..	..	..	..
	1978	67	72	48	5	4	6	3
Japan	1961	14	7	n.a.	..	..	—	..
	1978	32	8	7	..	3	—	..
Africa	1961	7	2,182	232	1	..	..	11
	1978	16	148	30	..	..	..	10
Latin America	1961	52	64	45	..	1	4	..
	1978	85	102	30	1	..	9	..
Caribbean	1961	12	81	5	..	..	..	..
	1978	207	83	7	7	7	1	3
Middle East	1961	4	49	14	..	..	2	33
	1978	30	142	23	..	1	..	106
Far East	1961	18	845	13	1	..	8	..
	1978	126	503	31	12	2	29	4
Total	1961	128	3,287	361	2	3	27	37
	1978	670	1,114	226	47	33	122	177
No. of banking establishments	1961	8	16	16	2	3	6	6
	1978	126	20	24	12	12	23	21

Source: R.M. Pecchioli quoted in de Laubier [1966].
n.a. = not available.
.. = no reported presence.

169

national boundaries. Financial institutions that do not join the international "club" either because they are intent on preserving exclusive access to their domestic market and preventing foreign banks from competing with them in that market, or because their governmental authorities prevent access of foreign financial institutions to the domestic market for noncommercial reasons, have to make the effort of acquiring the basic information and means of data processing necessary to offer a roughly comparable set of financial services to their clients that carry on business abroad, lest these clients transfer their assets and customs to foreign banks located in the markets with which they trade (if necessary, fraudulently, when existing currency regulations do not permit such transfer). This particular aspect of the internationalization process and its consequences on the competitiveness of financial institutions that remain outside the main stream of progress is particularly relevant to the prospects for developing efficient services under protection which is advocated by some spokesmen for developing countries.[8]

From Integration to Networking

One explanation which has been given for the tendency of service firms to establish abroad is that "...the cost of transporting services from one country to another is the cost of transporting either the providers or the receivers. It follows that the cost of transporting a unit of a service (in a conventionally traded unit) is in general higher than the cost of transporting a unit of a good. One reason for this is that the cost of transporting services must include the opportunity cost of time spent by providers or receivers of services in moving between countries. There is no such cost in trade in goods. For many services the transportation cost is too high for them to be traded among countries. Establishing a foreign affiliate in services is thus a way of reducing the transportation cost necessary for trade" [Lee and Naya, 1985, p. 22].

It is interesting that foreign direct investment also takes place in service sectors such as tourism, where normally it is the consumer rather than the producer who moves to the supplying market. In effect, the tourist services which are exported through foreign investment are not final consumer services. These can be produced more cheaply on the spot, particularly when they are labor-intensive and sourced in low-labor-cost countries. Rather, they are intermediate producer services of the kind that require large inputs of human and physical capital. Whereas physical capital may be available in the tourism-supplying country, especially if it consists of fixed assets such as buildings or construction equipment, human capital is not, or there would be little justification for foreign investors to incur risks. It should be noted in this connection that the human capital which is the motive force behind foreign direct investment in tourism often originates in activities not necessarily related to the tourist trade. For this reason, the staffing of foreign tourist ventures tends to reflect geographical patterns of comparative advantage based on specialized knowledge accumulated in these other activities. Thus, in large international hotels it is often found that the kitchen and catering services are managed by continental Europeans; the administration, procurement, communication, and advertising services by North Americans; and the financial and accounting services by British or, exceptionally, local staff. This may be a somewhat caricatural view of the international tourist trade, but it should at least serve to demonstrate that the service activities commonly lumped together under the heading of tourism are very diverse and that the best commercial results can be obtained by resorting to the acquired abilities of individuals from countries at different levels of economic development.

In a recent study, Jagdish Bhagwati stated that "...the enormous speed with which technological change has progressed in the communications and information sectors, commonly grouped under the 'telematics' rubrique, has shifted an ever increasing number of activities to the long-distance category where they may be executed 'over the wire' and hence become more readily tradeable and traded in consequence...But if tradeability of services has increased through 'long-distancing' trends in the provision of services, it has also increased for the very different reason that, where physical proximity continues to be necessary but has been traditionally difficult or impossible to achieve across countries, organizational innovations have appeared recently which have made such proximity feasible and even economical....Numerous construction firms have materialized in the post-OPEC 1970s to take, not just skilled but also entire teams of unskilled labour to the labour-scarce Middle East economies feverishly engaged in spending oil revenues. This innovation in organization fortuitously resulting from the OPEC-led change in the world economy, has made it possible for us to contemplate a transition of unskilled labour services, and hence of the category of services where the provider must necessarily move to the user, from its hitherto non-traded status to the tradeable category" [Bhagwati, 1986]. One can envisage, at least theoretically, that in an economic and sociopolitical setting where movements of persons from one country to another for temporary or permanent residence are greatly facilitated, as is already the case within the European economic community, the process of internationalization of services will increasingly extend to unskilled labor and, as a consequence, international trade in services will increasingly resemble international trade in goods, in the sense that relative factor endowments will constitute a major determinant of trade, though still with the essential difference that movements of factors will accompany movements of products rather than substituting for them.

The final stage in the internationalization process toward which current trends seem to lead is the "global network economy" described by Albert Bressand and Catherine Distler [1985]. Bressand and Distler describe a world where economic success depends increasingly on the synergy between the initiative of the entrepreneur and the mobilization of a set of networks.[9] Thus, they explain the success of Silicon Valley as the result of the joint action of innovative entrepreneurs and of financial, information, and human (scientific) networks on which the entrepreneurs can draw to assist them in starting their enterprises and carrying out their production plans. Interrelationships between economic agents carrying out identical or similar activities enhance each agent's effectiveness and provide stability to his/her operations. At the same time, the successive linking up of specialized networks of activity with one another creates the channels of communication through which each activity interacts with the rest of the economy, thus maximizing the efficiency of each network.

This aspect of networking described by Bressand and Distler, which relates to the organization of different *intra*functional relationships in concentric circles of *inter*functional relationships, is complementary to the networking phenomenon described by Leveson. The combination of the two gives rise to a new pattern of economic adjustment, when firms simultaneously develop their activities in different directions, mixing goods and services production, and apportioning their productive resources among activities which are not necessarily sequential as in traditional chain production systems or vertical integration structures (i.e., not necessarily linearly related), relying on other firms active in the same sector of activity or in other sectors of the economy to provide the missing links in their own production systems.

This evolving configuration of economic activity is naturally associated with the emergence of complex sets of products which Bressand has described as "complex packages of either goods, services, or a combination of both or *compacks*."[10] An important consequence of this modern form of production is, as Bressand put it, that "...an increasing proportion of comparative advantages is man-made." He added that "...thinking about trade in services should therefore be seen as an invitation to identify the proper framework that can account for the *creation* of comparative advantages and not simply their expression through trade. In this respect, we want to stress the link between *innovation* and the creation of comparative advantages. Once we start looking at trade (within as well as among advanced countries) as a matter of selling not 'goods' or 'services' but *compacks*, then we have to abandon the static framework of traditional trade theory. Rather than running regressions among a ready-made list of traded goods and services, we want to focus on the way in which corporations have combined goods and services together to create compacks that they can sell at home or abroad."

Another key factor in the development of the global market for services, and of increasingly complex networks of interconnected and overlapping productive activities, is the abolition of time. This is the consequence of the development of computer and telecommunication technology. Computer specialists calculate the period necessary to execute a given set of operations in *real time*, that is to say, the time it effectively takes, given the state of technology, to effectuate these operations. Real time has very little to do with time as human beings know it. The unit of time applicable to a computer is much smaller than the smallest unit of time perceptible by man. Moreover, the total time spent by a computer for carrying out a given set of operations does not contain any *wasted* time. There may be some "wasted" time in preparing and programming the computer for specific tasks, such as the time taken by a program designer to pick up a pencil and apply it to paper, but once the computer is functioning, it does not stop to do irrelevant things.

Now, each new generation of computer reduces the real time spent in data processing, and each advance in telecommunication technology increases the capacity and versatility of data transmission. These two factors combined considerably extend the reach of each economic agent, be it producer or consumer, to different sources of supply and different markets. In contrast to traditional forms of distant trade, point-to-point communication through modern networks (including satellite transmitters) is almost instantaneous, no matter what the physical distance is between two points. Due to the speed of transmission and to the increasing mobility of transmission equipment itself,[11] messages can reach their destination through alternative routes. In such a situation, ownership or control of a given telecommunication channel no longer represents a source of economic advantage. Modern computer and telecommunication technologies transform the character of distant trade in services, by reducing the need for the simultaneous presence of producer and consumer in certain activities. At the same time, however, by making it easy for distant travellers to maintain contact with their home office, they encourage producers and consumers alike to be more mobile. This further stimulates the process of globalization of service markets.

The growth of service activities worldwide also tends to abolish economic barriers between developed and developing countries, due to the central role played by services in the development process [UNCTAD, 1985b] and the consequent need for the latter countries to acquire the knowledge and experience generated in the former. One of the means through which such barriers are abolished is the development of the activities of transnational corporations in the field of services. There is an extensive literature on the activities of transnational corporations in both goods and services sectors, much of which is based on the data collected and the analysis conducted by the United Nations Center on Transnational Corporations (UNCTC).[12] Transnational corporations are a pet subject of inquiry and a preferred target of criticism for observers of the world economic scene who choose to present all contemporary economic issues in a North-South context. A typical example of this approach is that of Clairmonte and Cavanaugh [1984] who describe the activities of transnational corporations in the field of services as a move toward the "final frontier" of capitalism. These authors argue that "...the world economy is undergoing a momentus structural change. Services, moving to the centre of the stage, already account for two-thirds of world GDP. Internationalization is the crux of this transformation....A tiny number of large TNCs that entered the services sector are the driving force behind this internationalization, contributing to an accelerated liquidation of medium and small-scale firms that traditionally dominate the field....For several reasons the services sector was the last of the main sectors to fall under the hegemony of transnational conglomerates....At present, TNCs are impelling the service sector forward at a faster pace than any other sector" [p. 269–270]. Another noted observer, Deepak Nayyar, states: "There is a significant divergence between the corporate interests of transnational firms on the one hand, and the national interests of developing countries on the other. While a liberalized régime of trade in services would serve the economic interests of transnational corporations, the same cannot be said from the economic viewpoint of the developing countries" [Nayyar, 1986].

Such emotional statements about the role and influence of transnational corporations in the service sector reflect a preoccupation with the failure of many developing countries to adapt to the modern trend toward the globalization of markets. The increasing importance of theoretical and applied knowledge in production, distribution, and consumption processes, which constitute the essence of services activities, is only gradually being realized by governments whose primary concern up to now has been to move from the first to the second Fischer-Clark stage of economic development, namely industrialization. Corporate entities and countries possessing the required knowledge tend, however, to restrict access to it, respectively, to preserve their acquired rights to intellectual property and to safeguard the competitive position of their nationals. To overcome this difficulty, many developing countries attempt to impose free transfers of technology through their foreign investment regulations, or to encourage such transfers by failing to provide adequate protection of foreign intellectual property.

The process of internationalization of services taking place through the production and commercial networks controlled by large multinational enterprises is governed by two types of factors which are related to different characteristics of service activities. For services whose functions can be broken down into simple standardizable components, foreign market penetration is stimulated by the possibility to reap economies of scale, just as for manufactured goods. Further, when the functions in question can be broken down into sets of operations, each relying on a different mix of production factors, the expansion of productive activities on a global scale is stimulated by relative factor endowments, again just as for manufactured goods. The best example of this, to which reference has already been made, is the shifting of key-punching operations to low-labor-cost countries by major multinational enterprises engaged in computer processing of data either on a commercial basis or for their own account. For services which cannot be standardized, the stimulus to global expansion of business is the possibility it offers to spread risks among different markets and among different types of demand in each market. This need arises because there is no inherent continuity in the supply of nonstandardized services. The resulting uncertainty of returns from investment and productive effort places a high implicit cost on each individual service transaction. One way to reduce this cost is to build up confidence in the ability of the firm to meet the specific needs of various users, and such confidence or "goodwill" can best be secured by demonstrating this ability in a wide variety of situations, which in itself also stimulates globalization of activities.

Services and Developing Countries

Besides networking and transnational corporations, the changing structure of international trade relations is also a cause of internationalization of service activities. Presently, nonfactor services represent from one-fifth to one-third of total current foreign receipts and payments of major trading countries. In these circumstances, although the theoretical explanation of the gains from trade in services may be different than it is for goods, access to markets for services has become an integral part of the definition of "openness" of national economies. Concurrently, services have been introduced in the debate on trade protection versus trade liberalization not only among economists but also as a central issue in international economic diplomacy. Given the opposite views expressed on the issue by governments of developed countries on the one hand and governments of a number of developing countries (LDC's) on the other, the international debate has tended to revolve around the question of the role of services in the development process.

As pointed out by Henry Kierzkowski [1984], the analysis of the role of services in the development process is a "natural starting point" to the analysis of the economic role of services generally. "The tertiary sector plays a crucial role in the process of economic development. Secular trends in production, employment and productivity have been discussed and related to a number of theories. In the developed countries, the services sector has become the most important source of employment in national income, and this is also the case in many developing countries. But the role of the services industry is even more than that. Many services are a prerequisite for development rather than just its final product. Their adequate provision then becomes a crucial element in launching the economy on a dynamic growth path" [p. 39]. This problem is one of historical interest for industrialized countries and of contemporary interest for less-advanced countries. In the former case, public intervention or market mechanisms can be relied on as alternative sources for the adequate provision of services in national economies. In the latter case, market mechanisms for the provision of such services may be inexistent or inadequate, and this as well as the public good character of some services have been used as an argument for public intervention in the service sector in developing countries. Public intervention can take the form either of the direct provision of services by government administrations or enterprises, or of the protection of the domestic market against foreign competition in order to encourage the establishment and growth of infant service industries.

The policy options for developing countries in this area have been amply discussed by the United Nations Conference on Trade and Development (UNCTAD) and by many authors interested in the relationship of services to the growth prospects of developing countries.[13] The argumentation is developed around the theme of liberalization of international transactions in services which has commanded increasing attention in the international economic community since the GATT Ministerial Meeting of 1982. While this particular aspect of the question will be dealt with in the following chapters, it can be pointed out here that there is a greater or lesser degree of government intervention in the services sector in all national economies, and few economies escape the need to import essential services from abroad. However, policies that tend to exacerbate public intervention on the grounds that leaving the development of services to market mechanisms would merely result in turning the national economies concerned into "permanent importers" of foreign services and in deepening their dependence on transnational corporations active in this field, reflect an extreme view of the tradeoff that every government faces between allocating resources to the development of domestic productive capacity in as wide a range of activities as possible, and concentrating resources in activities where the domestic economy is best naturally endowed or best equipped to acquire and maintain a competitive position in world markets. Although services are seen as crucial elements in the formation and exploitation of economic interlinkages, the policy options with regard to production and trade in goods are essentially similar, and they have been debated for decades in similar terms.[14]

Whatever the origin of services, i.e., whether domestically produced or imported, one study has shown that for market economies to function at any level of development, there is a minimum percentage of total value added which must be available in each economy: for a sample of 30 countries ranging from the lowest to the highest income per capita in 1980, this minimum percentage has been calculated at 23%–27% of GNP [Nusbaumer, 1986]. As development takes place, i.e., as markets expand in scope and complexity, the distribution of services among different activities changes, some disappearing completely, some being internalized in goods-producing enterprises or in households, some becoming externalized, and the total proportion of services in the gross national product increases, partly as a result of a *net* externalization process. If this statistical analysis is any guide, it indicates that the development of economic interlinkages and hence the growth potential of national economies can be thwarted in countries that limit their reliance on imported services, and on the participation of foreign enterprises in domestic services production, beyond the reason where the domestic economy can supply adequate substitutes with its own means. The reason is not that domestic substitutes for imported services may be somewhat less efficient, i.e., entail a relatively high domestic resource cost at least in the initial stages of infant industry creation, but that some economies simply do not possess the knowledge and technology necessary to produce the required services at any cost, and may seriously impair their development prospect if they nevertheless endeavor to do so as a matter of policy.[15]

Notes

1. See, among others Sauvant and Zimny [1985]: "Thus the rise of FDI in services must be seen in the broader context of the internationalization of economic transactions. However, these developments would not have been possible on such a scale without rapid advances in international communications, including improved means of transportation and the spread of telephones, telex and, more recently, data communications."

2. Again, it is important to distinguish between standardizable and nonstandardizable service functions. For the former, since technology is not embedded (for capital) or embodied (for labor) in the factors of production, or only to a limited extent, a dissociation similar to that in the field of goods production is possible and indeed current, as exemplified by the spread of off-shore key-punching operations of multinational data-processing enterprises.

3. In the case of professional services, the immigration policies of recipient countries directly affect the possibility to do business there.

4. A case in point is the *Société Internationale de Télécommunication Aéronautique* (*SITA*), a private telecommunication network covering 295 airlines in 169 countries. Its purpose is to exchange traffic and passenger information in real time among its members. In 1985, 10 billion messages were carried over the network, which is composed of 28,700 terminals connected to 16,000 airline offices in 1,044 cities [Lambert, 1986]. The messages carried are basically of two types: first, those relating to flight reservations and in-flight communication between aircraft and their airline; second, more conventional messages of an administrative or commercial character, such as flight movements, ticket sales, lost luggage, etc. In recent years, *SITA* has entered the field of data processing covering reservation systems, tarification, boarding management, and tracing of lost luggage. The example of *SITA* shows how the development of telecommunication and data-processing techniques has enhanced the interdependence among commercial firms for access to and treatment of basic information, although these firms continue to behave competitively in the world market for air transport. In effect, the development of interdependent systems offers in itself a means of taking advantage of competitive opportunities which is neutral between individual competitors and therefore a form of public good of private sector origin. For other examples, see Leveson [1986] and Bressand and Distler [1985].

5. Most of the information under this heading is drawn from Leveson [1986].

6. For a detailed and thorough analysis of this aspect of the internationalization process, see de Laubier [1986].

7. A brief account of these developments and how they relate to the negotiating issues in the field of services (which will be dealt with in the next chapters) is found in Gavin [1985].

8. The examples of airlines and financial institutions are only two among many in the very broad-ranging process of internationalization of services. For a cross-sectoral analysis covering U.S. service industries, see Lee and Naya [1985], and Sauvant and Zimny [1985].

9. It is impossible in a few lines to do justice to the very thorough and searching analysis of the evolution of economic interrelationships from a linear to a network pattern carried out by these two authors. The following comments, therefore, only draw on some of their most

striking conclusions concerning what is admittedly a long-run, though fast-moving, process of transformation of modern societies and modern international economic relations.

10. The generation of compacks is described in Bressand [1985].

11. An important remaining physical constraint is the availability of an appropriate infrastructure for sending messages. Transmission and reception of messages also require physical equipment such as telephone lines and receivers. However, receiving equipment is increasingly mobile in some uses (e.g., portable telephone receivers), while radio and satellite communications reduce the need for *fixed* equipment.

12. See the bibliography for references to the many studies produced by the UNCTC.

13. See in particular UNCTAD [1985b], especially paragraphs 175–181; and UNCTAD [1986], especially paragraphs 89–90. Similar arguments are developed in Lanvin and Prieto [1986] as well as in Nayyar [1986].

14. As expressed by the UNCTAD secretariat, "Such a situation places developing countries in a dilemma. On the one hand, they require inputs of certain services for their development, if they wish to retain their competitive position in the production of manufactures and even agricultural products. On the other hand, acquisition of efficient, modern services from abroad can exacerbate their already dependent position" [UNCTAD, 1985b, paragraph 175].

15. The forced development of "self-reliant" service industries in many developing countries has been criticized on precisely these grounds. For a thorough discussion of the option between self-reliance and participation in the development of international trade in services, see the discussions in GATT [1986b].

7 TECHNOLOGY AND TRADE, TWO SIDES OF THE SAME COIN

Two recent developments of scientific research and corporate strategy are revolutionizing trade relations worldwide. The first is the simulation and standardization of thought processes currently being researched in Japan and the United States. The second is the networking phenomenon analyzed by Leveson and Bressand and discussed in the previous chapter. Although both developments are fairly recent and might therefore be considered to exert little impact on trade patterns, it would be an oversimplification to say that analyzing their consequences at this time is a purely futuristic exercise.

The pace of technological innovation and scientific discovery has accelerated markedly since the nineteenth century as the accumulation and diffusion of knowledge and work experience provided an ever wider base on which to build new experiments. In Japan, ICOT research on the so-called fifth generation computer takes place in the context of a 10-year program due to end in 1991. Already in 1985, ICOT scientists have begun to develop a machine capable of replacing man in the simplest and most straightforward decision-making situations. The ultimate purpose of the research is to free man's intellect from the preoccupation of solving simple problems, where the risk of error and the consequence of error are minimal, in order that it may concentrate on more complex tasks, requiring a degree of symbolization and synthesis which is likely to remain inaccessible to the machine for a long time.

The standardization of thought processes goes one step beyond the creation of what computer specialists call software packages, which are intelligent systems teaching computers how to perform certain jobs conceived by the human brain, to be sold and copyrighted when transcribed on physical supports such as magnetic tape, floppy disc, or even printed matter. In the ICOT model, the machine itself does the thinking. The standardization of thought processes is a sort of software of software. Contrary to simple software, it permits the solution of unpredicted problems in an almost unlimited set of possibles (within, for the moment, a limited range). As such, STP, as one might call the ICOT objective for short, is also the service of a service, where the service functions themselves, or—if one will—the organization and method services necessary to guide decision-making in situations where systems meet with unexpected difficulties in their functioning, are themselves transformed into a product which can be reproduced in unlimited quantities like software packages. The other term for the standardization of thought processes which has been used by the Japanese is industrialization of software, which clearly conveys the idea of a controlling force (the intelligent computer) producing on demand software packages that fit the particular needs of users in particular situations.

The major difference here with the standardization of goods is that the software product which can be reproduced at will can also be varied at will in accordance with certain basic systematic responses to complex probability scenarios. For such a system to function in practice, however, there is a need for continuous access to data both by users and by central computing headquarters. Initially at least, it may be expected that STP computers would be available only in certain locations, given the time lag necessary for miniaturization and development of consumer models. The centralization of worldwide operations of firms which will be made possible by the application of STP to their management, marketing, and financial functions is likely to provide an additional incentive for the expansion of multinational producing and trading activities in the goods and service sectors. STP would thus add yet another dimension to the tendency toward internationalization of corporate activities which already resulted from the development of telematics. It may at the same time be one further cause for concern for countries that fear the influence of transnational corporations on their technological choices, as well as on their prospects for developing a national scientific and technical base to meet the competitive needs of the future. There is no doubt that STP involves fundamental working assumptions which guide the decision-making process and which may be explicitly or implicitly introduced in the computer's intelligence. Would the computer know, for example, whether it is appropriate to tell a man to order a case of Coca-Cola in response to a problem of thirst? There are inevitable cultural problems in any manipulation of data, and these may be compounded by computer systems which not only provide technical solutions to problems but also guide the choices among different technical solutions.

The New Look of International Trade

In the words of Albert Bressand, "...studying trade in services is an invitation to think about the future of the trading system as a whole" [Bressand, 1986]. The technological and organization innovations described above and in the preceding chapter, i.e., STP, telematics, and networking, are giving rise to new forms of economic interdependence among nations, while the structure of international trade is changing through increased cross-border transactions and foreign direct investment in services. Interaction between goods and services in production, distribution, and consumption also modify the content of intercountry linkages, which no longer hinge on exchanges of individual items of trade but, more and more, on exchanges of complementary goods and service products and related functions. Furthermore, the development of cross-sectoral relationships in production and consumption which is characteristic of networking may lead to an overall increase of commercial risks due to possible domino effects of defaults in one part of the system, and to the fact that present-day regulatory systems are not geared to controlling cross-sectoral effects of the activities they regulate. All these factors argue for greater consistency between regulatory systems and in particular for enlarging the present world trading system which only applies to trade in goods, to cover both services as traded products and other aspects of economic interdependence such as foreign direct investment, protection of intellectual property,[1] transfer of technology, and international control of restrictive business practices.

Technology, therefore, increases the tradeability of services. In his study of data services, Bruno Lanvin [1986, p. 120] notes that "...by contributing to making technical and legal obstacles to trade in services more and more permeable, data services have undoubtedly been instrumental in increasing the importance of services as a whole in international transactions." It has thus become increasingly difficult to control the international movement of services in the form of data flows. Yet, direct barriers to the transfer abroad of raw data of national origin for storage or processing are being maintained by a number of countries, for a variety of reasons. Such barriers are equivalent to quantitative restrictions for goods and, especially, for essential raw materials including energy-generating materials, used in the production of goods. Consequently, the efficiency/ autonomy tradeoff, discussed earlier in relation to services generally, applies even more forcefully for data services. Developing countries, in particular, seek to acquire new technologies in order to reduce their reliance on knowledge developed elsewhere and thus increase their economic independence. This may be done by negotiating—and sometimes forcing—transfers of technology from more advanced countries, or by the autonomous (infant-industry) development of indigenous resources. In the field of information and data processing, control over domestic or foreign resources is more difficult to maintain in view of the ease with which data can be exported or imported through telematics. The best means available is to force all data flows out or into the country through designated points ("gateways"), where they are sifted in accordance with criteria related to their "stragegic" importance from a development perspective. Thus, technology, which increases the tradeability of services, also provides the means to increase barriers to such trade.

Efforts to control cross-border data flows are also associated with the objective of maintaining absolute decisional autonomy and sovereignty over all national policies affecting the exploitation and distribution of natural resources (including human resources), the management of socio-political relations and goals, and the preservation and development of cultural norms governing societal and economic choices. The rationale of this objective can only be questioned on subjective grounds, but it should be clear that the policies most appropriate to fulfill them are not necessarily autarchic or protectionist.

Maintaining control over objectives and the means to reach them is not synonymous with doing everything with available domestic resources since such resources may be either insufficient or inadequate. Leaving aside considerations relating to the preservation of political and social order or culture, in a market economy setting (which is relevant to all countries to the extent that they are participating in world economy through exports and imports of services) the economic efficiency of any country or region is predicated on the rational exploitation of the most abundant locally available resources. This often requires complementary inputs which may or may not be locally available, or which can only be created at such high costs as to jeopardize the country or region's comparative advantage. Thus, policies geared to the domestic creation of human-capital resources may have a stunting effect on economic growth. As opposed to trade in goods, trade in services introduces a new dimension to international competition, by involving movements of factors that can dramatically increase the production possibilities of countries which are willing to allow the importation of complementary resources. Conversely, the advantages of diversification and efficiency are foregone by countries which are not. However, it should be kept in mind that "...the transfer and trade in advanced technology is not a natural process. There is only a real transfer if there are capable and knowledgeable people on both sides of the process and if the recipient can use this know-how to increase his own acquired experience" [Ripper, 1984].

The efficiency/autonomy tradeoff implies that any international negotiations designed to expend the international exchange of services must somehow strike a balance between the development objectives of countries that attach importance to attaining a relatively high degree of self-reliance in production and trade in services, and the liberalization objectives of countries seeking to reach maximum trading opportunities from already established production and trading capacities in this field. The crux of the issue is whether there is scope and reason for subjecting national development policies to international competitive pressures. In other words, the question is one of the prominence or not of liberal trade policies over infant-industry policies of countries wishing to protect and build up their long-term development and competitive potential in services.

Trade Regulation in a New Environment

Definitions set parameters for action. The objectives of any understanding on the regulation of international services trade must therefore be defined so as to facilitate the liberalization of such trade while preserving the potential for development of services sectors in countries facing fundamental handicaps in the availability of accumulated knowledge and work experience. In this sense, there is a full analogy with trade in goods. A difficulty, however, is that exchange of services involves transactions which do not fall within the traditional definition of international trade; in common usage and in all economic literature to date, this term is understood to cover the movement of goods across national borders. Extended to services, it may be considered to cover only cross-border sales. Technically speaking, a great many services can be traded across borders but, as we have seen, even if this is so, a presence in foreign markets may still be necessary for a variety of reasons. First-hand knowledge of the working of foreign markets is an essential operational tool for certain services. Buildingup and maintaining consumer confidence may not be possible without personal contacts that narrow the psychological distance between the buyer and the seller. Such considerations lead to the conclusion that a definition of international transactions in services which excludes the direct sale abroad of services through a presence in foreign markets may unduly restrict the scope of any consideration of issues in this sector.

The International Monetary Fund defines an international transaction as a payment involving a change of ownership between a resident and a nonresident of a given country, whether or not the product (good or service) sold has actually moved from one country to another.[2] This payment criterion can usefully be applied to reach a new definition of trade specific to services which includes movements of factors accompanying the delivery of a service or constituting such delivery when the service is fully embodied in the factor. There are varying degrees to which factor movements are necessary. For example, whole teams of construction workers may be sent abroad to build dams, bridges, airports, etc., commissioned to nonresident contractors.[3] Engineers may need to go abroad to inspect construction sites and supervise work in progress. They may do so with a briefcase full of blueprints which could have been sent by mail or transmitted by satellite, so that their presence is only required for some aspects of the service function. Artists may go abroad to give live performances, although their presence is technically not necessary for them to be seen and heard, thanks to television.

Given the variety of situations, it is clear that the new definition of trade based on the IMF payment criterion would be far less simple and precise than that which applies to international transactions in goods. This can have an incidence on the scope and coverage of any international agreements on trade services. The practical application of such agreements would have to be defined for each type of service to which they apply, from the point of view of the degree of temporary presence in foreign markets required for the purpose of conducting trade operations in the services concerned. Despite such practical complications, however, the new definition of trade should not pose any real conceptual problems, insofar as the concepts of resident and nonresident do not do so themselves.

In addition to a temporary presence, a permanent presence in foreign markets is often needed to sell services. Such presence takes different forms, corresponding to different relationships between service producers and consumers: agent, representative office, branch, subsidiary, affiliate, or joint venture. The particular form of permanent presence adopted, of course, also depends on the possibilities offered by the laws and regulations of the host countries. Sales in the local market by established firms owned or controlled by foreign interests are transactions between residents of the same country. According to IMF definitions, they are not international transactions nor do they fit into the new definition of trade in services given above. Therefore, in order to include such transactions in the definition of trade, one would need to adopt an *IMF-plus* definition of trade. In the case of goods, transactions between residents are definitely considered as falling completely outside the concept of international trade. It is true that domestic sale/purchase transactions normally fall within the sphere of internal policy, and any government regulations, in this area are primarily related to national development objectives and macroeconomic demand management. Yet, services add a new dimension to these internal policies precisely because the parameters of international exchange are quite different for these activities. Where interlinkages between producers and consumers of different countries are an integral part of the texture of market interrelationships, that is, where the interface between different markets is no longer the sole external border, the result of increased trade in services is a form of *integration* between different national economies that goes much further than the economic *interdependence* resulting from the expansion of mutual trade in goods.

At the present time, most governments still view their policies in the field of foreign investment and establishment as totally distinct from their policies relating to international trade and payments. There is, therefore, a considerable political risk in proposing an IMF-plus definition of trade in services which englobes all forms of presence on a given market of foreign suppliers of services. Political sensitivities regarding foreign investment and establishment can be exacerbated by an approach to international regulation of service transactions which would appear to trample on the sacrosanct nationalist or cultural identity dogmas which subtend protectionist policies in the service sector of many countries.[4]

Nonetheless, the pressures of the global market—in other words, the forces at work in the process of internationalization of services—lead to the growing recognition of the advantages of services trade and other forms of exchange in this sector. On such force is the growing substitutability between trade and foreign direct investment in services. According to Sauvant [1986]. "...if the constraints inherent in the nature of services could be overcome, the potential for a substantial increase in trade in services would be high." Surmounting such constraints depends on the increasing use of transborder data flows which permit service transactions to take place at the same time but in different places. "As a result, the tradeability of certain service products increases considerably, affecting especially such key business services as banking, insurance, accounting, design and engineering, legal services, management consulting and, of course, data services themselves....One consequence of this broadening of options as regards the manner in which services can be made available in foreign markets may be that the need for foreign direct investment in certain service industries decreases. In the long run, therefore, the increased tradeability of certain services may have an impact on the level of foreign direct investment in services" [Sauvant, p. 8].

Given increased substitutability, this argument can be turned around: the circumstances in which firms will choose cross-border trade rather than investment will be more than ever governed by the regulatory environment Where the latter is hostile to foreign investment, some economic choices will be suboptimal. However, as firms compete for a share of the global market by playing one regulatory environment against another, the pressures for liberalization of investment policies on laggard governments are certain to mount. Such pressures may indeed come from domestic firms asking for "deregulation," rather than, as usually expected, from multinational enterprises or foreign governments representing their interests. Hence, taking into account that a definition of international transactions in services which excludes sales of services by foreign residents may unduly restrict the scope of any international liberalization effort, it is all the more necessary to pay special attention to reaching an appropriate balance in those terms between national sovereignty concerns regarding domestic economic management and the requirements of the global market.

In summary, for purely analytical purposes, it is clear that a "payments" approach to the delivery of services in foreign markets is preferable to a "movements" approach which only involves cross-border transactions. Moreover, the IMF-plus definition implies a form of competition extending to the acquisition of resident status (through establishment or investment) and to the benefits derived from such status (national treatment), thereby laying the ground for an approach to the liberalization of international exchange of services which fits contemporary economic realities.[5]

This being said, the question remains of whether given the fact that all services could at one point or another become tradeable in the sense of being produced in one place and being consumed in another, cross-border trade should not become the sole basis on which any liberalization of services transactions are undertaken. The fact of the matter is that the different technical means of delivering services blur the notion of "access to markets" as this is generally understood in the case of goods. Because of the many alternatives which exist to cross-border trade in services, the desirability of this or any other undimensional approach to the liberalization of international service transactions is much reduced, except perhaps regarding particular activities for which one type of delivery system is clearly dominant.

Scope and Coverage of International Trade Regulations

Another point at issue is which services should be the object of international liberalization efforts. There are three aspects to this issue. First, there is the distinction between "embodied" and "disembodied" services, which relates to the problem of tradeability just discussed. Second, there is the distinction between "factor" and "nonfactor" services. Third, there is the distinction between different service activities, the content and institutional setting of which evolve rapidly as a result of innovation and deregulation. All of these distinctions have been touched upon in earlier parts of this book, but it is worth coming back to them in the context of the consideration of possible international disciplines governing transactions in services, in view of the way they may affect the content of such disciplines.[6]

Balance-of-payments statistics distinguish between goods and "invisibles." The latter include three main types of transactions: (1) payments for services sold on an individual item basis, e.g., the transport of merchandise from one port to another, the sale of an insurance policy, the fulfillment of a particular consulting assignment; (2) payments of interest on loan capital, of dividends on equity capital, and of royalties and licence fees on copyrights, patents, and the like; (3) transfers to income earned abroad by migrant workers, and miscellanceous other transfers, official and private (grants, donations, gifts, etc.). Category 1 is usually referred to as payments for nonfactor services to distinguish them from payments for primary factors of production, that is capital (category 2) and labor (income transfers in category 3). Nonfactor services are treated as products, by analogy with goods, whereas factor services represent returns from work performed and rental of property, irrespective of whether the factors have been used for the production of services or goods. Thus, payment categories 2 and 3 are not linked to specific sales of individual service items.

It is easy enough, at least in conventional terms, to draw the line between a factor service and a good it produces, but it is more difficult to distinguish between a factor service and a service product because both are intangible. One way to do so is to establish a hierarchy of factor services, as discussed earlier (chapter 3) to the effect, say, that unskilled workers operating abroad are considered as performing factor services, while doctors, for example, deliver nonfactor services. Perhaps a more satisfactory way, less prone to subjective judgments, would be to count as nonfactor services any work performed that is directly linked to the delivery of a service product, such as the work of doctors but also of construction workers (purportedly unskilled or semiskilled jobs). Statistically, it would be difficult if not impossible to distinguish between these types of factor services, but this is not the issue. The issue is whether, and to what extent, failing a conventional definition of a service product (in contrast to the conventional definition of a good as a physical object) primary factor payments, and in particular foreign workers' remittances, should be considered as services for purposes of international trade discussions or negotiations.[7] However, this issue remains theoretically and statistically debatable.

The other problem, relating to the breakdown and classification of activities between different sectors, arises from the rapid pace of change in the production and delivery of different service functions. A case in point is banking.[8] In this field, the acceleration of financial innovation during the 1970s and 1980s has been associated with a number of key factors such as the sharp rise in inflation and increased volatility of interest rates and exchange rates, a sharp shift in the 80s of the geographic pattern of net flows of international savings and investments as reflected in the distribution of current account imbalances, a rapidly changing regulatory environment affecting national financial markets, new communications and computer technology applied to financial markets and financial transactions, growing competition in international financial markets, and the growth in the supply of new financial instruments in response to an explosion of demand, reflecting the desire of economic agents for new vehicles to perform the functions of transferring risk, enhancing liquidity, and generating debt and equity [BIS, 1986, pp. 7–8].

This example shows that the concept of banking services of yesterday no longer fits today's realities. Compounding the difficulty is the phenomenon of networking which rises to combinations of service functions being performed by individual firms which thereby fall under different jurisdictions in their domestic markets and abroad, e.g., credit card companies offering travel and other insurance and airline reservation services, tourism agencies offering food catering, vocational training, and public relation services [see Bressand, 1985]. In the light of such developments it becomes increasingly difficult to segregate certain service branches or sectors for discussion or negotiation, without involving technologically related functions traditionally associated with different regulatory environments involving the competence of different ministries in any given country.

Another question related to the concept of embodiment of services, but more specific to educational or entertainment services, is the extent to which these affect the value of traded goods in which they are contained— for example, films, blueprints, written or recorded teaching materials, diskettes or magnetic tapes containing computer software, etc. In many cases, the telecommunication infrastructure necessary to make possible the transport of the services over transmission lines as "disembodied" products is inadequate or nonexistent, and therefore the question of whether one is dealing with trade in goods or trade in services and which rules to apply becomes considerably blurred.[9] Another difficulty with the concept of tradeability of services is that many services are not identifiable as separate products. In other words, their effects on economic activity are not separable from the participation of the services user or consumer in the full deployment of these effects. This is the case for education services but also for a number of services requiring a degree of self-service by the user in the realization of its aims. An example is a consulting service whose efficiency depends on the faculty of assimilation of advice and of transformation of this advice into concrete economic results by users.[10] Among services that play such a societal as well as an economic role, one finds those which have the character of public goods. Since it is practically impossible to define units of such services or to think of them as independent products, their economic effects are not self-contained.[11]

Yet in different societies, and at different periods of a society's history, the distribution of services between the public and private domains varies, and international transactions in services vary accordingly. For example, in Europe, tax collection has been in private hands at different times ever since the Roman Empire, and for centuries Swiss soldiers have exported their defense services to warring states and principalities. Today, social security, telecommunications (including radio and television broadcasting), banking, air transport, and other services, falling or not falling into the category of public goods, are wholly or partly state-owned in some countries, wholly private in others. Some countries have entrusted the running of their customs administration to foreign private consulting firms.

The existence of different distributions of competence between the public and private sectors poses problems for the definition of appropriate competition rules. The first problem is a familiar one. It relates to the treatment of state-trading enterprises in a free-market setting when such enterprises produce services which are *not* public goods, such as banking services. The second problem relates to state monopolies which produce both public goods and marketable services. The classic example is public telecommunications. In countries where telecommunications is a state monopoly, the state provides the infrastructure and controls access to it by both suppliers and users. In such cases, the state may use or abuse its monopoly power, in order to make the marketable part of its operations pay for (or cover the losses of) the nonmarketable or public goods part. It can also dump services in foreign markets to capture these markets for future exploitation or simply to maintain prestige (state-owned airline and shipping lines have often been accused of such behavior.) Such behavior, of course, affects the conditions of competition of suppliers of marketable services in the international market. It should be kept in mind, however, that the separation between marketable and public goods elements in the output of state-controlled enterprises is not simply an economic problem. The allocation of certain services to the public domain often connotes ideological preferences regarding the social responsibility of the state, and this, of course, varies from country to country. These considerations are at the root of some of the difficulties which may be expected in arriving at an international consensus on what may be considered as "reasonable motivations" for maintaining strict control over the delivery of certain services and insulating them from international competition (see chapter 8).

Finally, in addition to services regulated by the state, there are also services, notably in the professions, for which demand is relatively saturated in given economic conditions or at least growing slowly, and which at the same time undergo relatively slow technical progress. Examples are legal, accounting, and medical services. Such service activities are often organized into cartels with the blessing of public authorities. One justification for allowing this type of behavior is that these services are considered as containing a large public good element, in the sense that their beneficial effects (by way of preserving law and order or the health of the population at large) extend far beyond the immediate benefits which may be obtained from the private consumption of their output (the resolution of a law case or the curing of a sickness). As long as scientific or technological progress is slow, entry into the professions can continue to be restricted; whatever progress is made is then expected to be integrated into the production methods of the service providers concerned. On the other hand, innovation often disrupts established working habits and leaves room for newcomers operating somewhat on the fringe of established rules. In such circumstances, the development of more competitive conditions both at the national and at the international level becomes feasible.

Notes

1. Work on international protection of intellectual property has been going on for a long time in what is now the World Intellectual Property Organization (WIPO). However, this work is based on the Paris Convention dating back to 1883, therefore totally out of step with recent technological and economic developments, i.e., with modern information technology and the growth of international transactions in services. The issue of counterfeiting has been brought to the attention of trading nations in the framework of GATT by a few major industrial countries, as one instance of the dangers for orderly trading relations of the pilfering of innovation made possible by new techniques, but there are others that may have more serious consequences for the future of foreign direct investment. The matter is currently under consideration in the GATT Uruguay Round of multilateral trade negotiations, launched in Punta del Este in September 1986.

2. IMF [1977]; see especially paragraphs 31, 32, 200, and 319.

3. As argued earlier in this book, the part of construction work which consists in the manufacture of fixed assets is not, properly speaking, a service. Nevertheless, the example of construction engineering projects carried out by foreign building contractors is sufficiently current to merit attention in formulating a new definition of trade which fits the reality of service exchange in the global market. Some contractors, notably major Korean firms, owe their successful export performance to the fact that they deliver complete service "bundles," including engineers, surveyors, etc., and all grades of skilled and semiskilled labor needed to complete construction projects. In such instances it could be argued that only local low-skilled labor used for the actual erection work is engaged in manufacturing operations.

4. Note, however, that for the first time in history, the international regulation of some aspects of investment policies has been placed on the agenda of the new round of multilateral negotiations decided by the Ministerial meeting of the Contracting Parties of GATT in Punta del Este, Uruguay, in September 1986. The Uruguay Round is surely not expected to result in major adjustments in national investment policies, but it nevertheless represents an important first step in strengthening international economic cooperation in this area.

5. At the present time, there are still major differences among services with regard to the degree to which they can be traded across borders without loss of efficiency. This applies not only to the technical possibility of supplying the services but also the possibility of adapting the contents of each service product to the specific needs of individual users and consumers. Sometimes it may be possible to deliver services abroad by gaining access to local distribution systems: for example, to telecommunication networks. In other cases, service providers may need to move to consuming markets (e.g., tourist guides, consulting engineers, visiting scholars, etc.); some form of legal extraterritoriality may be involved, for instance for consulates, military bases, etc. In still other cases, the possibility to contract for the sale of services with local brokers or agents, even if 100% locally controlled, is sufficient to ensure effective access to consuming markets (travel agents, security brokers, local advertisers, etc.); or, a degree of foreign management control may be a sine qua non condition for efficient operation (franchising, international hotel chains, etc.).

6. The question is whether international disciplines should be guided by the traditional classifications of economic activities found in contemporary national accounting systems or

should, on the contrary, be sufficiently flexible to take into account the likely evolution of technology and market innovation in a changing world (see *infra*).

7. The International Monetary Fund differentiates between "labour income" and "unrequited transfers" on the basis of the length of stay of the worker in the foreign country, i.e., or more than one year [see IMF, 1977, paragraphs 59, 60, 200, and 207]. But this does not permit a distinction between work performed in service activities and work performed in goods-producing activities.

8. The information in the ensuing paragraphs is largely drawn from BIS [1986].

9. "Defining services trade involves two tasks—defining 'services' and defining 'trade'. Each task can be handled easily in the abstract, but it nevertheless may be quite difficult to qualify and classify particular transactions" [Ascher and Whichard, 1986].

10. A useful distinction between various services from the point of view of their identity as separate products, or of the varying degrees in which they produce indirect effects on the economic efficiency of users, through the participation of the latter and the influence they exert on the context in which the latter's producing activities are performed, is found in Gadrey [1986].

11. For example, a radio program can be heard by 1 or by 1 million listeners and a new army unit can add to the welfare of 50 million citizens or to none, without the cost of the radio program or of the army unit's being affected one way or another. Note that the marketability of a radio or television program can be enhanced by restricting the geographical range of the radio or television signal and/or by technically restricting access to it through, for instance, image coding. Similar possibilities exist for other public goods; for example, police protection can be higher in high tax-paying areas of a city than in others.

8 A NEW FRAMEWORK FOR TRADE IN SERVICES: RATIONALE, METHODOLOGY, AND SCOPE

All the considerations in the first six chapters of this book have butted against the fact that international services transactions have up to now developed in haphazard fashion. That is to say, dynamic corporations have extended their reach into foreign markets on the basis of bilateral cooperation with host government, or of home-to-host government agreements concerning the conditions under which they could operate, or by learning to live with or evade the government regulations they faced in host countries. As the global market for services expanded and diversified both geographically and through innovative networking between and within corporate entities, and as the processes of production of goods and services became more interlinked and mutually dependent upon information resources, the resulting complexity of interrelationships between production units and producing nations has increasingly called for the breaking of the straight-jacket of bilateral and sectoral arrangements. These arrangements can no longer provide the across-the-board security and predictability of commercial relations necessary for realizing the full economic potential of technological innovation in the field of intangible knowledge-based activities—services—and in new, cross-sectoral fields of activity which combine the production of goods and services. It is the growing

195

consciousness of these new developments in the economic sphere which is at the root of the proposal by the governments of the most advanced countries to establish a binding multilateral framework of disciplines designed to limit the protective impact of national policies, so as to facilitate the development of a global services market, and to insure its coherence with the global market for goods which has gradually (though still far from fully) been evolved under the aegis of the General Agreement on Tariffs and Trade (GATT).[1]

GATT and Services: A Bird's Eye View

Before looking at the issues that these proposals raise, let us examine briefly the content of GATT and its possible relevance to international transactions in services. A more detailed examination of GATT principles and rules will follow in the next section.

Basically, GATT is a set of principles and rules with which governments have agreed to abide in formulating and implementing their trade policy. It establishes a preference for certain trade policy measures (tariffs) and bans others (quantitative restrictions) except in certain circumstances (safeguards and exceptions). It provides for transparency and surveillance. Commitments entered into are binding and, when not honored, can give rise to compensation. Multilateralism (most-favored-nation treatment and nondiscrimination) is the rule, i.e., trade benefits granted to any country, whether a member or nonmember, are extended to all members, save in special situations, e.g., preferential trade arrangements and special and differential treatment of developing countries. Complaints can be lodged against alleged breaches of obligations, through a consultation and dispute settlement mechanism. GATT also embodies long-term economic growth and trade liberalization objectives, to be implemented through joint action by member governments, but the contractual relationship established between them does not carry any specific obligation to liberalize trade nor to negotiate to that end. Essentially, GATT does not dictate the protection policies of governments; it dictates *the way in which* protection is applied and insures no back-tracking from the degree of trade liberalization achieved through negotiation.

This short-hand description of how GATT operates should suffice to indicate the reasons why GATT is seen by many as the preferred framework within which the question of the establishment of new multilateral disciplines governing trade in services should be debated. Up to now, problems arising with regard to such trade have almost exclusively been dealt with bilaterally, and where some international disciplines exist (e.g., in OECD)[2] they have only been applied by a limited number of countries and have not been effectively enforceable. Strictly bilateral arrangements involve discrimination which undermines the stability and predictability of the global market.

The fact is, however, that the binding character of GATT commitments and the surveillance and dispute settlement mechanisms provided for in the General Agreement on Tariffs and Trade have caused concern in some countries, that the inclusion of new disciplines on services trade in the GATT might lead to unwarranted forms of supranational control over national policies in the service sector which have nothing to do with the protection of the domestic market against foreign competition or even with economics.

The desire to preserve national policy goals from any outside influence reflects a growing consciousness of the role of services, either as facilitators of market processes or in social relations. Preoccupations range from the fear of domination of production and distribution channels to preservation of cultural heritage, including political ideology and the existing pattern of industrial relations. These concerns translate, among others into negative attitudes toward foreign direct investment and establishment. Infant-industry considerations have also become more prominent in some countries as policy-makers began to realize the impact of services on national production and trade, including trade in goods. As tradeability of services increases, possible future export gains from this source draw increasing attention, leading to defensive attitudes toward foreign competition in countries where it is felt that their full export potential is not yet developed, and where such development may be impaired by foreign domination of the domestic market. Further, the trade priorities of many countries remain limited to the field of goods, both because these still account for the greater part of their exports and because, in many cases, these exports have faced restrictions abroad. Any trade negotiations should, in their view, focus on dismantling these restrictions. On the other hand, protectionism in services is not a major concern for these countries, most of which are currently net importers of services. Finally, the lack of interest of some countries in multilateral negotiations on services reflects a certain degree of unpreparedness on their part, as well as misgivings about the extent to which major trading partners might request from them trade concessions in the field of services in exchange for concessions in the field of goods and, worse still, make the "rollback" of protectionist measures taken by them in recent years conditional upon such concessions on services.

Most of these concerns have been taken into account in the decision by Ministers meeting in Punta del Este, Uruguay, on 15–20 September 1986, to launch negotiations on trade in services as part of the Uruguay Round of Multilateral Trade Negotiations (MTN). The objectives of services negotiations are defined as follows in that decision:

> Negotiations in this area shall aim to establish a multilateral framework of principles and rules for trade in services, including elaboration of possible disciplines for individual sectors, with a view to expansion of such trade under conditions of transparency and progressive liberalization and as a means of promoting economic growth of all trading partners and the development of developing countries. Such framework shall respect the policy objectives of national laws and regulations applying to services and shall take into account the work of relevant international organizations [GATT, 1986].

While part of the MIN, services negotiations are not taking place within the legal framework of the General Agreement on Tariffs and Trade, which leaves open the question of the eventual status of any agreements reached in this area, i.e., whether or not they will be included in that legal framework and so constitute an integral element of the enlarged world trading system. Countries that hesitate to assume binding obligations regarding the effects of their policies in the area of services on other countries' trade are therefore protected against the risk of legal complaints about such effects, at least for the duration of the negotiations.

Could GATT Apply?

Much discussion took place in the preparatory phase to the Uruguay Round about the legal competence of GATT to deal with trade in services. Apart from purely legalistic arguments concerning the coverage and scope of the General Agreement on Tariffs and Trade as an international treaty, the more fundamental issue this raises is whether, and to what extent, the principles and rules that govern international trade relations in the field of goods since the World War II are generally relevant and practically applicable to trade (or "trade" in the wider definition proposed earlier in this book) in services. While the resolution of this issue will depend on the outcome of the negotiations, which are only starting at the time of writing, the experience gained with the operation of GATT principles and rules provides a sound basis for some a priori judgments on the matter.

Basic Principles

Most of the principles embodied in the General Agreement existed before GATT was negotiated, and they may therefore be viewed as universal concepts extending far beyond the reach of this particular treaty. They are (1) most-favored-nation (MFN) treatment, whose characteristic is automaticity and unconditionality; (2) nondiscrimination, which is basically the same concept but is neither automatic nor unconditional;[3] (3) transparency and surveillance, which gives to the GATT Contracting Parties[4] the right to be informed of and to criticize individual contracting parties' trade policies; (4) national treatment, which guarantees that trade concessions made at the border are not nullified by internal measures such as tax discrimination or local content legislation; (5) multilateral reciprocity; (6) safeguards; (7) dispute settlement, or the possibility to obtain redress against actions that nullify or impair any party's rights under the General Agreement—this is a unique feature of GATT; (8) special and differential treatment for developing countries.

All those principles could conceivably be included in a framework for trade in services, as indeed they could be applicable in other fields. However, some of them may need to be carefully defined for the purposes at hand, e.g., there exist at present several definitions of national treatment in different legal instruments (General Agreement; GATT Agreement on Government Procurement; OECD; U.S.-Israel Trade Agreement).[5] Moreover, it is clear that the *practical* relevance of the principles depends on the coverage of any arrangement in respect of the inclusion of various types of service transactions (i.e., cross-border only, or also transactions involving a presence in foreign markets and/or primary factor movements) as well as of various types of measures (i.e., services-specific measures only, or also generic measures such as fiscal, monetary, and immigration measures).[6]

Access Rules

The second element contained in the GATT system (which includes the General Agreement itself and the nontariff measure agreements negotiated in the Tokyo Round; see GATT [1969 and 1980] consists of specific rules to insure security and predictability of market access for traded goods. These rules govern the type of protective measures that governments can or cannot take and the conditions under which they must be applied. Their aim is to prevent arbitrary distortions of competition and to encourage governments to base their trade policy on the use of market mechanisms rather than administrative fiat. Thus, customs tariffs are allowed but quantitative restrictions are not (except as safeguard measures); export subsidies on industrial goods are banned; countervailing and antidumping duties may only be imposed after proof of injury; etc. The applicability of these specific rules to services would depend on the practical possibility of extending trade policy measures designed for tangibles to intangibles. This is the main criterion by which the technical relevance of existing GATT rules may be judged. Other considerations are also relevant, of course, notably whether there are reasons for protecting services more than goods. Such reasons may exist, and some of them may not be very different from justified "general exceptions" already provided for in Article XX of the General Agreement. However, the types of reasons that have been invoked in international discussions, i.e., non-economic motivations for service regulations, mostly fall outside the existing GATT framework.[7]

Since movements of services across borders can only be apprehended by payment flows and it is difficult to identify comparable units of services, neither price-related border measures such as tariffs nor quantitative restrictions can readily be used to restrict imports, and the unit price effect of subsidies or dumping practices is at best elusive. Hence it is difficult to choose among traditional trade policy tools one which would have the least disruptive effect on services trade. It would seem that existing restrictions on such trade mainly take the form of limiting market penetration as a factor of time, turnover, or some other indicator. Many existing GATT rules would thus need to be reexamined, readjusted (for example, rules on transit could be adjusted to cover information flows), or substituted for by more technically relevant ones, in order to provide governments with clear markers as to what means of protecting their domestic service markets would be allowable under a multilateral framework.

The main problem is that no single measure might be appropriate for all types of services, as is the case with tariffs for goods. If that were so, it would not be possible to avoid separate agreements or codes covering sector-specific rules for the implementation of the general principles outlined above. But the situation need not be so desperate. After all, there is at least one *numéraire* that applies to all types of transactions: money. A properly defined levy on standard monetary aggregates might play a role similar to that of tariffs on goods. It would have the advantage of being equally applicable to services traded on a cross-border transactions basis and on an investment/establishment basis.

The nonstorability and nontransportability of many services also remain sources of difficulty in dealing with access to markets. Despite recent developments in information technology, some of the essential environment-creating functions of services cannot be performed without a presence, and therefore any restrictions on presence are restrictions on the ability of service firms and factors to compete internationally. Thus the granting of material treatment is a *concession*, rather than a condition of market access (as it is in the GATT system). For reasons already mentioned, foreign direct investment, establishment, and factor movements are sensitive subjects which many governments are not keen to see multilaterally regulated. Nevertheless, restrictions on foreign presence (permanent or temporary) may act also as de facto denials of national treatment in the traditional GATT sense of the term, i.e., as internal barriers nullifying the benefits of border concessions. For example, prohibition of the establishment of representative offices of foreign insurance companies may nullify and would certainly impair the benefits which could be expected from the liberalization of cross-border sales of insurance policies. Thus, the question is at least raised of how far investment and establishment could be included in the institution-building and liberalization process? At the present time it seems purely rhetorical to conceive of a full-fledged inclusion. The other question is, then, what is the minimum required to permit market forces to operate on equitable terms? These are questions which have so far remained totally outside the frame of reference of GATT and which deserve new and, no doubt, particularly close attention.

Exceptions and Motivations

Given the special role that services, or at least some of them, play in the socioeconomic and political structures of some countries, it may be necessary to take into account the motivations behind certain regulations, although care should be taken not to assume that each type of service has the same "status" in all economies (e.g., several governments have given over their customs and excise services to foreign private surveillance enterprises, and there have been cases of governments relying on hired foreign military personnel for their defense). In the GATT, nontrade motivations are dealt with as "exceptions," but in international discussions on services so far the suggestion has been made that certain regulations might be defined as being intrinsically "reasonable" or "legitimate." The real issue is who bears the burden of proof.

Under the "General Exceptions" provisions of the General Agreement,[8] contracting parties have the right to take, subject to certain conditions, any measures necessary to secure compliance with laws and regulations "...which are not inconsistent with the provisions of this Agreement," i.e., essentially dealing with matters not covered by the Agreement. Thus there is no need for the contracting parties concerned to request permission to take such measures, or to volunteer evidence that these meet the conditions laid down in Article XX of the Agreement, because the laws and regulations to which the measures relate are deemed to fall within the sovereign domain of the contracting parties concerned. However, the exercise of this right can be challenged by any other contracting party, on two grounds: either (1) the measures are claimed to be consistent with the GATT obligations of the contracting party maintaining them, i.e., they do not meet the conditions laid down in Article XX, thereby constituting a *prima facie* case of nullification or impairment of benefits accruing to that other contracting party under the General Agreement; or (2) the measures, though consistent with the provisions of Article XX, are nevertheless claimed to nullify or impair benefits accruing to the complaining party under the General Agreement, i.e., to unduly affect its trade interests. In the first case, "...it is up to the contracting party against whom the complaint has been brought to rebut the charge" [GATT, 1980, p. 216]. In the second case, the contracting party bringing the charge "...would be called upon to provide a detailed justification" [p. 216].

The right to take measures in the sovereign domain is thus circumscribed by three main conditions: (1) that the measures are "necessary" to implement national laws and regulations; (2) that they do not constitute a means of arbitrary or unjustifiable discrimination or a disguised restriction on international trade; (3) that they do not unduly affect the trade of other contracting parties. Broadly speaking, the sovereign domain includes all areas of national policy for which no specific obligations are laid down in the General Agreement. The conditions stipulated in Article XX are, in themselves, obligations, and the drafters of the Agreement have deemed them sufficient to avoid situations where measures consistent with Article XX would give rise to nullification or impairment of the benefits of other contracting parties. Hence, the second case in the preceding paragraph is not expected to arise frequently, if at all, and normally it would be up to countries maintaining measures in the sovereign domain to rebut charges that these are not in conformity with their obligations.

This feature of the GATT dispute settlement mechanism has the distinct advantage that it avoids the need to specify the contents of the sovereign domain, except in broad outline. (There are other provisions of Articles

XX which are more specific than the one referred to in the preceding paragraphs.) For the mechanism to operate efficiently, the conditions that circumscribe the sovereign rights of contracting parties in policy areas falling outside the scope of the Agreement must, of course, be very carefully defined. This would apply even more forcefully in the case of a multilateral agreement on trade in services, since there appear to be many more circumstances where national regulations in the service sector may indirectly affect other countries' trade interests. (The various types of regulations affecting the operation of foreign firms or foreign-controlled supply interests in domestic markets, whether or not these must be considered as trade restrictions, are illustrated in table 8–1.)

In order to provide a firm foundation for countries to continue to regulate services in sensitive areas such as cultural identity, health care, consumer protection, etc., it has been suggested, as an alternative to the GATT approach, that the circumstances where there are "legitimate" grounds for allowing countries to take measures necessary to secure compliance with their relevant laws and regulations, irrespective of their effects on other countries' trade interests, should be defined through negotiations.

The first difficulty of approaching the problem in this way is that generally agreed criteria for defining "reasonable regulations" which are applicable to different national regulatory systems may turn out to be so vague as to defeat the purpose of the approach, by providing legal cover for protectionism, that is, what one country sees as a restriction, another country could always present as a reasonable regulation: one man's meat is another man's poison. A further difficulty is that, once a given national regulation was identified as conforming to the agreed criteria, it would become practically "untouchable," even if with the passage of time it was found to generate adverse trade effects for the trading partners of the country concerned. In principle, the trade problems posed could be solved through negotiations, but in practice legitimacy is a powerful argument for inertia.

Negotiating Techniques

In the context of international negotiations on services, the foregoing observations are relevant for the choice of technique most suited to creating the maximum leverage for the expansion of service transactions on a global scale. One way of solving the dilemma between respecting national policy objectives in regulating services activities while providing for a mutually satisfactory degree of trade liberalization among all trading

Table 8–1. National regulations that affect significantly the competitivity of foreign-owned service firms

Activity	Import prohibitions or restrictions	Local content requirements	Local preference in public procurement	Cultural or ethical standards	Other standards (health, safety, technical, professional, etc.)	Limitations on establishment	Restrictions on local operations	Limitations on employment of foreigners	Exchange control
Advertising	Yes	Yes	Yes	Yes	No	Yes	No	Yes	Yes
Banking	No	Yes	Yes	Yes	Yes	Yes	Yes	Yes	Yes
Construction-Engineering	Yes	Yes	Yes	No	No	No	No	Yes	Yes
Franchising	Yes	Yes	No	No	Yes	No	No	Yes	Yes
Insurance	No	Yes	Yes	No	No	Yes	Yes	No	Yes
Leasing	Yes	Yes	No	No	No	Yes	No	Yes	Yes
Legal services	No	No	No	No	Yes	Yes	Yes	No	No
Telecommunication and data services	Yes	Yes	Yes	Yes	Yes	No	Yes	No	No
Tourism	No	No	No	No	No	Yes	Yes	Yes	Yes
Air transport	No	Yes	No	No	No	No	Yes	No	Yes
Shipping	No	Yes	Yes	No	Yes	No	Yes	No	No

Source: United States. 1985. U.S. National Study on Services, Appendix IV. Geneva: GATT.

partners is to follow the negotiating process depicted in figure 8–1. According to this plan, the selection between regulations which may be considered reasonable in terms of legitimate national goals, and those whose adverse effects on trade are judged to be disproportionate to these goals, is an essential first step in the negotiations. However, rather than attempting to define objective criteria, the negotiations would address each regulation case by case. All existing regulations affecting the sale and purchase of services both nationally and internationally would be notified in the initial stage of the negotiating process (box A).

Thereafter, negotiations would begin to segregate between reasonable and other regulations, which would be apportioned to boxes B and C, respectively. Regulations placed in box C would be "untouchable," and their incidental trade effects could not in principle give rise to complaints

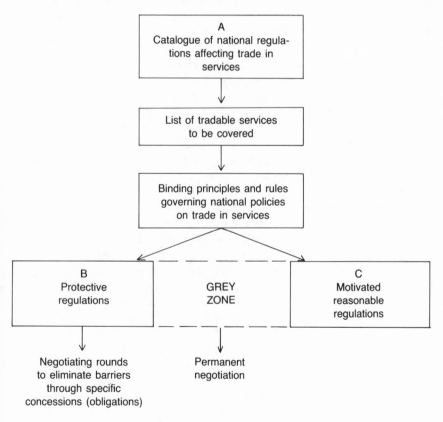

Figure 8–1. A plan to negotiate on services

by the affected countries. On the other hand, regulations in box B would be considered as being either a priori protective in intent, or as having protective effects that go far beyond those which may be inevitable in light of the nontrade objectives being pursued. All regulations in box B would be open for negotiation with a view to reducing or eliminating their protective effects. General principles and rules applying to international transactions in services would be limited in their scope and coverage to these same regulations. There would inevitably subsist a "grey zone" between boxes B and C, which would include all national regulations considered appropriately motivated or reasonable by the governments maintaining them, and inappropriately motivated or "protectionist" by other governments. The process of selecting among these grey-zone regulations, those which should be put in box B or C, would be the object of permanent negotiations among interested governments on a "less-than-consensus" basis, that is, subject to some form of supranationality: at the end of the day, majority rule would determine whether they should finally fall in box B or box C.

Finally, the overall negotiating process would start with a "standstill" commitment, involving a freeze on any existing regulation that appears in the inventory (box A), as well as an understanding that any regulation which has not been notified for inclusion in the catalog and which cannot subsequently be proven to be reasonable is by definition forbidden and must be withdrawn.

There are, of course, other ways of tackling the problem of national regulations that fulfill legitimate national goals. From a free trade point of view, any restriction to the free interplay of market forces has a negative impact on world welfare. Governments maintaining regulations that have restrictive effects on trade must therefore be ready to justify the need for such regulations. An alternative negotiating plan based on this concept is presented in figure 8–2. This plan does not involve an initial process of negotiation to determine the reasonableness of regulations. It begins by defining the multilateral disciplines that should govern international trade in services, whatever the regulations at national level. It goes on to assume that any national regulation is a potential source of trade restriction and distortion, and must therefore be submitted to international scrutiny *from that standpoint*. Provided certain conditions are met—as with regulations governing production, distribution, and trade in goods contained in Article XX of GATT—the *presumption* would be that the regulations in question are not protective in character, and/or that their negative incidence on the free flow of trade are justified by the goals they are intended to pursue. Yet, this contention could always be challenged,

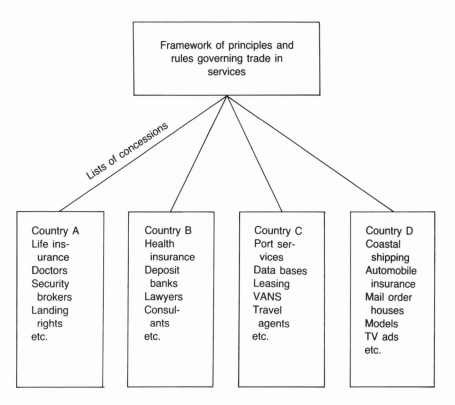

Figure 8–2. An alternative plan to negotiate on services

and there is no category of regulations as such which could ever be considered as a priori untouchable.

In this approach, there is no need for any a priori analysis and classification of regulations, and therefore no temptation to legitimize existing regulations in terms of supposedly sacrosanct national goals. For example, technically speaking, it may be desirable to define very strict rules for the establishment of banks and insurance companies, on the ground that in the given structure of banking and insurance markets consumers need specific kinds of protection related to that structure. However, if the structure of the banking and insurance markets changes, e.g., from a monopoly or near-monopoly situation to a truly competitive situation, the consumer protection requirements that defined the sovereignty rules in a situation of market control by a few dominant banks or insurance companies should change accordingly. Existing regulations are a reflection of existing market structures. With the evolution of the latter, the concept of reasonable regulation must be adapted to the new circumstances. The principles and rules embodied in the new multilateral framework to be negotiated must provide the flexibility to do so.

This second negotiating plan assumes that existing structures and regulatory frameworks are not necessarily most conducive to a welfare-creating competitive environment. Consequently, it does not attach particular value to existing sectoral regulatory frameworks in the field of services, so that sectoral trade agreements that lean on such frameworks are not a priority, if they are at all desirable. The analysis conducted in the preceding chapters has shown that service activities relate to specific functions and each service act is to be regarded as producing a specific service product. Such service products can be exchanged as such both nationally and internationally. Trade in services (taking the definition of trade in the broadest sense) can therefore be seen as a lucrative process of exchange of different service acts, just like shoes can be exchanged against machine tools in the international market. Thus, it is perfectly conceivable that in a negotiation between two countries with different exporting and importing interests in the field of services, landing rights for foreign airlines may be exchanged against the right of foreign consulting engineers to participate in public works projects. In each case, of course, the fundamental principles that guide government policies in granting and seeking access to other countries' markets would be those contained in the multilateral framework of principles and rules governing all international transactions in services, in the same way that trade concessions in the field of goods are governed by the GATT.

One potential difficulty with the second approach is the quantification of concessions made. This difficulty would also arise within sectoral agreements, mainly because in trade negotiations one is always dealing with the creation of trading opportunities rather than with the allocation of existing benefits. Nevertheless, it is conceivable that concessions in the same sector of service activity may be more easily comparable than concessions made in different sectors. The only solution that can be found to this problem is to leave it to the service industries concerned, rather than to government officials, to assess the magnitude of the benefits expected from specific trade concessions. In sum, the object of trade negotiations is to define parameters of change in trade policies which provide traders with reasonable profit expectations, rather than to give hard and fast assurances of trade benefits. In a multilateral trading system, it is often the case that a concession granted to country A is made better use of by exporters from country B, with the result that the would-be beneficiaries who have lobbied to obtain it fail to register any additional export earnings. That is the rule of the game of trade liberalization on a nondiscriminatory basis. The reverse and positive side of this coin is that trade opportunities opened up by concessions negotiated by third countries in a given market can benefit countries which have not had to concede any reciprocal access in their own market in return. Multilateralism is the science of "free rides."

The plans described in figures 8–1 and 8–2 are only two of many possible approaches to the negotiation of multilateral agreements on services. In general, the objective of multilateral trade negotiations is to provide the basis for a mutually beneficial expansion of trade among participating countries, and as a result, for a more efficient allocation of world productive resources. It must be recognized, however, that considerations of economic efficiency do not always prevail over considerations of economic independence, in view of the imbalances in the distribution of global wealth that may result from free-trade-oriented policies. Moreover, the choice between economic efficiency and economic independence rests on more complex arguments than does the theory of free trade in services. Indeed, as we shall see again below, while comparative advantage applies to a certain extent, in the modern world absolute advantage plays an increasingly important role in determining the direction of trade.

Other Issues

State intervention in service production and trade poses particularly acute problems in some service sectors. Market access is restricted by state monopolies in telecommunications, banking, insurance, transport, and other fields in certain countries. In these cases the question is not simply one of motivations for regulations but also of the possibility of the monopolies abusing market power.

An international agreement on trade in services would also need to address some aspects of *labor migration*, in particular where equitable competitive opportunities imply that firms operating abroad can temporarily employ staff from their home country to perform specific service functions and/or carry out specific service projects, e.g., construction contracts. The broader issue of labor movements may also need to be tackled, at the request of labor-exporting countries. Here, the problem would be to distinguish between primary factor movements unrelated to specific service outputs and those that are related, and different solutions may be called for in either case.

The *treaty-making power* of central governments also deserves particular attention, insofar as in certain federal states the regulation of major service sectors such as banking, insurance, and professional services falls within the competence of political subdivisions. This is not a new problem in the GATT, but it has not been handled consistently. Article XXIV: 12 of the General Agreement states:

> Each contracting party shall take such reasonable measures as may be available to it to ensure observance of the provisions of this Agreement by the regional and local governments and authorities within its territory.

Article 7 of the GATT Agreement on Subsidies and Countervailing Duties[9] and Articles 3, 4, 6, and 8 of the Agreement on Technical Barriers to Trade[10] also recognize that there are limitations on the responsibility of central governments for measures taken by local governments. Until now, however, the Contracting Parties of GATT have not formally given an interpretation of the scope of these provisions. Yet it does not seem conceivable that service sectors falling under local jurisdiction in certain countries could be excluded from the coverage of an international agreement on that account alone.

Special and differential treatment (S&D) for developing countries is another issue to be considered. A priori, the need for such treatment would appear to depend on the type of arrangement concluded, but it may be expected that some developing countries would insist on the inclusion of S&D provisions in any agreement as a general safeguard against requests for fully reciprocal concessions from their developed trading partners.

In this section, the applicability of some key GATT principles and rules to services has been examined, mainly to demonstrate their relevance. It should be clear, however, that even if theoretically possible with some adjustments, the simple extension to services of the present world trading system for goods embodied in GATT would represent too much of a change in the distribution of responsibilities for economic management between national authorities and the international community, to be acceptable to most governments—not to mention the strains and tensions to be expected from the forced merging of cultures which would inevitably result from complete free trade in services.

The Story of the Shoe

There is still one fundamental issue to be resolved before one can legitimately embark on a trade liberalization exercise in the field of services, and that is, *what is there to trade?* So far in this book we have examined in general terms whether the traditional theory of comparative advantage could be extended to services, the various problems posed by the operation of service sectors at national level, and the extent to which these could be dealt with under an essentially trade-oriented approach which would take as a starting point the multilateral trading system embodied in GATT. If it is found that there is some room for comparative advantage theory and that the issue of national sovereignty, particularly in regard to economic and social development objectives, can be handled satisfactorily in a multilateral agreement on trade in services, then we can move to the last step in the analysis of tradeability in services, namely to define in concrete terms those services that compete in the global market, either as specialized inputs or as products in their own right, on the basis of the particular primary factor endowments of the countries producing them.

   In order to do so, we must go back to the analysis presented in the earlier chapters of this book, relating to the role of knowledge in the production of services. As indicated there, knowledge is the most important component of many service activities; in fact, it is one characteristic of services that distinguishes them from goods,[11] unless goods themselves embody an overwhelming proportion of advanced services, e.g., so-called high technology goods.[12] This being said, for purposes of trade theory it is necessary to relate the knowledge-content of services to their tradeability in a more precise way. Lest it can be proven that the theory of comparative advantage is totally irrelevant, there must be distinct elements in the knowledge-content of services which are tradeable in the traditional sense of the word, that is, which can be beneficially exchanged on the basis of differences in natural resource endowments. Only if international trade in services can at least partly be conducted on this basis can such trade be described as a plus-sum game, in the sense that it allows a more efficient allocation of world resources and therefore an overall increase in world productivity from which all participants in the game can benefit. How, then, can one reconcile the general observation that the acquisition of knowledge and the control of information confer an absolute advantage on those that own or control these resources, with the requirement that the exchange of products obtained from the harnessing of these and other resources procures net economic benefits?

   This question can best be answered by looking at the history of production. A detailed statistical account of the secular evolution of the components of physical output in specific sectors or in particular national economies would be beyond the scope of this book. However, a cursory reading of economic history gives a fairly reliable idea of this evolution, whether one is dealing with agricultural, industrial, or service products.

Figure 8–3 gives an illustration of the process by schematically retracing the history of the shoe. There are two cross-sectional diagrams in the figure, A and B, representing, respectively, the cost composition of a shoe in the "early industrial age" and in "modern times." In diagram A, where the shoe is fairly standard and basically utilitarian, the main components are leather, labor, some simple technology specific to the making of shoes, and a little bit of design. In diagram B, the share of leather in the total value has fallen, either as a result of economies in the use of this raw material due to technological progress, or because of the substitution of leather by other synthetic materials—also the result of technological developments in related fields. The second main component, labor, is also reduced compared to situation A, as a result of the capitalization of production and of other sources of productivity gains such as improved labor relations, labor discipline, and improvements in the skills of individual workers. The share of shoe-making specific technology in the total is approximately equal to what it was in situation A, given the fact that the operations performed remain relatively simple and the scope for innovation in this area is correspondingly limited. On the other hand, in diagram B the share of design is considerably higher than in diagram A. This is attributable to a number of factors, among which are the following: (1) the higher income elasticity of demand for shoes is the main markets for the product, which results in increased competition among suppliers through product differentiation; (2) the greater availability of designers due to the higher general level of education in the population; (3) the

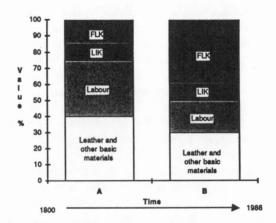

Figure 8–3. The story of the shoe

greater supply of talents induced by higher producer margins, in turn made possible by technological progress in physical production; and (4) the sheer need to compete with low-cost producers from developing countries, which forces traditional producers in industrialized countries to aim for the upper brackets of the shoe market in order to remain in business.

Now, what is interesting from the point of view of international trade is the relationship between the two main types of service components in the total cost of the shoe depicted in figure 8-3. These components can be described first as product-specific technology on the one hand, i.e., in this example the specific techniques applied to stitch shoe soles to uppers, etc.; and second as general-purpose technology which in this case is design, aimed at making the product attractive to consumers in various income brackets and usage brackets, i.e., relating the product to fashion and function. In terms of our previous analysis, the first type of technology can be described as *locked-in knowledge* (LIK), in the sense that the technology is directed and inextricably linked to the production of a specific product or category of products. The second type of technology can be described as *foot-loose knowledge* (FLK), meaning that this type of technology is not specific to the manufacture of a given product or category of products but can be used in a much more general way in other fields of production. This is the case of shoe design. Shoe designers are essentially artists who draw forms adapted to particular market needs or market prospection efforts. Their art is not exclusively related to the demands of shoe buyers but can easily be applied in other fields, e.g., automobile design. Indeed, their ability to design shoes is not linked to their understanding of the dynamics of the materials used in shoemaking or of the specific requirements of a variety of users: this is the job of the "shoe engineer," who identifies the materials best suited to particular requirements and the shapes best able to stand up to wear and tear and stress factors in particular usages.

FLK is essentially fungible, as are the production factors possessing and applying such knowledge. It can be obtained from any general, publicly accessible, or state-owned education system, from publicly accessible information networks including communication media, and through "learning by doing" in different social environments. Given this relatively accessible character of foot-loose knowledge, it is unlikely that the possession or nonpossession of such knowledge will in the long run affect the localization of production (value-added) in any particular area, country, region, or continent of the world. The one thing that can be said about it, however, is that those who possess it first possess an absolute advantage in production. This advantage may be of relatively short or relatively long duration, depending on the ease of entry into the "world of knowledge" which breeds FLK. In countries where the education system lags behind the most advanced in both content and coverage (curricula and percentage of the population), the gap in FLK tends to be temporarily filled by imports (foreign diplomas and foreign technical assistance delivered locally). Between countries at comparable levels of scientific and technological development and access to information, the absolute advantages conferred by FLK are usually short-lived.

LIK can also, in certain cases, confer an absolute advantage in production on those who possess it and indeed, this is the reason why owners of new production technology seek protection of their right of "being first" through intellectual property legislation. But LIK differs fundamentally from FLK, precisely because it is (1) related to specific outputs (shoemaking technology is of no use in woodworking); (2) closely interlinked with the use of given proportions of primary factors (physical capital and labor), and therefore dependent on the relative endowments of different countries with these factors.[13] Viewed in this light, LIK is a source of comparative, not absolute, advantage in international trade.

FLK, LIK, and International Economic Relations

The story of the shoe shows how comparative advantage theory can be extended to modern production methods, particularly to the increasing interlinkage between services and goods. It shows that production is a continuum, not a sectorally differentiated process. At the same time, it brings out the limits of a simple extension of the theory; beyond those limits, the theory of absolute advantage takes over. This has implications for the localization of value-added, as already stated, but also for the structure of business corporations, and for the nature of intercorporate relationships.[14] It also has implications for the rate of globalization of markets both in the goods and services fields: the greater the proportion of FLK in any given production process, the faster the rate of globalization: the suppliers of FLK components of goods and services will move to any location where physical and LIK components can be produced cheapest.

From the point of the production of services proper, the distinction between LIK and FLK is of particular interest due to the fact that together, they constitute an overwhelming share of total value-added in most service activities. It is true that individuals operating in FLK-rich environments have a tendency to seek protection against new entrants through regulatory mechanisms whose ultimate aim is to make their markets captive. This is typically the case of doctors, veterinarians, lawyers, accountants, architects, etc. Where locked-in knowledge is at stake—for instance, in engineering technology—limitation of access is attempted through the establishment of so-called intellectual property rights (copyrights, patents, etc.) which by themselves confer a marketable value on inventions at least for the time that the protection of such rights applies. However, despite some successful attempts by professional associations to protect or cartellize FLK, there is an inherent tendency for FLK-rich services to locate anywhere in the world, and to operate on a global basis from any location. Operators establish in places where the regulations governing the exercise of their activities are more liberal. In so doing, they exert strong pressures for deregulation in the bastions of corporatism being upheld in certain countries or regions. By contrast, services with a high content of LIK tend to find their more natural location in countries or areas where complementary factors are more readily available. Indeed, it is the complementarity between this type of knowledge and primary factors that gives it its locked-in character. This relationship is obvious in the field of manufacturing, but it is also evident in some service activities such as telecommunications and data processing. In these cases, the comparative advantage in the production of complementary equipment has a determinant effect on the geographical location of the corresponding locked-in knowledge and not vice versa. Thus, computer software cannot be developed in readily marketable forms without computers being available to test it and adapt it to user requirements.

In sum, the question of the tradeability of services discussed earlier in this book should be related to the relative shares of locked-in and foot-loose knowledges in given service activities. Paradoxically, it is precisely the type of knowledge (foot-loose) that depends least on the location of complementary factors which may be the least easily tradeable in the *traditional* sense of this term. Owners of such knowledge possess an often short-lived absolute advantage which they wish to exploit by delivering directly, through the temporary presence or permanent establishment of production factors in consumer markets, the services in which this knowledge is embodied. Therefore, issues of right of establishment, investment, and migration of individuals in foreign markets, as well as the relationship of intellectual property rights to trade in services, can only usefully be addressed in terms of the distinction between FLK and LIK. Because there is a preference for delivering FLK-rich services abroad through movements of factors rather than through cross-border trade, even if such trade is feasible, in many cases foreign direct investment is not an alternative to trade in the traditional sense of the term: it is the only *acceptable* way of gaining a foothold in foreign markets.

Table 8–2. Legal protection for computer programs, March 1986

Nation	Copyright	Trade secret Unfair comp.	Trademark	Patent
Argentina	Maybe	Yes	Yes	Unclear
Australia	Yes*			Unclear
Austria	Yes	Yes	Yes	No (3)
Belgium	Probably	Very limited		No
Brazil	Unclear (2)	Yes	Yes	Sometimes
Canada	Yes (2)		Yes	Unclear
China	Unclear (1)			Unclear
Denmark	Probably (2)	Limited		
Dominican Republic	Yes*			
Egypt	Unclear			
Finland	Probably (2)	Yes		Unclear
France	Yes*	Unclear		Perhaps
Germany [Fed. Rep.]	Yes*	Yes		No (3)
Germany [Dem. Rep.]	Unclear			No
Hong Kong	Yes			
Hungary	Yes*	Yes		
India	Yes*			
Indonesia	No			
Ireland	Unclear			
Israel	Yes*	Yes		Maybe
Italy	Yes	Limited		Unlikely
Japan	Yes*	Maybe		Sometimes
Malaysia	Yes*	Very limited		Unclear
Mexico	Yes	Yes	Yes	No
Netherlands	Yes (2)	Yes	Yes	Unclear

New Zealand	Probably			Unlikely
Nigeria	Maybe			Unclear
Norway	Maybe (2)		Yes	
Philippines	Yes*			
Panama				Yes
Poland	(2)			No
Portugal	Yes*			
Singapore	Maybe	Probably	Limited	See U.K.
South Africa	Yes	Yes	Yes	Sometimes
South Korea	(1)	Limited	Sometimes	
Spain	(1)	Maybe		
Sweden	Maybe (2)			No (3)
Switzerland	Unclear (2)	Maybe	Yes	No
Taiwan	Yes*		Pending	
Thailand	Maybe*			
U.S.S.R.	(2)			
United Kingdom	Yes*	Yes	Yes	Sometimes
United States	Yes*	Yes	Yes	Sometimes
Uruguay	Maybe			
Venezuela	No	Limited		
Yugoslavia				No

Source: (C) *Computer Law Newsletter*, R. P. Bigelow, 1985, 1986.
Robert P. Bigelow, Warner & Stackpole, 28 State St. Boston, MA 02109
Notes:
* Special legislation passed or decree issued.
1. Legislation pending.
2. Legislation proposed.
3. Perhaps, if included in process.

The fact that, generally speaking, FLK is readily accessible to potential competitors is another reason for preferring direct delivery. One form of access to FLK is general education dispensed by the state or by private educational institutions, whose services are within the financial reach of a large section of the population in affluent societies. For example, a large part of designers' or advertisers' skills consists of a general education base plus some specialized studies or training.[15] Other examples are literary works, which are written using a commonly accessibly form of knowledge, namely language and grammar, and where only ideas are original. FLK confers an absolute advantage onto those in which it is embodied only to the extent that they provide some part of the total knowledge product in the form of innovation. Sometimes even the innovative part of FLK can be easily copied and imitated: this is the origin of counterfeit goods, and the reason why counterfeiting is more pronounced in the field of fashion goods than in technical goods that embody a higher proportion of LIK. As we have seen, given that FLK knowledge has no "natural" location (the contrary would be tantamount to assuming that intelligence is unevenly distributed among the human races), the only way to retain the value-added derived from the exercise of FLK-based activities in given locations is to artificially lock it into the legal stronghold of patent and copyright laws (table 8–2).[16] Further, given the fact that foreign direct investment is a preferred way of exploiting the absolute advantage conferred upon the owners of FLK, there is an evident relationship between this form of delivery of services abroad and the existence of adequate property laws in the countries hosting such investment. Where cross-border trade is an alternative to foreign investment, it is only likely to take place in situations where intellectual property rights enjoy a minimum of protection.[17] On the other hand, where FLK-based foreign direct investment takes place, it may in itself become a source of increased trade both through imports of components required for the operation of branches and subsidiaries of firms established abroad, and of exports of these branches and subsidiaries to third countries from their foreign base.

The distinction between LIK and FLK also contributes to a better understanding of the changing structures of production in modern societies. In any production process, FLK is the part most likely to be externalized. Firms in whose production structure it is integrated first seek to commercialize separately the services of their FLK departments in order to maximize returns on in-house FLK-producing capacity; then at a later stage they divest from FLK departments as a means of saving on fixed costs. Thus the process of dismembering traditional corporate structures begins by the divestiture of FLK operations.[18]

In conclusion, to the question put earlier, "What is there to trade in services," we are now in a position to answer that (1) although FLK constitutes a large part of the value-added in many services, there are in some services elements of LIK which confer a true comparative advantage onto countries endowed with the relevant complementary factors (labor-intensive work of data entry in databases, cheap crew labor in sea transport, etc.); the FLK element, if it escapes counterfeiting, confers an absolute advantage onto those who own it, and they will attempt to exploit it by delivering the services abroad directly; (2) to the extent that services are incorporated in goods (compacks), the LIK element is fully tradeable on a comparative advantage basis. These conclusions lend force to the idea that multilateral disciplines governing international trade in services should be coherent with the disciplines already established for trade in goods. In effect, the elaboration of existing concepts in this area is only necessary to cover the exchange of FLK-intensive service products.[19]

Notes

1. The GATT, founded in 1948, now has 92 member countries or "contracting parties" representing over 80% of world trade in goods. For a brief account of the history and main provisions of GATT, see GATT regular publications listed in the bibliography.

2. When the Organization for Economic Cooperation and Development (OECD) was established in 1960, the member countries agreed that the free international movement of private capital flows and the removal of obstacles to the international exchange of services and current payments were desirable objectives. These principles were embodied in two legal instruments adopted in December 1961: the Code of Liberalization of Capital Movements (CLCM) and the Code of Liberalization of Current Invisible Operations (CLIO). The coverage of both Codes is extensive, but individual member governments can maintain reservations or derogations with respect to individual items. A procedure exists for the periodic review of such reservations or derogations with a view to the gradual extension of the scope of liberalization, and the contents of the Codes themselves have been revised from time to time to this end. However, the Codes do not establish a legal framework similar to GATT with binding obligations and a dispute settlement mechanism to enforce them. For a brief description of the working of the Codes, see GATT [1986a].

3. The principle of nondiscrimination applies more directly to trade regulations such as quantitative restrictions, or to technical regulations such as mandatory product standards, where the control on trade flows exercised by public authorities must not differentiate between products that meet the conditions set in the regulations.

4. The contracting parties acting jointly: the full membership of GATT is the Agreement's supreme decision-making body. Between their regular sessions, the Contracting Parties are represented by the Council. Membership in the Council, though in practice covering some two thirds of the total membership of GATT, is open to all contracting parties.

5. In the General Agreement on Tariffs and Trade, national treatment is defined as follows:

The contracting parties recognize that internal taxes and other internal charges, and laws, regulations and requirements affecting the internal sale, offering for sale, purchase, transportation, distribution or use of products, and internal quantitative regulations requiring the mixture, processing or use of products in specificed amounts or proportions, should not be applied to imported or domestic products so as to afford protection to domestic production.

The reference to "products" is deemed to restrict the application of this provision to traded goods. The Agreement on Government Procurement, on the other hand, extends national treatment to both products and suppliers:

With respect to all laws, regulations, procedures and practices regarding government procurement covered by this Agreement, the Parties shall provide immediately and unconditionally to the products and suppliers of other Parties offering products originating within the customs territories (including free zones) of the Parties, treatment no less favourable than:

(a) that accorded to domestic products and suppliers; and

(b) that accorded to products and suppliers of any other Party.

Products, in this context, also means goods, but in view of the anticipated extension of the Agreement to service contracts, this provision would presumably also cover the latter. The OECD definition of national treatment relates only to the operation of multinational enterprises. It reads as follows:

That Member countries should, consistent with their needs to maintain public order, to protect their essential security interests and fulfil commitments relating to international peace and security, accord to enterprises operating in their territories and owned or controlled directly or indirectly by nationals of another Member country (hereinafter referred to as "Foreign-Controlled Enterprises") treatment under their laws, regulations and administrative practices, consistent with international law and no less favourable than that accorded in like situations to domestic enterprises (hereinafter referred to as "National Treatment") [OECD, 1984].

In the U.S.-Israeli Free-Trade Agreement, concluded in 1985, national treatment is defined as follows:

Each Party will endeavour to assure that trade in services with the other nation is governed by the principle of national treatment. Each Party will endeavour to provide that a supplier of a service produced within the other nation is able to market or distribute that service under the same conditions as a like service produced within the first nation, including situations where a commercial presence within the nation is necessary to facilitate the export of a service from the other nation or is required by that Party. (For example, in the area of commercial banking, the concept of a commercial presence refers to the activities of representative offices, but not to agencies, branches or subsidiaries of commercial banks.)

6. It may, for example, be necessary to distinguish between national treatment and equivalent treatment, given the fact that in certain circumstances the sheer granting of equal operating rights to dependencies of foreign firms is not sufficient to equalize conditions of competition. In such cases, national treatment may be a necessary, but not a sufficient condition for effective market access.

7. The third element in GATT is the shared objective of trade liberalization, whereby

contracting parties recognize the desirability of entering into periodic negotiations for the reduction of customs duties and other obstacles to trade. Trade liberalization has been a gradual process since the founding of GATT, and it can be deemed unlikely that an initial round of negotiations on services would result in very drastic reductions in the existing arsenal of restrictions in most contracting parties. Certainly, the relative urgency of liberalization of trade in services on the one hand, and of establishing a viable framework within which such liberalization can be undertaken, on the other, would have to be carefully weighed.

8. The conditions laid down in Article XX of the General Agreement are as follows:

Subject to the requirement that such measures are not applied in a manner which would constitute a means of arbitrary or unjustifiable discrimination between countries where the same conditions prevail, or a disguised restriction on international trade, nothing in this Agreement shall be construed to prevent the adoption or enforcement by any contracting party of measures: [follows a list of measures] [GATT, 1969].

9. Footnote 1 to Article VII reads as follows:

In this Agreement, the term 'subsidies' shall be deemed to include subsidies granted by any government or any public body within the territory of a signatory. However, it is recognized that for signatories with different federal systems of government, there are different divisions of powers. Such signatories accept nonetheless the international consequences that may arise under this Agreement as a result of the granting of subsidies within their territories.

10. The limitations on central government authority are reflected in the way that obligations contained in these articles are formulated, i.e., "Parties shall take such reasonable measures as may be available to them to ensure that local government bodies [or non-governmental bodies] comply with the provisions of...etc." In GATT parlance this is called "second-level" obligations.

11. This characteristic has been recognized even by analysts who stress the heterogeneity of services: see, for example, Gibbs [1986]: "...in spite of their striking heterogeneity, there is perhaps a single, important component which is common to a large number of services. This is the amount of knowledge and information which they embody—in banking and insurance, shipping and accounting, trading and advertising, franchising and data processing, not to mention the vast range of professional services such as legal advice, consulting and engineering, technical design and health and education services. In all of them, the most common component is the amount of knowledge and information they contain."

12. A precise definition of such goods has never been given, and indeed there has been intensive discussion in various fora, notably OECD and GATT, on what is meant by them and how they differ from ordinary goods. While it is true that a clear borderline between high-technology goods and other goods is difficult to draw, in terms of the analysis of this book a common-sense definition would be that high-technology goods are those that contain, as stated in the text, an "overwhelming" proportion of services. In the absence of statistical conventions, overwhelming can be described as anything between 50.1% and 99.9% contained services in total value.

13. The question of relative endowments in skilled labor poses a problem of interpretation. This type of labor is in a sort of grey zone between natural factor endowment and acquired absolute advantage. On one hand, it might be argued that the natural level of skill of population differs from one country to another, but this idea is both morally abhorrent and contrary to observation. On the other hand, easy access to general knowledge is a result of a

long-standing accumulation process which may have been facilitated by the disposal, at the initial stages of the process, of valuable natural resources, which almost by definition are unevenly distributed among the populations of the earth. In a recent article on the tradeability of services, Peter Zweifel [1986] writes: "...in traditional theory, comparative advantage is mainly a matter of relative marginal cost of production. New demand theory, applied to international trade, results in a more general view. First, a rich country stands a better chance of being able to export some of its services than a poor country because it can afford more product differentiation...second, the problem of correctly identifying relevant characteristics [a notion corresponding to that of functions used in this book] should not be underestimated. Some characteristics (such as religious knowledge) may not be relevant in the partner country. Moreover, services processes of the repair type always start from a particular endowment point...again, a rich country's producers *with all their marketing and information-gathering facilities at their disposal, will have an advantage on this score.* Their services are more likely to produce all the characteristics (often latently) desired by consumers." The underlined part of the foregoing quotation corresponds to what in the text is described as foot-loose knowledge (FLK). In the same study, Zweifel states: "...in the case of financial services, any comparative advantage less-developed countries may have in terms of cost will be at least partially undermined by Western countries' *comparative advantage in terms of product development.*" This example corresponds to what in the text has been described as locked-in knowledge (LIK).

14. In this connection, see Bressand [1986] and the discussion on networking in chapter 7.

15. In the absence of a general education base, the skills are, of course, only within the reach of an elite. When that happens, customers are more likely to move to the country or place of residence of service producers than the reverse. Religious pilgrimage is a case in point.

16. An extreme example of the latter is the recent attempt by French culinary pundits to obtain copyright protection for cooking recipes developed by them.

17. Product-specific technology may involve a combination of LIK and FLK and may therefore also be a candidate for intellectual property protection. LIK proper, on the other hand, is only transferable where there exists the right combination of physical factors to make use of it, and may be less in need of intellectual property protection on a large scale. It is, of course, difficult to make a hard-and-fast distinction between FLK and LIK in the case of new products, where not only the conceptual elements but also the technical elements of the production process contain a large amount of innovation.

18. See Bressand [1986]. The explanation of the process of dismembering traditional corporate structures, described by Bressand with reference to the "hollow corporation" concept put forward by Brandt and others [1986], stops short of an analysis of the components of externalized services. The distinction between FLK and LIK made above is believed to follow the line of Bressand while providing a more rigorous explanation of the origin of the process. A concrete example of the externalization of FLK is the marketing by Canadian Railways of their rolling-stock management system.

19. For example, rules on customs valuation had never foreseen that the value of information contained in physical information stores such as floppy disks and magnetic tapes could be a million times superior to the value of the disk or tapes themselves. Yet, customs valuation rules to this day exclude the value of contained information from the dutiable value of imported tapes, disks, etc. Similarly, telecommunication transmission charges usually exclude the value of transmitted information from the basis of assessment of the charges. These anomalies can only be explained by the fact that when customs valuation rules were drafted some 40 years ago, nobody had any idea of the technological progress that would be

made in informatics and telematics. The persistence of such rules to this day reflects the exercise of negotiating power by countries which are major exporters and processors of information, an FLK-intensive service product which is a major source of absolute advantage for multilateral enterprises originating in these countries.

9 BY WAY OF CONCLUSION
OR EPILOQUE

This book has dealt with the role of services in present-day international economic exchange. The focus of attention has therefore been on those factors affecting the worldwide expansion of service activities on the one hand, and the worldwide expansion of productive activities which are either complementary to services, or which use increasing proportions of services as inputs into complex products, on the other. Much attention has been devoted to describing the channels through which international transactions in services take place as well as the motive forces behind competition in the world market. Emphasis has been placed on the role of knowledge and work experience as determinants of the competitive advantage of individuals, firms, and countries. After an initial analysis of the role of these factors, which have been variously described as technology, scientific progress, or cultural ascendency, as opposed to the role of physical factors of production with which various regions or countries may be endowed—labor, land, and capital—an attempt has been made to define more precisely the role of knowledge and work experience in determining the location of value-added in the global market. It has been found that general, easily accessible knowledge which is in some sense the common heritage of mankind, is essentially fungible and as such cannot constitute a "natural" endowment of any particular population of the earth, although the means to acquire, store, and process such knowledge, to the extent that they rely on physical factors, may be unevenly apportioned among different populations. On the other hand, it has been shown that knowledge and work experience which is more specifically related to the production of specific outputs, and which for this reason depends more on the availability of specific complementary physical factors, is part and parcel of the factor endowments that underlie the comparative advantage of different social entities. Thus, the basic question, "Where does comparative advantage in services lie?" has been answered.

The second most important question in analyzing the role of services in the global market has been tackled at the outset, through the explanation of microeconomic production processes, in order to bring out what constitutes the basis for the production of value in service activities and how this value can be measured. The approach, which has consisted in giving priority to this aspect, was prompted by the implicit understanding that international trade in services would not take place unless some additional macroeconomic benefits were expected from it. (Trade is not a zero-sum game.) Hence, it was essential to identify the main sources of economic gains in trade in services as a guide to policy for both governments and the private sector. The main source identified in this book is optimum use of knowledge factors in production, taking into account natural physical factor endowments.[1]

The preceding analysis has also laid the foundation for dealing with the question of the tradeability of services. This question has two aspects. First, there is the semantic aspect, where the problem is to find a definition of trade in services which reflects the technical requirements of the sale of services in foreign markets, namely the need for a presence of the seller at the point of sale, and how this relates to the traditional notion of trade as it applies to the physical transfer of goods from one location to another. Secondly, and more interestingly, there is the problem of determining which services are more likely to be exchanged internationally and what are the forces at work on the supply and demand sides which bring about such international transactions. There are, in fact, two answers to the latter question, one from the standpoint of demand and the other from the standpoint of supply. In the first instance, as pointed out by Zweifel [1986, p. 12], ". . . from a basic consumer's point of view, there is even more scope for trade in services than for trade in goods. Domestic goods, once acquired, can be mixed freely by their owner. This is not true of services, which opens a great potential for imported services producing exactly the characteristics combination desired by the consumer." In other words, the specificity of demand, and the tendency of many services, particularly sophisticated or knowledge-intensive services, to be geared to the needs of individual consumers or groups of consumers, are permanent sources of product differentiation, which enhances trade. In this case, there is a perfect analogy with trade in differentiated goods. Associated with the different preferences of consumers in different countries, or in different economic circumstances within the same country, is the fact that there is a natural tendency for services to be adapted to the needs of consumers thanks to the direct market relationship which is established with the service producer, which itself derives from the intangible character of service products (themselves better described as service *acts*, as indicated earlier).

From the point of view of supply, tradeability of services is increased to the extent that services can be standardized. In this case, there is no difference with undifferentiated goods, which in Zweifel's terminology provide conventional "characteristics"—or in the present author's terminology, functions—and can therefore be broken down into readily identifiable units whose price depends on the quantities offered for sale and demanded, taking into account the income level of consumers and the possible applicability of Engel's Law to particular service products.[2]

Before taking a longer-term view of the implications of the increased share of services in total world production and trade, two comments on the effects of the internationalization of service activities on the economies of individual countries will serve to illustrate the concerns expressed by a number of governments, particularly of less-developed countries, regarding the possible consequences of the liberalization of international service transactions. Again using Zweifel as a reference [1986, pp. 19–21], the analysis of the basis for trade from the demand side of the equation shows that "...consumption equilibrium will be compatible with balance-of-payments equilibrium only in special cases...[the equilibrium condition that revenue from exports and expenditures on imports will balance] will not be satisfied in general as soon as international trade in induced by a desire to reshuffle characteristics, resulting in a flow of services (or differentiated goods)." Since the services most in need in less-developed countries are of the more sophisticated, knowledge-intensive, differentiated type, there appears to be some a priori justification for the fears expressed by the former countries. The choice open to them is then either to accept the status of net importers of services as a price to pay for participating in the world networks of information and financial flows (which allows them to maintain the necessary market linkages for exporting and importing goods on the most economic terms), and for reaching world efficiency levels in the production of goods and services for which they have a comparative advantage; or to develop their own service production capacity under protection, at the risk of increasing the technological gap between their economies and those of more advanced and more market-oriented countries.

Also relevant to the development of international transactions to services is that of quality norms or standards. Such standards can be defined in various ways depending on the services concerned. In the case of professional services they are often referred to as qualifications. In the area of financial services they may be referred to as solvency requirements. In engineering they are called state of the art. In the military world they are called strike or defense capability. In all these examples, and there are many others, standards define minimum performances required by service *providers*. This is not equivalent to performance standards for service products. But the depth of the bow of a lift attendant in a Tokyo department store may be an exception. In fact, for fully standardized service products the borderline between performance and design standards is somewhat blurred, since performance is associated with strictly defined acts of the service agents which, as in the case of the Japanese elevator girl, can be visibly identified. Generally speaking, however, it is difficult to reduce service acts to such menial proportions; therefore, the only control that can be exerted on the quality of service products is through control of the modalities of supply.

The fact that setting minimum performance standards addresses itself to the suppliers has three distinct effects on the international movements of services. In the first instance, it may limit the possibility to transact services across borders, insofar as the importing country setting the standards has no direct control over the performance of the supplier. This is a fundamental problem: for example, in allowing sales of insurance policies by companies established abroad and which are not subject to the same solvency standards as in the insurance-importing country. The same applies also to differences in professional qualifications when governments fail to recognize the equivalence of foreign diplomas earned by doctors, lawyers, accountants, and the like. The second effect is to restrict the movement of factors of production. This effect is specific to international transactions in services insofar as there is a need for a simultaneous presence of service providers and users in the place of consumption, as in the examples given above of doctors, lawyers, etc. It may be more severe than the previous effect, because even with equal quality standards suppliers of services may find it more difficult to sell services across borders, especially nonstandardized services, due to the difficulty of adapting the contents of the service product to the specific needs of consumers. One must also take into account the "natural" mistrust of unknown firms or individuals in a type of commercial relationship where face-to-face contacts are a condition of success. Third, both in the case of cross-border or on-the-spot transactions, quality norms limit the operation of the price mechanism, in that suppliers of services cannot enter markets that maintain higher standards than their own at any price. Quality norms, in fact, also have important restrictive effects on trade in goods when they relate to service components such as cultural messages, e.g., in labelling.

In a longer-term perspective, the tradeoff between protection and efficiency is the same for services as it is for goods. All countries in the process of development face the same challenge of either building up local production capacity at a certain economic cost or relying on foreign supplies. But in dealing with services, one must also realize that in the long run, cultural and political values are also fungible, and therefore it may be totally unrealistic to repulse sociopolitical influences embodied in tangible and intangible products, on the ground that accepted traditional moral values are superior to those which may evolve with the greater interdependence and networking of economic activities worldwide. To drive the point home, suffice it to consider the role of the city as a "services bundle." It has long been recognized that there are external economies in locating production facilities in areas where there is already a high concentration of demand in the form of physical numbers of population and income per head, and where the intermingling of productive activities catering to the needs of those consumers permits the exploitation of economies of scale, both in the production of essential services[3] and in the distribution and exploitation of market information. Now, in the same way that the development of city life has been seen as a step forward in the development of civilized relations among human beings, and in the "melting pot" function of urbanization as a factor in national cultural integration, the globalization of service transactions can be seen as a step in the same direction on a worldwide scale.

Cultural differences have found expression in different art styles. Art, therefore, is the optimum form of service, in that it expresses in summary and readily communicable form a complete set of economic, political, racial, and linguistic parameters as they impinge on the development of given social entities. The worldwide growth of services production and trade cannot but lead to an explosion of art, though perhaps coupled with a certain harmonization of art forms. A paradox, if one remembers the words of Théophile Gautier [1924]: "*Il n'y a de vraiment beau que ce qui ne peut servir à rien.*" In analyzing the role of services in modern societies, we have come full circle from identifying the dynamic economic role of services, to singling out their hedonistic utility as art. Such are the vagaries of research.

If anything can be said for this intellectual process, it is that more thinking and more research are needed to understand fully the workings of modern societies, dominated as they are by the most "unproductive" kinds of activities which Adam Smith could think of. However modest the conclusions of such thinking and research may turn out to be, they should help future generations put contemporary developments in proper perspective. For economists of this generation, it is enough to try and open vistas into the brave new world of the twenty-first century.

Notes

1. In order to make the general language of the text clear in terms of day-to-day experience, the previously used example of low-cost key-punching in developing countries may be repeated to point out that literacy is one general knowledge factor, which can be put to most efficient use by employing abundant literate labor resources in some countries, for purposes of data entry in data bases exploited on computers manned by highly skilled labor in relatively capital-rich and labor-scarce countries.

2. The gradual disappearance of domestic services can be attributed to the incorporation of those services in standardized goods (household appliances) which provide the same characteristics (in Zweifel's terminology) more reliably and more cheaply, but it can also be interpreted as an effect of the average consumer's higher income, which makes him turn away from the "inferior good" represented by the obnoxious presence of surly maids.

3. Utilities, telecommunications, transport, wholesale and retail trade, financial and insurance services, as well as the services of government in the form of fiscal administration, police protection, legal protection (courts and tribunals), and networking through the close interconnection between the central administration of states and top business executives represented in professional associations.

BIBLIOGRAPHY

Abramowitz, 1957. *Resource and Output Trends in the U.S. since 1870.* Occasional Paper 53. New York: National Bureau of Economic Research.

Aho, Michael C., and Aronson, Jonathan David. 1985. *Trade Talks, America Better Listen!* New York: Council on Foreign Relations.

Ames, Brian. 1986. A researcher's guide to statistics on production, trade and employment in services. Unpublished paper.

Arndt, H. W. 1984. Measuring trade in financial services. *Banca Nazionale del Lavoro Quarterly Review,* June.

Aronson, Jonathan David, and Cowhey, Peter F. 1984a. *Trade in Services, A Case for Open Markets.* Washington, D.C.: American Enterprise Institute.

—————. 1984b. Computer, data processing and communication services. *Third Annual Workshop on U.S.-Canadian Relations, October 19–20, 1984.* Ann Arbor: Unpublished.

Ascher, Bernard, and Whichard, Obie G. 1986. Improving services trade data. *Services World Economy Series No. 1.* Oxford: Pergamon Press.

Atinc, T., Benham, A., Cornford, A., Glasgow, R., Skipper, H., and Yusuf, A. 1984. International transactions in services and economic development. *Trade and Development,* No. 5. Geneva: United Nations Conference on Trade and Development.

Austin, Ray. 1985. Business needs for innovation in the service Sector. *Symposium on the Service Sector, Hanover, May 13–15 1985.* Hanover: Unpublished. (See Pestel, Eduard.)

231

Ba, Boubacar. 1986. Réflexions sur la question des services dans le contexte africain. *Group of Experts on the Economics of Services: United Nations Conference on Trade and Development.* Geneva: Unpublished.

Bank for International Settlements (BIS). 1986. *Recent Innovations in International Banking.* Basle: BIS.

Baker, A.M. 1986. Liberalization of trade in services—The world insurance industry. *Services World Economy Series No. 1.* Oxford: Pergamon Press.

Balassa, B. 1979. A stages approach to comparative advantage. *Economic Growth and Resources,* vol. 4, I. Adelman (ed.). London: Macmillan.

Barcet, R., and Bonamy J. 1986. *La productivité dans les services, prospective et limite d'un concept, Deuxièmes journées annuelles d'étude sur l'économie des services.* Geneva: Institut universitaire d'études européennes, unpublished.

Bartlett, Bruce. 1985. Supply-side economics: Theory and evidence. *National Westminster Bank Quarterly Review,* February.

Barton, John H. 1984. Coping with technological protectionism. *Harvard Business Review,* November-December.

Baudet, Emmanuelle. 1986. L'internationalisation de la publicité: l'heure est aux alliances et à la créativité. *Séminaire sur l'internationalisation des services FAST/PROMETHEE/CEPII/CEPS:* Brussels: Unpublished.

Becker, Gary S. 1962. Investment in human capital: A theoretical analysis. *The Journal of Political Economy,* Supplement: October.

Benz, Steven F. 1985. Trade liberalization and the global service economy. *Journal of World Trade Law,* March–April.

Berekoven, Ludwig. 1985. "The market for services—Relevant characteristics, empirical findings, *Symposium on the Service Sector, Hanover, May 13–15 1985.* Hanover: Unpublished. (See Pestel, Eduard.)

Berr, Claude J., and Reboud, Louis. 1985a. Pour une politique communautaire des services. *Revue du Marché Commun,* May.

—————. 1985b. Rapport introductif. *Journées d'études sur le concept d'obstacles non tarifaires et son application aux échanges de biens et de services.* Grenoble: Unpublished.

Bhagwati, Jagdish N. 1986. *International Trade in Services and its Relevance for Economic Development.* Oxford: Pergamon Press.

—————. 1984. Splintering and disembodiment of services and developing nations. *The World Economy,* June.

Brandt, Richard, et al. 1986. The hollow corporation. *Business Week,* March.

Brender, Anton, and Oliveira-Martins, Joaquim. 1984. Les échanges mondiaux d'invisibles: une mise en perspective statistique. *Economie prospective internationale,* 3ème trimestre, n⁰19.

Bressand, Albert. 1983. Mastering the Worldeconomy. *Foreign Affairs,* 61(4).

—————. 1985. Services in the new world economy: In search of a conceptual framework. *Symposium on the Service Sector, Hanover, May 13–15 1985.* Hanover: Unpublished. (See Pestel, Eduard.)

—————. 1986a. International division of labour in the emerging global information economy: The need for a new paradign. *Séminaire sur l'inter-*

nationalisation des services FAST/PROMETHEE/CEPII/CEPS. Brussels: Unpublished.

————. 1986b. Le capital-risque américain: leçons pour l'Europe des stratégies d'intégration des services. *Séminaire sur l'internationalisation des services FAST/PROMETHEE/CEPII/CEPS*. Brussels: Unpublished.

Bressand, Albert, and Distler, Catherine. 1985. *Le prochain monde*. Paris: Seuil.

Brown, H.P. 1949. Some aspects of social accounting—Interest and banks. *Economic Record*, August.

Bulthuis, R., van Holst, B., and de Wit, G.R. 1985. *The Service Sector and Technological Developments*. Rotterdam: Netherlands Economics Institute.

Canada. 1984. *National Study on Services*. Geneva: General Agreement on Tariffs and Trade.

Canton, Irving D. 1984. Learning to love the service economy. *Harvard Business Review*, May–June.

Carter, Robert L., and Dickinson, Gerard M. 1979. *Barriers to Trade in Insurance*. Thames Essay No. 19. London: Trade Policy Research Centre.

Cash Jr., James I., and Konsynski, Benn R. 1985. IS redraws competitive boundaries. *Harvard Business Review*, March–April.

Chant, John F. 1984. The Canadian treatment of foreign banks: A case study in the workings of the national treatment approach. *Third Annual Workshop on U.S.-Canadian Relations, October 19–20, 1984*. Ann Arbor: Unpublished.

Clairmonte Frederick F., and Cavanagh, John H. 1984. Transnational corporations and services: The final frontier. *Trade and Development*, No. 5. Geneva: United Nations Conference on Trade and Development.

Clark, Colin. 1957. *The Conditions of Economic Progress*. London: MacMillan.

Commission of the European Communities. 1984. *FAST, 1984–1987, Objectives and Work Programme*. Brussels: EC Commission.

Corden, W.M. 1971. *The Theory of Protection*. Oxford: Clarendon Press.

Daly, Donald J. 1984. Technology transfer and Canada's competitive performance. *Third Annual Workshop on U.S.-Canadian Relations, October 19–20, 1984*. Ann Arbor: Unpublished.

Deardorff, Alan V. 1984. Comparative advantage and international trade in investment in services. *Third Annual Workshop on U.S.-Canadian Relations, October 19–20, 1984*. Ann Arbor: Unpublished.

Deardorff, Alan V., and Stern Robert M. 1985. *Methods of Measurement of Non-Tariff Barriers*. Geneva: UNCTAD (document UNCTAD/ST/MD/28).

de Laubier, D. 1986. Les firmes européennes et l'internationalisation des services commerciaux. *Séminaire sur l'internationalisation des services FAST/PROMETHEE/CEPII/CEPS*. Brussels: Unpublished.

————. 1986. L'internationalisation des services financiers. *Economie prospective internationale*, $2^{\text{ème}}$ trimestre, n°26.

Denison, Edward F. 1962. Education, economic growth and gaps in information. *Journal of Political Economy*, October.

————. 1974. *Accounting for United States Economic Growth, 1929–1979*. Washington, D.C.: The Brookings Institution.

————. 1979. *Accounting for Slower Economic Growth: The United States in the 1970s*. Washington, D.C.: U.S. Government Printing Office.

De Vany, Arthur S., and Saving, Thomas R. 1983. The Economics of Quality. *Journal of Political Economy*, 91 (6).

Dickinson, G.M. 1978. *International Insurance Transactions and the Balance of Payments*. Etudes et Dossiers n^{0}16. Geneva: "Association de Genève."

————. 1986. Changing international insurance markets: Their implications for EEC insurance enterprises and governments. *Séminaire sur l'internationalisation des services FAST/PROMETHEE/CEPII/CEPS*. Brussels: Unpublished.

DiLullo, Anthony J. 1981. Services transactions in the U.S. international accounts, 1970–1980. *Survey of Current Business*, November.

Distler, Catherine. 1986. Logiciel et services informatiques. *Séminaire sur l'internationalisation des services FAST/PROMETHEE/CEPII/CEPS*. Brussels: Unpublished.

Economic Consulting Services Inc. 1981. *The International Operations of U.S. Service Industries: Current Data Collection and Analysis*. Washington, D.C.: Unpublished.

Edvinsson, Leif. 1985. *Services Internationalization: Trade in Thoughtware*. Stockholm: Consultus International AB.

————. 1986. The new business focus. *Deuxièmes journées annuelles d'étude sur l'économie des services*. Geneva: Institut universitaire d'études européennes, unpublished.

Ertel, Rainer. 1985. What are services? Defining annotations. *Symposium on the Service Sector, Hanover, May 13–15 1985*. Hanover: Unpublished. (See Pestel, Eduard.)

Ewing, A.F. 1985. Why freer trade in services is in the interest of developing countries. *Journal of World Trade Law*, March–April.

Feketekuty, Geza. 1984. Negotiating strategies for liberalizing trade and investment in services. *Third Annual Workshop on U.S.-Canadian Relations, October 19–20, 1984*. Ann Arbor: Unpublished.

————. 1986. About trade in tourism services. *Services WorldEconomy Series No. 1*. Oxford: Pergamon Press.

Findlay, Christopher. 1985. A framework for services trade policy questions, *Pacific Economic Papers*, September.

Fischer, Allan. 1933. Capital and the growth of knowledge. *Economic Journal*, September.

————. 1939. Primary, secondary and tertiary production. *Economic Record*, June.

Fontela, Emilio. 1984. The international division of labour and the development of information and communication technologies, *International Conference "1984 and After: the Social Challenge of Information Technologies", Berlin, November 28–30 1984*. Unpublished.

Freeman, Harry L. 1985. Potential of the services sector in job creation. *Symposium on the Service Sector, Hanover, May 13–15 1985*. Hanover: Unpublished. (See Pestel, Eduard.)

Gadrey, Jean. 1986a. *Société de services ou de self-services?* Baltimore: Johns
    Hopkins European Centre for Regional Planning and Research.
————. 1986b. Productivité, output médiat et immédiat des activités des
    services: les difficultés d'un transfert de concepts. *Deuxièmes journées annuelles
    d'étude sur l'économie des services*, Geneva: Institut universitaire d'études
    européennes, unpublished.
Gasiorowski, Mark J. 1985. The structure of third-world economic interdepend-
    ence. *International Organization*, 39 (2).
Gautier, Théophile. 1924. *Mademoiselle de Maupin (Préface)*. Paris: Fasquelle.
Gavin, Brigid. 1985. A GATT for international banking? *Journal of World Trade
    Law*, March–April.
General Agreement on Tariffs and Trade. 1969. *Basic Instruments and Selected
    Documents*, Vol. IV. Geneva: GATT.
————. 1980. Understanding regarding notification, consultation, dispute
    settlement and surveillance. *Basic Instruments and Selected Documents.*
    Twenty-sixth Supplement. Geneva: GATT.
————. 1985. *GATT, What it is, what it does*. Geneva: GATT.
————. 1986a. *Summary of Information Made Available by Relevant
    International Organizations: OECD*, MDF/17/Add. 4. Geneva: GATT.
————. 1986b. *Exchange of Information on Services: Minutes of Meetings*,
    MDF/- series. Geneva: GATT.
————. 1986c. Ministerial declaration on the Uruguay Round. *Document
    MIN/DEC*. Geneva: GATT.
————. Yearly. *GATT Activities*. Geneva: GATT.
Gershuny, Jonathan, and Miles, Ian. 1981. *The New Service Economy: The
    Transformation of Employment in Industrial Societies*. London: F. Pinter.
————. 1985. Will the service economy save us from unemployment? *Services
    WorldEconomy Series No. 1*. London: Pergamon Press.
Giarini, Orio. 1980, *Dialogue on Wealth and Welfare*. London: Pergamon Press.
————. 1981. Développement économique et richesse des nations: le retour à
    l'économie de l'offre. *Revue économique et sociale*, August.
————. 1985a. The consequences of complexity in economics: Vulnerability,
    risk and rigidity factors in supply. *The Science and Praxis of Complexity*. The
    United Nations University.
————. 1985b. Patterns to the wealth of nations: Some key issues and defini-
    tions on the service economy. *Symposium on the Service Sector, Hanover, May
    13–15 1985*. Hanover: Unpublished. (See Pestel, Eduard.)
————. 1986. Foreword. *Services WorldEconomy Series No. 1*. Oxford:
    Pergamon Press.
Giarini, Orio, and Loubergé, H. 1978. *The Diminishing Returns of Technology*.
    London: Pergamon Press.
Gibbs, Murray. 1985. Continuing the international debate on services. *Journal of
    World Trade Law*, May–June.
————. 1986. Services, development and TNCs. *The CTC Reporter*, No. 21,
    Spring.

Goldberger, Arthur S. 1959. *Impact Multipliers and Dynamic Properties of the Klein-Goldberger Model.* Amsterdam: North–Holland.

Grey, Rodney de C. 1984. Negotiation about trade and investment in services. *Third Annual Workshop on U.S.-Canadian Relations, October 19–20, 1984.* Ann Arbor: Unpublished.

————. 1986. *A Not-So Simple Plan for Negotiating on Trade in Services.* Ottawa: Grey Clark Shih and Associates Limited.

Griffiths, Brian. 1975. *Invisible Barriers to Invisible Trade.* London: Trade Policy Research Centre.

Grossman, Gene M., and Shapiro, Carl. 1984. Normative issues raised by international trade in technology services. *Third Annual Workshop on U.S.-Canadian Relations, October 19–20, 1984.* Ann Arbor: Unpublished.

Grubel, Herbert G. 1975. *Intra-Industry Trade: The Theory and Measurement of International Trade in Differentiated Products.* London: MacMillan.

Herman, B., and van Holst, B. 1981. *Towards a Theory of International Trade in Services.* Rotterdam: Netherlands Economic Institute.

————. 1984. *International Trade in Services: Some Theoretical and Practical Problems.* Rotterdam: Netherlands Economic Institute.

Hill, T.P. 1977. On goods and services. *The Review of Income and Wealth*, December.

Hindley, Brian, and Smith, Alasdair. 1984. Comparative advantage and trade in services. *The World Economy*, December.

Hufbauer, G.C. 1966. *Synthetic Materials and the Theory of International Trade.* London: G. Duckworth.

International Air Traffic Association (IATA). 1978. *The IATA Traffic Conferences.* Geneva: IATA.

Institute for New Generation Computer Technology (ICOT). 1984. *Outline of Fifth Generation Computer Project.* Tokyo: ICOT.

Inman, Robert (ed.). 1985. *Managing the Service Economy, Prospects and Problems.* Cambridge: University Press.

International Monetary Fund (IMF). 1977. *Balance-of-Payments Manual*, 4th edition, Washington, D.C.: IMF.

Jao, Y.C. 1985. Hong Kong's future as a financial centre. *The Three Banks Review*, March.

Jones, L. 1984. A comment on comparative advantage and international trade in services. *Third Annual Workshop on U.S.-Canadian Relations, October 19–20, 1984.* Ann Arbor: Unpublished.

Jotuni, Perti. 1986. Educate and innovate. *The Finnish Business Challenge.* Hensinki: Union Bank of Finland, Ltd.

Kamarck, Andrew W. 1976. *The Tropics and Economic Development: A Provocative Enquiry into the Poverty of Nations.* Baltimore: Johns Hopkins University Press.

Kanamori, Hisao. 1985. *The Japanese Economy and the Microelectronics Revolution.* Tokyo: The Japan Economic Research Centre.

Keesing, Donald B. 1967. The impact of research and development on U.S. trade.

Journal of Political Economy, February.

Keesing, Donald B., and Sherk, D. R. 1971. Population density in patterns of trade and development. *American Economic Review*, December.

Keppler, Horst. 1986. *Die Bedeutung des Dienstleistungssektors für die Entwicklungsländer*. Munich: Weltforum Verlag.

Kierzkowski, Henryk. 1984. *Services in the Development Process and Theory of International Trade*. Geneva: The Graduate Institute of International Studies.

Kim, Inchul. 1985a. *Discussion Materials on Service Policies for Developing Countries*. Seoul: Korea Development Institute, unpublished.

—————. 1985b. *Growth and Trade in Services: Korea's Perspective*. Seoul: Korea Development Institute, unpublished.

Klein, Robert W. 1973. A dynamic theory of comparative advantage. *American Economic Review*, March.

Koulen, Mark, 1985a. Trade in banking services. Geneva: Unpublished.

—————. 1985b. Trade in Insurance Services. Geneva: Unpublished.

—————. 1985c. International trade in data services. Geneva: Unpublished.

Kozma, Ferenc. 1985. L'exportation des systèmes complexes de produits et de services et la coopération triangulaire Est-Ouest-Sud. In *Croissance, échange et monnaie en économie internationale*, Mélanges en l'honneur de Monsieur le Professeur Jean Weiller, Paris: Economica.

Kravis, I. B. 1956. Availability and other influences on the commodity composition of trade. *Journal of Political Economy*. April.

Krommenacker, R. J. 1979. GATT and trade-related services. *Journal of World Trade Law*, November.

—————. 1984. *World-Traded Services: The Challenge of the Eighties*. Dedham, MA: Artech House.

Kumar, Prem. 1985. Keynote address, *Colloquium on the Proposed New Round of Multilateral Trade Negotiations and Developing Countries, New Delhi, December 12–13 1985*. Unpublished.

Kuznets, Simon. 1960. *Six Lectures on Economic Growth*. New York: Free Press.

Lambert, Sophie, 1986. SITA, le plus vaste réseau du monde. *01 Informatique*, April.

Lanvin, Bruno. 1986. *The Impact of Trade and Foreign Direct Investment in Data Services on Economic Development: Some Issues*. Geneva: Unpublished preliminary draft.

Lanvin, Bruno, and Prieto, Francisco. 1986. Les services, clé du développement économique? *Revue Tiers-Monde*, January–March.

Leamer, Edward E. 1984. *Sources of International Comparative Advantage, Theory and Evidence*. Cambridge, MA: MIT Press.

Lecraw, Donald J. 1984. Some economic effects of standards. *Applied Economics*, 16.

Lee, Chung H., and Naya, Seiji. 1985. *The Internationalization of U.S. Service Industries*. Unpublished.

Le Grelle, Bernard. 1985. European state service monopolies and the establishment of a new service industry: International courier services. *ICC Symposium*

"*Public and Private Enterprise: Striking the Balance to Promote Competition*",
Frankfurt, November 14–15. Unpublished.

Leibenstein, Harvey. 1966. Allocation efficiency vs. x-efficiency. *American Economic Review*, June.

Leveson, Irving. 1985a. *The New Global Economic Balance*, New York: Hudson Strategy Group, Inc.

————. 1985b. *The Service Economy in Economic Development: Perspectives from the United States.* New York: Hudson Strategy Group, Inc.

————. 1985c. The networking economy. *Services WorldEconomy Series No. 1.* Oxford: Pergamon Press.

Llewellyn, David T. 1985. The changing structure of the U.K. financial system. *The Three Banks Review*, March.

Liberalization of Trade in Services (LOTIS). 1986. *International Information Flows.* London: British Invisible Exports Council.

Machlup, Fritz. 1984. *The Economics of Information and Human Capital*, Vol. III. Princeton: University Press.

McMahon, C.W., and Worswick, G.D.N. 1961. The growth of services in the economy. II. Do they slow down overall expansion? *District Bank Review*, March.

Malmgren, Harold B. 1985. Negotiating international rules for trade in services. *The World Economy*, March.

Marquand, Judith. 1980. *The Role of Tertiary Activities in Regional Policy.* Brussels: EC Commission.

McMeans, Dave. 1985. Services data: Expanding our understanding. *Business America*, March.

Mincer, Jacob. 1962. On-the-job training: Costs, returns, and some implications, *Journal of Political Economy*, October.

Modwel, Suman Kumar. 1985. Should services be included in the proposed new round of multilateral trade negotiations? *Foreign Trade Review*, Autumn.

McFarlan, F. Warren. 1984. Information technology changes the way you compete. *Harvard Business Review*, May–June.

Nayyar, Deepak. 1986. International trade in services, implications for developing countries. *EXIM Commencement Day, Public Annual Lecture.* Bombay: Export-Import Bank of India.

Nusbaumer, Jacques. 1984. Some implications of becoming a services economy. In *Communication Regulation and International Business*, J.F. Rada and G.R. Pipe (eds.). Amsterdam: North-Holland.

————. 1985a. Services and the international economic agenda. In *International Geneva 1985*. Lausanne: Payot.

————. 1985b. Services in the international economy: Issues and prospects, *Symposium on the Service Sector, Hanover, May 13–15 1985.* Hanover: Unpublished. (See Pestel, Eduard.)

————. 1987. The *Services Economy: Lever to Growth.* Boston: Kluwer-Nijhoff Publishing.

Organization for Economic Cooperation and Development. 1978. *National treat-*

ment for foreign-controlled enterprises established in OECD countries. Paris: OECD.

————. 1983a. An exploration of legal issues in information and communication technologies. *ICCP*, Paris: OECD.

————. 1983b. *International Trade in Services: Banking: Identification and Analysis of Obstacles*. Paris: OECD.

————. 1983c. *Banking and Electronic Fund Transfer*. Paris: OECD.

————. 1984a. *International Trade in Services: Insurance: Identification and Analysis of Obstacles*. Paris: OECD.

————. 1984b. *International Investment and Multinational Enterprises, Revised Edition*. Paris: OECD.

————. 1985. *Software, An Emerging Industry*. Paris: OECD.

Pang, Eng Fong, and Sundberg, Mark. 1985. *ASEAN-EEC Trade in Services: An Overview*. Canberra: ASEAN-Australia Joint Research Project.

Pauli, Gunter. 1986. *Newsletter*, May–June, Brussels: European Services Industries Forum.

Pestel, Eduard. 1986. *Perspektiven der Dienstleistungswirtschaft: Beiträge zu einem internationalen Dienstleistungssymposium der niedersächsischen Landesregierung vom 13.15 Mai 1985 in Hannover*. Göttingen: Vandenhoech & Ruprecht. (Contains German translations of unpublished memoranda presented to the *Symposium on the Services Sector, Hanover, May 13–15 1985*.)

Pipe, Russel G., and Brown, Chris (eds.). 1985. *International Information Economy Handbook*. Springfield, VA: Transnational Data Report.

Pollack, Andrew. 1986. Document processors help eliminate the paperwork. *International Herald Tribune*, September 5.

Porter, Michael E., and Millar Victor, E. 1985. How information gives you competitive advantage. *Harvard Business Review*. July–August.

Posner, M. V. 1961. International trade and technical change. *Oxford Economic Papers*. October.

Psacharopoulos, George. 1984. The contribution of education to economic growth: International comparisons. In *International Comparisons of Productivity and Causes of the Slowdown*. John W. Kendrick (ed.). Cambridge, MA: Ballinger.

Rada, Juan F. 1984. Advanced technologies and development: Are conventional ideas about comparative advantage obsolete. *Trade and Development*, No. 5. Geneva: United Nations Conference on Trade and Development.

————. 1986. *Information Technology and Services*. Geneva: International Labour Organization.

Rada, Juan F., and Pipe Russell G. (ed.). 1983. *Communication Regulation and International Business*. New York: North-Holland.

Rafferty, Peter J. 1986. *International Trade in "Other" Services: Trends, Transportability, Implications*. Geneva: International Management Institute.

Rajan, Amin, and Cooke, Geoffrey, 1986. The impact of information technology on employment in the financial services industry. *National Westminster Bank Quarterly Review*, August.

Reboud, Louis, and Berr, Claude, 1984. *Le marché commun des services.* Grenoble: C.U.R.E.I.

Richardson, John. 1986. A sub-sectoral approach to services' trade theory. *Services WorldEconomy Series No. 1.* Oxford: Pergamon Press.

Riddle, Dorothy, I. 1986. *Service-Led Growth, The Role of the Service Sector in World Development.* New York: Praeger.

Ripper, Mario Dias. 1984. *Transfer and Trade in Advanced Technology.* Geneva: Graduate Institute of International Studies, unpublished.

Roessler, Frieder. 1985. The scope, limits and function of the GATT legal system. *The World Economy,* September.

Rothman, Matt. 1986. The leading edge of "white-collar robotics." *Business Week,* February 10.

Ruffini, Pierre-Bruno. 1983. *Les banques multinationales.* Paris: Presses universitaires de France.

Salvaggio, Jerry L., and Nelson Richard, Alan. 1986. The development and adoption of information technologies: Two approaches to the emergence of service economies. *Service World Economy Series No. 1.* Oxford: Pergamon Press.

Sampson Gary P., and Snape, Richard H. 1985. International trade in services: A framework for identifying the issues. *The World Economy,* June.

Sapir, André. 1985. North-South issues in trade in services. *The World Economy,* March.

Sapir, André, and Lutz, Ernst. 1980. *Trade in Non-Factor Services: Past Trends and Current Issues.* Washington, D.C.: The World Bank.

——————. 1981. *Trade in Services: Economic Determinants and Development-Related Issues.* Washington, D.C.: The World Bank.

Sauvant, Karl P. 1986. Presentation to the GATT meeting on services. Geneva: Unpublished.

Sauvant, Karl P., and Zimny, Zbigniew. 1985. FDI and TNCs in services. *The CTC Reporter,* No. 20, Autumn.

Saxonhouse, Gary R. 1983. Services in the Japanese economy. In *The Future of the Service Economy,* Wharton School, University of Pennsylvania.

Schott, Jeffrey J., and Mazza, Jacqueline, 1986. Trade in services and developing countries. *Journal of World Trade Law,* May–June.

Schultz, Theodore, W. 1984. A comment on education and economic growth. In *International Comparisons of Productivity and Causes of the Slowdown,* John W. Kendrick (ed.). Cambridge, MA: Ballinger.

Shelp, Ronald Kent. 1981. *Beyond Industrialization: Ascendency of the Global Service Economy.* New York: Praeger.

——————. 1985. Entrepreneurship in the information society. *The Heritage Foundation.* Washington, D.C.: Unpublished.

Shelp, Ronald Kent, Stephenson, John C., et al. 1984. *Service Industries and Economic Development: Case Studies in Technology Transfer.* New York: Praeger.

Skolka, Jiri. 1985. Division of labour and services. *European Research Seminar*. Leuven: Unpublished.

Services Policy Advisory Committee (SPAC). 1985. *Services Trade: An Agenda for International Trade Negotiations*. Washington, D.C.: SPAC.

Spiegel, Murray R. 1961. *Theory and Problems of Statistics*. Schaum's Outline Series. New York: Schaum Publishing Co.

Spero, Joan Edelman. 1985. *The Politics of International Economic Relations*, 3rd edition. New York: St. Martin's Press.

Stern, Robert M. 1984. Global dimensions and determinants of international trade and investment in services. *Third Annual Workshop on U.S.-Canadian Relations, October 19–20, 1984*. Ann Arbor: Unpublished.

Stigler, George J. 1962. *The Theory of Price*. New York: MacMillan.

Suzuki, Shigeki. 1986. Databasing takes off. *Journal of Japanese Trade and Industry*, No. 3.

Tempest, Alastair. 1986. Advertising and the liberalization of services. *European Association of Advertising Agencies*. Brussels: Unpublished.

Tucker, Ken, Seow, Greg, and Sundberg, Mark. 1983. *Services in ASEAN-Australian Trade*. Canberra: ASEAN-Australia Joint Research Project.

United Kingdom Department of Trade and Industry. 1984. *National Study on Services*. Geneva: GATT.

United Nations Conference on Trade and Development (UNCTAD). 1984. *Insurance in the Context of Services and the Development Process (document TD/B/1014)*. Geneva: UNCTAD.

——————. 1985a. *Production and Trade in Services: Policies and their Underlying Factors Bearing Upon International Service Transactions (document TD/B/941/ Rev. 1)*. Geneva: UNCTAD.

——————. 1985b. *Services and the Development Process (document TD/B/1008/ Rev. 1)*. Geneva: UNCTAD.

——————. 1985c. New and emerging technologies: What impact on developing countries? *UNCTAD Bulletin*, February.

——————. 1986. *Problems of Protectionism and Structural Adjustment, Part II (document TD/B/1081 (Part II)*. Geneva: UNCTAD.

United Nations Centre on Transnational Corporations (UNCTC). 1980. *Transnational Reinsurance Operations*. New York: United Nations.

——————. 1982. *Transnational Corporations and Transborder Data Flows: A Technical Paper*. New York: United Nations.

——————. 1983. *Transborder Data Flows: Access to the International On-Line Data Base Market*. New York: United Nations.

——————. 1986. *UNCTC Work on Services and TDF*. New York: United Nations.

United States, Department of Commerce. 1951. *National Income 1951 Edition*. Washington, D.C.: USGPO.

——————. 1984a. *A Competitive Assessment of the United States Data Processing Services Industry*. Washington, D.C.: USGPO.

————. Department of the Treasury, 1984b. *Report to Congress on Foreign Government Treatment of U.S. Commercial Banking Organizations, 1984 Update.* Washington, D.C.: Department of the Treasury.

————. General Accounting Office. 1985. *The Difficulty of Quantifying Non-Tariff Measures Affecting Trade.* Washington, D.C.: USGAO.

Vernon, Raymond. 1966. International investment and international trade in the product cycle. *Quarterly Journal of Economics.*

———— (ed.) 1970. *The Technology Factor in International Trade.* New York: Columbia University Press.

————. 1979. The product cycle hypothesis in a new international environment. *Oxford Bulletin of Economics and Statistics,* November.

Vickrey, William S. 1964. *Microstatics.* New York: Harcourt, Brace and World.

Wallich, Henry C. 1984. U.S. Bank deregulation: The case for orderly progress. *The Banker,* May.

Walter, Ingo. 1985. *Barriers to Trade in Banking and Financial Services.* Thames Essay No. 41. London: Trade Policy Research Centre.

Wassenbergh,, H. A. 1986. *Regulatory Reform in International Air Transport.* Boston: Kluwer.

World Telecommunication Forum. 1985. *The Washington Round.* Geneva: ITU.

Yeats, Alexander J. 1985. On the appropriate interpretation of the revealed comparative advantage index: Implications of a methodology based on industry sector analysis. *Weltwirtschaftliches Archiv,* Band 121, Heft 1.

Zweifel, Peter. 1986. On the tradeability of services. *Deuxièmes journées annuelles d'étude sur l'économie de service.* Geneva. Institut universitaire d'études européennes, unpublished.

INDEX

Advantage, absolute, 52, 59, 214
  comparative, 48 ff
Ames, Brian, 101 ff
Arndt, 120 ff
Art, as a service, 229

Banks, functions of, 109
  statistical methods for calculating, 117 ff
  technological innovation, 114
Bhagwati, Jagdish, 106, 171
Brender, Anton, 61
Bressand, Albert, 61, 123, 172, 183, 191

Capital, physical and human, 15–16
Characteristics, of services, 60
Classification of services, 39–41, 68
Compacks, 40, 61, 172–173
Comparative advantage, 48 ff
  revealed, 60
  and specialized knowledge, 171
  and innovation, 172–173

Consumer services, and participation of
  users, 155
Conventions, for classification and statistical
  purposes, 44
Council of Europe, and protection of
  personal data, 128

Data privacy, 128
Deardorff, 50
Deregulation, 188
Development, economic, and services,
  35–36
Disembodied services, 21, 106, 189, 191
Dispute settlement, GATT mechanism,
  201–202
Disutility, 5

Economies of scale, 14
Edvinsson, Leif, 93
Efficiency, and trade, 49
  in use of knowledge, 49, 148

243

and economic autonomy, 185, 229
Electronic fund transfer, 114, 115
Embodiment, of services in goods, and
    direction of trade data, 105
Endowments, factor, 48
External economies and diseconomies, 6,
    123
Externalization, of consumer services, 152 ff
    and development, 177
Externalities, and linkage functions of
    services, 102

Factor proportions, in services, 15 ff
Final services, 43
Financial services, 130
FLK (foot-loose knowledge), and
    professional services, 148, 213 ff
Freedoms of the air, 137
Functions, and utility, 17
    relations supplier-user, 34
    of services, and classification, 40, 41,
    93 ff

Gateway system, for data flows, 137, 184
Giarini, Orio, 155
Goods, services content of, 45 ff, 105

High-technology goods, 89, 211
Hindley, Brian, 53–55
H-O-S (Hekscher-Ohlin-Samuelson), and
    trade in services, 53, 57–59

IMF-plus definition of services transactions,
    104, 188
Index number problems, 9
Information, and knowledge, 25
Innovation, in banking services, 111
ISIC, 68, 101
Insurance, facilitation function of, 129–130
Intangible, character of services,
    as basis for definition, 7–8, 67
Integration, and interdependence, 187
Intellectual property, and trade in services,
    166
Interdependence, economic, 35, 187

Intermediate services, 18, 42
Intermediation, financial, 120
Investment, and trade in services, 165

Kierzkowski, Henryk, 176
Knowledge, as production factor, 14, 17
    and comparative advantage, 214
    content, as a basis for classification, 44
    and economic progress, 24
    effect on localization of production, 213
    specialized, and classification of services,
    42
    and trade, 59
    tranferable, 42

Labor services, definition of, 8, 86 ff
Lanvin, Bruno, 63, 163, 183
Leamer, Edward, 56 ff
Leverage, effect of services, 63
LIK (locked-in knowledge), 213 ff
Localization of production, effect of
    knowledge on, 213
Lutz, Ernest, 55

Marx, Karl, 42
Monopolies, PTT, and social rôle of, 124
Motivations, for national regulations, 192

Natural endowments of factors, 49
Nayyar, Deepak, 174
Networking, 181
Networks, and information technology,
    122–123
Nontraded goods, 34

Output, per man, services and goods,
    12–13

Packages, of services, 167
Personal data, protection of, 126–128
Primary services, 42
Processing, degree of, in services, 41 ff
PTTs, 123 ff

Public goods, as government services, 156
  as information bases, 168

Quality, of goods, 9
  of services, 16
  and education base, 18
Quantification, of trade concessions, 208

Regulations, and classification of services, 98
  reasonable, 201 ff
Ricardo, David, 15, 22–23, 42, 48

Sapir, André, 55
Sauvant, Karl, 187
Self-service, 191
Service acts, 8
Skill, levels of labour, and the definition of services, 90
Smith, Alasdair, 53–55
Standardization of services, and trade, 59
Standards, and international service transactions, 228
  of value, 15
Stigler, George, 48
STP (Standardization of thought processes), 182
Supply, characteristics, 7
  side analysis of value, 17
SWIFT, 115, 167

Technology, and trade in services, 51–52
Telematics, 122
Three-factor theory, revisited, 19 ff
Thought processes, standardization of, 182
Thoughtware, 93
Trade, in services, theory of, 29–35, 50 ff
  compared with trade in services embodied in goods; 48
  wholesale and retail, 150
Tradeability, 91 ff, 215, 226
Transactions in services, IMF classification, 103–104
Transborder data flows, 122, 128
Transnational corporations (TNC's), in banking, 112
  and abolition of barriers, 174

Units, conventional, in services, 28
Universal banking, 113
Utilities, public, 92
Utility, general, 5
  of services, 13, 16
Uruguay Round, 198

Value, market, 15
VANS (value-added network services), 123–124

X-efficiencies, 123

Zweifel, Peter, 226–227